Singin' the Blues

Neil Nixon

A Foxake Production

First published 2000, Terrace Banter
This edition 2006

Produced and distributed by
Hayloft Publishing Ltd, Kirkby Stephen,
Cumbria, CA17 4DJ

tel: (017683) 42300
fax. (017683) 41568
e-mail: books@hayloft.org.uk
web: www.hayloft.org.uk

ISBN 1 904524 36 2

A catalogue record for this book is available
from the British Library

Printed and bound in the EU

Dedication

For 'Alan' Ross

b. James Allan Ross

26 May 1942 - 2 Nov 1999

466 Games for Carlisle United 1963-1978

A hero

THANKS!

The strange thing about writing an honest account of following a football club that's plumbed the depths and known shameful episodes is that this book couldn't have happened without the help of some of truly decent people. So let's give them some credit:

David Steele: Is the greatest living authority on Carlisle United. He also checked this book for factual accuracy, something that was a problem with the last edition. David applied himself to the task, working against time and for less money than he really deserved. He's a decent, honest and caring man and a credit to the club and city he has served for years. Tactful too, with regard to the swearing he said only: 'It's your book.' I doubt he'd write one like this. I hope he puts his matchless knowledge down on paper someday. When he does you'll all find yourselves behind me in the queue.

Jenny Dunlop: Is a talented artist who takes a very personal interest in her commissions and managed to interpret my rough instructions for the Foxake fox into something better than I imagined. She doesn't follow football but still nodded and smiled sweetly through my attempts to explain the Conference, the play offs and the deadline for the book. It's to her credit that she worked so hard to capture an attitude and an idea that wouldn't usually be part of her life.

Tim Pocock: And I lost touch years ago. He was the editor of *So Jack Ashurst Where's My Shirt*. A great Carlisle fanzine still fondly remembered. Some of the words here started life in his fanzine and he was happy for me to publish them in a book. Thanks Tim, again!

Jane Nixon: Is a psychotherapist who deals every day with tales of obsession, depression and powerless-frustration. Once she's dealt with my obsession with Carlisle United she goes off to deal with her clients who - by and large - are more balanced and live more productive lives. How she's put up with me for well over two decades I can't begin to imagine. 'I love you,' is never enough in such circumstances. 'I love you more than I loved Alan Ross,' comes closer.

Introduction

Carlisle United and I have both changed in the time covered by this book. There are times I've needed Carlisle and times they've needed me. When the need has been greatest we've never let each other down. As a child I needed heroes, I found Alan Ross. Years later, Carlisle needed anyone with a pulse and spare change. I was equal to the challenge, paying up when I knew that the other side of the turnstiles offered the sight of Mike Graham and Eric Gates heaping shame and disgrace on the once proud blue shirt. Paying up again when the sad assortment of under-paid chancers on the pitch left us feeling that most of our money was going into the chairman's pocket. If you were there, you'll know the commitment it took to survive in those situations.

This book is the truth. Or, more accurately, the 'truth.' It is an honest account of my undying devotion, told the way I saw it. I've checked little more than spellings and dates because this is not a definitive history. It is a history of opinions, the story of one fan, his team and a love that will last as long as both exist. The opinions and memories are mine and mine alone. I've got reasons for my opinions and these are made clear but sometimes - such as my take on the strange creature that was Paul Bannon - I know I'm in the minority. So, take these descriptions and opinions for what they are. The way I saw things.

If you are one of the players singled out for a literary hammering, you'll certainly see it differently. Just remember, these are my opinions. I paid to watch, now I'm telling it as I saw it. One fan sees a missed sitter as a brave attempt, another sees the money wasted on Eric Gates' wages.

I've pulled a few punches, but not many. People who sold or took drugs get mentioned, but not named. Imagine you were one of these people and you'd gone straight to the point that the lives, mortgages or the safety of a few oil rigs now rested on your decisions, you'd probably want your teenage recreational habits left out too. 'Nuff said. I've gone easy where people disappeared from my life and vanished without trace. I've also taken it easy when people disappeared from my life and both of us were glad to see the back of each other. Since I couldn't contact these people, I chose to say nothing about them.

But mainly this book is about one man and his team. And, it is a 'true' story.

Prologue
Why Carlisle United?

I could take you to where I was born but it wouldn't be wise to stand around. For starters, if we stood on the exact spot where I emerged into the world we'd be run down by traffic. There used to be a hospital of sorts in Workington, now, so I'm told, the location of the maternity ward is part of the traffic system. Assuming we did get run down looking for the spot that isn't there anymore, the ambulance crew would pour what was left into the back and head off to the new hospital at Hensingham near Whitehaven, a little further down the coast and a little closer to Sellafield.

I've heard loads of stories about Workington, most of them told by people who lived in or around Carlisle. One memorable tale involved the baby born in the same hospital as me. Like many babies it came out with a look of naked fear in its eyes and gave all of the onlookers a brief sense that this new life had lived before. Unlike most other babies it didn't descend into a weeping mass and slowly adjust itself to the new surroundings. Flopping off the delivery table, the little bundle of life crawled to the window as the doctors and its amazed mother watched in awe. Forcing its feeble limbs into action it hauled itself up to peer through the open top of the window, taking in the incomparable Workington skyline with its grim stonework and grey skies. With a deep breath the baby groaned, 'Oh shit.' Some story, oh how we laughed. And the moral of this story is... you don't have much when you're born in Workington, but you do have a choice about where you'd like to be.

I had a hell of a lot more than most. Middle class parents with attitudes that were light years ahead of the times. I've even got pictures of my Dad changing my nappy and pushing the pram with his young son on board. If that doesn't sound too exciting you've got to consider that I grew up on the borders of West Cumbria and men just didn't do those kind of things then. Soon after my birth, with my Mum ill and me still helpless in hospital, my Dad did more than push a pram. He took me and my carry-cot and marched out of the hospital determined to organise better care than I was getting from the nearest available nurse every time I cried. This wasn't so much a criminal act as full-blooded blasphemy by the standards of the time and the place. But, if you find yourself in Workington, remember, you've got a choice!

Quite a few people have made choices about being in Workington. There's the hospital for starters, which chose to move a few miles down the road. They chose to close the steelworks in 1982 and for decades, people who live within striking distance of Borough Park, home of Workington Reds, have been choosing to head up the A596 to watch Carlisle United play football. Workington means 'working town'. Which, with the kind of grim northern humour that sees a decent laugh where your average punter sees only the terminal illness, is really pretty funny. Workington, the 'working town' in which I was born, is an unemployment black-spot and has been for most of my life. If you want to meet a guy from Workington with a job, head for Kent. That's where I live these days.

We're big on grim humour, West Cumbrians. If you want a real laugh, try this one on for size. Workington Reds used to be a football league team. When the Premiership was the First Division and the Fourth Division was as low as you could go, Workington were stalwarts of the bottom flight. Young people out there might be confused at this stage. After all, those ex-league teams all end up in the Conference, Southport, Hereford, Doncaster, Scarborough if they're not there when you read this they'll be back in the league, right? Well, no, not exactly. If you've got time to spare on a Sunday morning you could try looking for Workington's result. You'll need a decent paper, one that prints hundreds of results. Work your way down, and down, and down, and... a magnifying glass might help. To put this in perspective, if you see a national paper that prints Workington results, there will probably be more results on the page than there were spectators at that Workington game. But that isn't the real grim joke. Hang on for a few minutes, there's a real corker coming.

Workington were, by common agreement, crap, when I was growing up. Like your average kid I took an interest in football, knew my local teams and gradually learned players' names, details of the strip, the name of the ground and a few other facts that mattered. Soon enough, I was off to games and into an experience that would follow me through every stage of my life.

Workington Reds had their moments - whilst the rest of the world went mad for colour, drugs and free love in the sixties, Workington got seriously high with a finish in the play off positions of the Third Division. The good news is, this is the old Third Division - the one we all know and love as League One. The bad news is that Workington were in a play off place over twenty years before anyone invented the play offs. By the seventies, Workington, the town, was dying on its feet and the team were doing their best to stay in step. I was in my apprenticeship as a football supporter then. The period when quoting football facts and figures as you fish the gristle out of the gloop on your school dinner plate is worth something by way of status. Workington had their uses.

SOME OTHER KID - 'It's right, they used Roker Park as a ground in the World Cup when they had it in England.'

ME - 'Isn't big enough, you're making it up.'

SOME OTHER KID - 'Am not, my Dad went. He's been to all the grounds.'

ME - 'He's never been to Workington.'

SOME OTHER KID - 'Eh?'

ME - 'Hardly anybody goes. I saw in the paper, there were 973 there last Saturday, only game in the whole league with less than a thousand.'

I'd like to think that kid was impressed. Then again, I'd like to think my second hand Honda is a Lambourghini.

The writing was on the wall when Barrow, then in Lancashire, now in Cumbria, baled out of the league in 1972. Workington and Barrow didn't share a county then but there were some obvious similarities. Geographically speaking both towns are on the road to nowhere, which is a pretty good summary of the football they played. If the 1000 odd spectators who braved the merciless Solway winds to watch Workington Reds were treated to anything it was a decent pie at half time. The few away supporters who struggled along the single carriageway of the curving A66 to watch a grisly encounter had it slightly better. There was always the prospect of a near certain away win to cheer their long journey home. If Workington Reds had their moments in the mid-seventies it was when they were at home tucked up in bed with their wives. They were fucking about on the pitch too, but that wasn't anywhere near as much fun.

By 1977 Workington were noted the length and breadth of the country as re-election specialists. This is another historical detail that may need explaining. Before we had automatic promotion and relegation to and from the Conference we had re-election. Any team finishing in the bottom four of the league would have to apply to a meeting of the whole lot for the right to stick around in Division Four for another year. On the positive side for the league clubs this meant that everyone who had a few pals could lean on them for a favour and the end result was that, most of the time, all the league clubs stayed as league clubs and the part-timers didn't get a look in. By the end of this system Hartlepool would emerge with the all time record having applied for re-election fourteen times. Barrow bit the dust in 1972 when their eleventh application was turned down in favour of admitting Hereford United. The down side of this system was that you didn't need to finish bottom to get booted out, and every bottom four finish was remembered.

By 1977, the era of punk, when being hopeless, working class and belligerent was cool, Workington's hopeless, working class and occasionally belligerent football was doing them no favours. In front of crowds that would have looked thin standing around a big bonfire they were reduced to spiralling long balls, kick and run attacks and furious last ditch defending. The predictably pathetic finish didn't impress anyone and the club ran out of favours with their seventh attempt at re-election. Apart from anything else, if it was down to the other clubs to vote on Workington, anyone with experience of the lower flight knew the length of the return trip along the A66. Anyway, it was obvious. The last refuge of a hopeless team was the long ball game, supplemented with crunching tackles and blatant attempts to break up the opposition's rhythm. It was poor entertainment and a symptom of everything that was wrong with an increasingly cynical game. I warned you there was a real corker coming. In 1977 The Football League finally decided they had no place for Workington and their cynical long ball game. So they kicked them out and let in Wimbledon! Eleven years later 'The Dons' turned over the mighty Liverpool to win the FA Cup with a performance built on the long ball game, supplemented with crunching tackles and blatant attempts to break up the opposition's rhythm.

The dismissal hurt the faithful few although in truth it was part of a trend. In 1978 Southport were also ejected from the league. Barrow, Workington and Southport, three small seaside towns in the North West all dying on their feet, were replaced by Hereford, Wimbledon and Wigan, all inland and with some upwardly mobile pretensions in the seventies. If any of the ex-Workington players watched Wimbledon's march to cup glory in 1988 perhaps they felt a deep envy of those in the leafy London suburbs. Their envy could have been justified. If you're going to play a game which involves hoisting the ball into the air and racing to get on the end then the balmy and still confines of South London are a more promising location than rain lashed, gale hammered, Workington.

In the mid-seventies the generally hated A66 trunk road was widened to make a fast and efficient link to the M6 motorway. The thinking behind this involved better communications and new opportunities for business in Workington. At least, these were the arguments given in response to the complaints about the damage to the scenic beauty of the Lake District that resulted. Within ten years of the widening and upgrading, manufacturing industry and league football had fled down the improved road seemingly never to return to Workington. Maybe if they'd taken the turnstiles out of Borough Park in 1977 and slapped them on the end of the A66 they could have ensured that people got in and nothing else got out. In the 'working town' where I was born even the footballers are part-timers these days.

As my conversations swing round to football and, inevitably, Carlisle I'm often asked 'why Carlisle United?' This book is about the reasons, and they're not always simple. But remember one thing. If you wonder why I support Carlisle United, you never saw Workington!

Blue Nightmare

Carlisle United has been home to some great players over the years. We've seen international class in the ranks. Some future internationals - Bowles, Beardsley - have played their way up. Some others - notably Eric Gates - have plumbed the depths at the end of once great careers. Let's face facts. The minor international sides in the UK have sometimes fielded transparent shite in their ranks and for every George Best that turned out for these teams there are countless plodders who would struggle to catch the great man on one of his weaving runs. The ever-expanding international game means that any pile of rocks that can raise a flag is now fit to negotiate a World Cup stuffing, in return for a smattering of TV money. This situation has given Faroe Island fishermen and Cypriot cabbies a handful of international caps to flash off in the bar. Being an international footballer isn't all glamour and improbable pay cheques.

But, in a world where anyone with a pulse and exotic parentage might become an international footballer there is one man, and one man only, who can rightfully claim to have earned international caps whilst playing for Carlisle United. That man is Eric Welsh and, naturally enough, he played on the wing for... Northern Ireland. His country called him four times in the sixties whilst he was also on the books at Brunton Park. To this day, whenever men gather in earnest huddles, strangle pints and argue about legendary encounters in that green and pleasant land that lies on Warwick Road the name of Eric Welsh remains a legend.

Intense conversation and ale strangling also go hand in hand when men gather to debate football statistics. Put a Cumbrian in such situations and the other assembled anoraks will accost him in a predictable way about Carlisle United.

ANORAK - 'Nickname?'

CUMBRIAN - 'The Cumbrians.'

ANORAK - 'Ground?'

CUMBRIAN - 'Brunton Park.'

ANORAK - 'Most capped player?'

CUMBRIAN - Eric Welsh.

Hell, it's easy. There is no other candidate and history teaches us no-one will ever threaten Welsh. But there is a difference between this and other questions. We've seen the ground, we heard chants of '1-0 to the Cumbrians'. But Eric Welsh is simply a legend. Virtually no-one around on the terraces these days saw Welsh play. And, with each passing year, his status as 'most capped and the only capped' seems secure. Brunton Park appears cursed for those with international aspirations.

In recent years Jason Priestley - a goalie and no relation to the Jason Priestly you might be picturing - trained with the England under 21 squad. Within minutes he was in the local papers keeping goal for Carlisle City where a walk to catch a missed shot might find a goalie retrieving a ball from the jaws of a watching dog. In 1994 the Jamacian Christopher Dias was briefly touted as an international addition to the Carlisle squad. Maybe he put an XR3-i through the front window of Bulloughs, maybe he ran foul of all the newsagents he asked for some 'erb' but Dias doesn't appear in any history of the club. Fair enough, he never appeared on the pitch. To this day you'll meet Blues who deny that the man ever existed.

Troubled by the lack of an international, and suspecting that pictures of Eric Welsh were simply fakes concocted along with fuzzy alien snaps and the Ben Nevis Yeti portrait that once adorned the *Sunday Sport,* a Cumbrian once went in search of the great man. It was a long and troubled journey broken only by transport cafe fry-ups and furtive encounters with hunched figures in doorways. Glancing anywhere but into his eyes, they would engulf the Cumbrian in a hale of bad breath and mutter through broken teeth that Welsh could be found 'fifty miles to the West in a street that bears no name.'

After several long days of useless directions the Cumbrian finally came upon the legendary Eric Welsh. The venue was a smoke filled room. The Cumbrian felt his blood run cold as a nightmare of epic proportions unfolded before him. The 'room' was a theatre, Welsh was on stage and his 'act' said it all.

He started slowly. A glance, some general patter, a grunt or two and then the killer line.

'I played football for Northern Ireland... and I was on the books at Carlisle at the same time!' Howls of laughter, loud slaps on legs, the audience collapsing onto the floor in tears. Welsh went for it without mercy.

'Seriously, I played for Carlisle and I played international football in the same week!' More laughter. Suddenly it became clear to the Cumbrian. Welsh is the new Frankie Howerd. An act capable of reducing the hardest heart to hysterics with a routine built on nothing. The Cumbrian stood rooted to the spot as the crowd howled through two hours of unrelenting comic genius. The following morning, their sides aching, the crowd would attempt to explain to their work-mates how the man had amused them almost into unconsciousness.

'Tell us a joke he told you,' the work-mates would howl.

'Well, it was about Carlisle and being an international and... look, if you'd been there you'd understand.'

The Cumbrian was there, and he did understand. The following night he told what he had learned in a Cumbrian pub. 'Eric Welsh is real,' he whispered, 'I saw him, I heard him speak.'

'So what is he doing now?' asked the other Cumbrians.

'He's, ermmm... well... he's a legend.'

'AWWWWW, for fuck's sake, we knew that already,' roared the Cumbrians.

But Eric Welsh is real, he lives, he breathes and he once played international football whilst he was signed to Carlisle. Eric Welsh is a legend. And I know this because... I was that Cumbrian.

1 Alan Ross

Mentioned for the first time in this chapter:

These are my opinions not facts. Others - especially those mentioned below - are likely to disagree.

Chris Balderstone: Stylish and unflappable midfielder. Once dubbed 'The best player never to appear in the first division.'
Frank Barton: Free ranging midfielder with notable skills in holding possession, sneaking up on the blind side of opposing players and laying off accurate balls.
Bob Hatton: Confident and prolific goal scoring centre forward.
George McVitie: Speedy winger, deadly on the break and crowd favourite, especially with the younger end of the support.
Alan Ross: Tall, skinny and agile Scots goalie. Holder of all time appearance record for Carlisle United with 466 games to his name, including one outfield substitute appearance.
Graham 'Tot' Winstanley: Imposing centre half, central to success of 'classic' Carlisle teams of early seventies.

I'm sure there is such a thing as love at first sight but if it's going to work, really work, you've got to put the effort in. That's true for most things in life - marriage, bringing up kids and the really important stuff, like football. This book is a love story about one football team and a fan. I'm not the most devoted supporter Carlisle United have ever seen. I fled South years ago and I'm still here. But I am loyal and my support for the club has lasted through great days and dark depressing slides to the very brink of existence. Like Elton John I'm still standing. Well, I don't stand exactly like him but let's not sink into those cheap gags this early in the proceedings eh?

Like most kids I liked football. Like most kids I was also a pretty average playground performer. I was surprisingly keen on long stints in goal. At seven years old in the playground of Allhallows School, Fletchertown, I did have my moments. Mainly hurling myself against the tarmac in the teeth of another Cumbrian winter wind as my shot stopping capabilities between the two drains on the canteen wall held the other team at bay. The post-match analysis occasionally revolved around my attempts to be the best playtime goalie.

Once in a while the whole show gravitated to the 'Rec' or the sloping field that doubled as a recreation ground for the village. This was serious and official stuff in which Mr Bell, the headmaster and Dad of my best mate Geraint, doubled as ref. You could tell it was serious because we got to wear the football boots we'd cadged, borrowed or inherited.

This Rec had its attractions. Mainly the minimal chance that I'd break bones or come up with concussion after a mis-timed dive. I was eight or nine, at the height of my powers as a contender to replace Gordon Banks in the England goal. One incident sticks in my mind. We were on the Rec and I was having a good game. As another well timed rocket headed in my direction I threw myself up and took the ball as it dipped for the corner. Skidding and rolling within sight of a clump of thistles I held on tight and staggered up without once letting go. This move put bruises on your elbows but it looked great when Gordon Banks did it.

On that day I remember clearly that Mr Bell's reaction was to say 'You're a regular Gary Sprake.' Sprake was the goalie in Don Revie's Leeds team who were in the infancy of their dominance of the English game. He was also well into his eleven year stint as a regular keeper for Wales. For all this, I remember this little incident because the thought of being Gary Sprake didn't appeal then or now. If I was going to 'be' anyone that afternoon I'd have settled for Gordon Banks, Alex Stepney or... Alan Ross. Never mind that Sprake was the only one to whom I had any kind of resemblance with his tufty shock of blond hair, and famed ability to drop the odd clanger.

Alan Ross was the regular first choice keeper at Carlisle United. My images of Ross included only the vaguest ideas of how he moved and how he shut out the best the Second Division could offer. Ross and the other Carlisle players slowly assumed a legendary status in my life. Their absence from all but the local papers was probably a factor in this. I never saw them play on television so, whilst the legend that was Gordon Banks appeared in stark black and white on telly at the back of the leaking disaster that was the Stoke City defence, the legend that was Alan Ross only moved in my mind. His saves and his command of his area were described by the people to whom I looked up. Geraint's big brother Gavin for one. Gavin had been to Brunton Park. He once lovingly drew a picture of the ground which ended up in my pocket and stayed there for almost a year. It was in my coat pocket on the day that I finally made it through the turnstiles. In a crude way the sketchy picture of an empty football ground was all the more powerful for its lack of detail. I had to put in the spectators and the action on the pitch and in my mind the blue shirts of Carlisle swept up the pitch like a whirlwind.

If my generation added anything to football support - apart from an impressive capacity for mindless violence - it was a genuinely unrealistic element in our romantic love of local teams. Anything was possible in those days. Hell - England held the World Cup. The deal, on the fringes of rural West Cumbria, was that you supported some big team of achievers and also got behind the local team - Carlisle or Workington.

In the period between England's World Cup triumph in 1966 and their ignominious exit in 1970 I became a fully-fledged football fan and a blooded member of the active support of Carlisle United. This period certainly had its humour value to outsiders and I took stick from people who really knew what they were on about. In the playground things could get dodgy if you couldn't tell the truth from fiction. There were loads of stories flying around. Some were complete bollocks:

There was a match between 'Fleccy' [Fletchertown] and Leeds and Fleccy won.

Others, believed to be bollocks, were completely true:

Carlisle got stuffed by a bunch of non-leaguers the season they won the Third Division.

I'd figured the non-league stuffing as complete bollocks on the grounds that everyone who told me the story struggled to name the team in question. It's true, Carlisle United 0 Crook Town 1, 14 November 1964.

At the same time I was getting a sense of the excitement of a real game from the few people I knew who - like Gavin Bell - went to Brunton Park. He'd been often enough to run through players' nicknames and he had the time to describe the action. Gavin, Geraint, and their headmaster Dad would occasionally go to Brunton Park together. Geraint and I were inseparable at the time and we'd gone through several important firsts together from discovering Thunderbirds to staying over at each other's houses. It was natural enough that I'd take in my first game in their company. The only realistic alternative was a trip to the dreaded Borough Park and ninety minutes in the company of Workington Reds.

If Gavin Bell's stories of Carlisle United fired my imagination ahead of the first visit there was an equal importance in the things I heard about Workington. Laura Irving from the village had grown up with my Mum. Sometimes she baby-sat me and my sister. When she did, I remember her husband Bob heading off to Workington and never coming back happy. His face looked bleak enough on one occasion and I assumed Workington had lost. In fact they'd managed a 1-1 draw. Laura asked Bob whether it had been a decent game and he could only look into the middle distance and mutter, 'Poor... poor.' That is 'poor' in a solid Northern accent with a deep sound and flat 'ooh' in the middle leading to an 'R' sound that stumbles from your lips and falls into a great sorry puddle on the floor. Gavin Bell and others who had been schooled in the arts of Workington watching would tell it like that. I remember an argument about consistency in football and Gavin chipping in with a one liner about Workington being the most consistent team he'd ever seen, seven times he'd been and they were never less than complete rubbish.

So there was no choice, it had to be Carlisle. On 31 March 1970 I finally made it through the turnstiles to see players who had already assumed a legendary status in my eyes. The game, against Bristol City, was the second last home encounter of the season and had been rendered meaningless by the hopeless mid table position of both clubs. In the end we finished two points above them so a reversal of the score that night would have reversed our two mid table positions, nothing more.

Then again, the team I went to see had got within 90 minutes of Wembley and actually went to West Brom in the second leg of their League Cup semi-final carrying a 1-0 lead. They had sold out the 27,500 places at Brunton Park for a storming FA Cup fifth round collision with Middlesborough. They may have lost this clash by the odd goal in three but earlier in the same competition, they'd seen off top-flight opposition from Nottingham Forest. In that season Carlisle had continued to impress the football world with their ability to raise their game to the big occasion and pull passionate performances from an improbably thin first team squad. This level of performance was fairly new to the long time fans but my growing awareness of the club went hand in hand with these great days. The third place finish in Division Two in 1967 had almost pitched them into the top flight and their mid table finishes in the following years had maintained a reputation as a tough and well organised outfit with clear potential.

On that first venture through the turnstiles, I drank in a heady mix of atmosphere, excitement and potent football skill. In reality this marked just about the lowest point of the season. The team played out an encounter they knew to be unimportant on a cool midweek evening in front of six thousand of the truly committed, a smattering of Bristolians... and me. The things that most astonished me, were the sounds, sights and smells and the fact that I heard one fan around my own age chanting, 'Alan, Alan, Alan... Clarke!!!!!' as in Alan 'Sniffer' Clarke Leeds and England centre forward. In those days you could get into any part of Brunton Park quite easily and we headed in at the 'Waterworks' end before wandering round to the Scratching Shed. Both were known haunts of away fans but the red scarved Bristol contingent were in short supply and we mixed easily enough. The Waterworks was, then as now, the only section of the ground lacking any roof and the icy blackness of the sky above amazed me. The piercing white of the floodlights in an evening kick off spreads a light that puts a gloss on the night sky as you look up into the blackness. This more than anything else stuck with me from that night, well that and the way the pitch almost glowed. A stage fit for legends.

In my mind Carlisle were inspired and superior to anything Bristol City could manage and I expected the skilful moves from televised games: thirty-yard rocket goals, stunning saves and George Best levels of possession and control. What I recall most clearly is the pace, the sounds of tackles and the closeness to the action from our place hanging over the perimeter wall. With space to wander on the terraces Geraint and I had found a position as close to the pitch as possible, within sight of his dad and big brother but still our own place. Winger George McVitie ran flat out with awesome power, and as he ran at the Waterworks End goal I could hear the churning of the turf and the ball skidding just ahead of him. In all of the times I'd stuck my oar in at school in football arguments I'd never imagined these sounds or sights. More than anything it was the power and pace of the game that caught me that night.

And finally, there was Alan Ross. My goalkeeping career had progressed to owning a proper football kit and 'training.' The training consisted of persuading anyone gullible enough to bang a succession of shots in my direction as I threw myself at supersonic speeds through the air to deflect them with as much needless overacting as I could manage. The action pictures of great goalies in *Shoot* were a useful source of tips here. But the truth was my goal keeping career amounted to playground action and odd occasions when my uncles or a work friend of my dad's would humour me punting a few shots my way on the lawn. Well, that and the gloves. The same low grade gloves from a proper clothes shop that every other playground goalie wore at the time. Useless for the most part but handy for taking the sting out and deflecting screaming under-pumped footballs in winter.

So, back to Alan Ross. I knew everything about goalkeeping down to the properties of pathetic gloves until the night I saw Alan Ross play. Ross was class. Gavin said so, Geraint agreed and the local papers made it obvious. The reports I read so carefully described the teamwork and flashes of inspiration that had turned over the likes of Nottingham Forest and West Brom. Each member of the outfield would get occasional praise. One day 'Tot' Winstanley would head off the line, another time a well timed Bob Hatton strike would have left the opposition goalie sprawling and hopeless. The one man who always seemed to get a mention was Ross. By the time I saw him in action I'd learned to cherish newspaper lines like, 'Ross pulled off a fine save.' If the icy sky, churning of feet on the turf and the pace and fury of the whole spectacle was inspiring, the real revelation was Ross. This man was known to be a top quality keeper. He'd trained with Scotland, others named him as a player who could transfer into the First Division some day. But none of these things made him a revelation that first night. What stunned me was the fact that the great Alan Ross didn't wear gloves! That night he did it all with bare hands. I heard well struck balls smack off his palms, saw him deflect one hit high at a corner with his bare fingertips and never once saw him flinch.

I saw Chris Balderstone run the midfield with skill and commitment that ignored the meaninglessness of the match. I saw George McVitie storm off after loose balls and bury one in the Bristol net. I grumbled at the absence of Bob Hatton and 'Tot' Winstanley, howled for at least three penalties and came home happy that we'd won 2-1. None of these, however, looked like football on the telly. Down low to the pitch it was fast and furious and I had to take some cues from the crowd because I couldn't see all the action in front of the Warwick Road end. The one thing I did see in spectacular detail was the legendary Alan Ross in full flight. Gloveless, lightning quick, brave beyond belief and almost unbeatable. Most of what I'd imagined about the game was little more than a combination of school boy wish, television clips and *Shoot* action shots. The real thing wasn't a disappointment but it was different to expectations. Ross was a revelation. Better than I could have imagined. He stood just yards away from me as the game rumbled around the mid-field and I saw him read it, position himself and dive into action when it came his way.

Your average football addicted schoolboy has a favourite player to go with the favourite team and I'd veered from Balderstone to Hatton to Ross in the gristle from the gloop lunch-time conversations. But all that was in the past. As of 31 March 1970 there was only one player in the frame for me and that man was Alan Ross. A lifetime of support later he has no rival. I'd like to think that I detected in his inspired touches that night a clear sign that he would go on to make 466 appearances for Carlisle, setting an all time record for the club in the process and continually scuppering the best efforts of highly rated strikers. Then again I'd like to think that the six numbers on my lottery ticket will come up the next time there's a triple roll over.

My lifetime of admiration for the man comes down to one thing. In his performance that night I saw him do the things I thought I could do, the things I wanted desperately to do. Alan Ross had it. Whatever it took to be a great goalkeeper was there in that average game in the mid-table of the old Second Division. The man on the pitch was doing the things that one schoolboy standing yards away could only dream of doing. His commitment, positioning and the fact that he loved the job were a genuine inspiration. The man was born to keep goal for my team and - from that day to this - my life is better because of him. And it is because of those experiences and people like Alan Ross that many of us go to football matches. And it is because of those experiences and those people that we should go and keep on going.

When I left Brunton Park that night I knew one thing for sure. I was going back.

2 Stan Webb

Mentioned for the first time in this chapter:

These are my opinions not facts. Others - especially those mentioned below - are likely to disagree.

Peter Beardsley: Yup, he started with us!
John Gorman: Speedy full-back, tough tackler, good distributor of the ball and sometime assistant to Glen Hoddle and Howard Wilkinson in the England management team. And a Scotsman.
Matt Jansen: Slender and slippery forward, possessed of obvious class even as a teenage prodigy in the United reserves. Amongst his many claims to fame is the fact that he turned down a move to Manchester United twice before his 21st birthday.
Dennis Martin: Fast winger, former West Brom player and long-term favourite at Brunton Park.
Bobby Owen: Attack minded midfielder, signed from Manchester City.
Keith Walwyn: Muscle-bound striker, almost two decades ahead of his time here, but mentioned in this chapter all the same.
Stan Webb: Short lived but well remembered striker signed from Middlesboro 1971, sold to Brentford 1972.

'Stan Webb, might be a reet mongul features but he gets goals.' Keith Easterbrook had spoken and I knew he had a point. A polite translation of his words might read, 'Stanley Webb bears an uncanny likeness to a person with educational problems but his abilities in front of goal suggest that all his faculties are in good working order.'

Keith was a couple of years older than me, lived in a house 100 yards up the road which his parents had bought from my uncle Tom and messed around with me and what passed for a gang around our way. We weren't exactly kindred spirits. Time would show just how far apart we were. Keith went on to join the police and eventually got a job in the motorcycle division where his life was cut short at 36 at an accident black spot on the road to Cockermouth. It was, as I recall, the job he'd always wanted. I went on to write a 'comedy' novel in which a trio of psychopathic thugs beat the police to a pulp and, in the heat of one battle, ate a constable. I found an audience, mainly outside Cumbria, who thought the whole thing inspired and hilarious. Not exactly the job I'd expected when I was eleven.

But back to Stan Webb - I felt confident enough to talk about personalities, skills and specific games. Still in the company of Geraint and his family I was making a few trips to Brunton Park. By the summer of 1971 Geraint and I had graduated to heading off there together and stumping up a mighty fifteen pence to stand in the boys pen in the front left hand corner of the Warwick Road end. With programmes at 5p, this was just about affordable. Throw in crisps and Bovril and we had a great day out. By now I was getting used to the games, the pattern of play, the genius that was Alan Ross and a few other favourites in the team.

Webb truly was a strange phenomenon and holding a discussion about him with Keith I was growing in confidence as a Carlisle supporter. Hell, I knew plenty about Webb because I'd heard the rumbles and grumbles coming out of the Warwick. One book on United reports a famous Webb incident. I wasn't there but it must have been a hell of challenge that left Stan stunned on the pitch. The guy usually bounced off gorillas in the opposition defence with no obvious ill effects. He was upended by one of his former team mates as Carlisle played away at Boro. Even the Cumbrians joined in the fun with a chant of, 'Don't bother with the trainer, just go and get the vet.'

I remember one great Webb performance I saw from the boys pen. The end of the 1970/71 season left us with no hope of promotion but every hope of finishing impressively. Our last game was at home to Sheffield Wednesday and we hammered them 3-0 with our Stanley finding the net twice in a typically deceptive performance. Webb had a diminutive presence, the face of a cheerful schoolboy from some inbred pre-war back street community and a haircut that suggested his barber still had a pudding basin in the back. There were times he'd run straight at goal and the defenders forced to stop him would misjudge their tackles. I was still naive enough to think pushing up against the perimeter wall was smart and so for me the boys pen offered a view at little more than pitch height and turned Stan Webb into a bizarre spectacle. On occasion Webb's body would appear to be heading in one direction whilst the ball would leave his feet and head off at an angle. The trick, and maybe the legend has grown in my mind over the years, was that Webb's legs would then follow the ball whilst his upper body would continue to look as if it was heading off in the other direction. Defenders acting on instinct could be thrown in the split second it took them to register that Webb's body wasn't wired in the same pattern as everyone else. The confusion might be short lived but it left enough time for Stan to bang in a shot.

He also helped me to put arguments together concerning Carlisle. I could counter Keith's 'Reet mongul features' line with several of my own. I wasn't smart enough to work out what it was about Webb that was so unusual. I was sharp enough to listen to the old timers on the edge of the Warwick who would scream, pass comments and impart wisdom that was eagerly snapped up by some of the youngsters in front. As I recall it, the main difference between Webb and several of the others was that Stanley's slips were often greeted with gasps of despair along the lines of 'fuckin' pillock.' You might get the same abuse hurled at someone else but on the rare occasions that Frank Barton lost the ball in the same circumstances it might be: 'Barton, you fuckin' pillock.' The difference - and it matters here - is that people were hacked off with a skilful player like Barton because they figured he could help it. Webb, and for all I know the guy is about to win a Nobel prize for a great discovery, was given the benefit of the doubt on the grounds that he couldn't help it.

It just felt so damn good to be encouraging Webb. I was starting to get some sense of community. Not understanding exactly why I found his unpredictable goalward runs so bloody entertaining, I'd listen out for Webb talk and hear a mixture of encouragement, abuse and strange comments along the lines of 'the lad' not being able to help it. In short, he might have been a nutter but he was our nutter. In 1982 I saw one other man in a Carlisle shirt with a facial expression that suggested he would struggle to hold a newspaper the right way up and a touch on a football that suggested some bizarre genius lurking beneath the surface. I remember thinking then he might be another Stan Webb. He was Peter Beardsley. The new Stan Webb! What the hell did I know?

As a bizarre footnote to the enigma that was Stanley Webb the generally trustworthy *Lads In Blue*, Paul Harrison's history of the club records his birth date as 6 December 1917! Making the man 53 years old on his United debut. It's probably a slip in the editing. Then again it fits somehow that a mistake in the most comprehensive history ever published would centre on Stan Webb. Maybe the date is accurate. Maybe Webb is/was subject to different laws of nature. Where Stan Webb is concerned nothing would truly surprise me.

Webb went on to Brentford in 1972 and I couldn't tell you what happened after that. He and a handful of others made a real impression on me that 70-71 season and after Webb's great game I was over the wall for the first time onto a pitch and running for the tunnel to mob the side that had finished fourth in the old Second Division. I grabbed myself a lump of turf and spent time over the next few days in a futile attempt to grow it at home. Geraint already had a lump that was struggling for life at his place.

The fourth place finish made little difference then. Today we'd have been in with a late season shout at securing promotion and I'd have been in for some serious begging at home involving distant relatives, Wembley tickets and a massive financial outlay on the part of my parents. The one thing that finish did secure was a feeling of involvement between the team and me. I could recount Webb talk in Keith Easterbrook's attic bedroom. I knew the players and their strengths and weaknesses. I'd seen a young full-back called John Gorman come on that season and I was already praising him to people who'd listen. Since most of these listeners were not regulars at games I had one over on them.

Geraint had gone one better. He was being ferried around in his parent's new car - an 1100 formerly owned by Robert Owen from Manchester. Bobby Owen had signed for Carlisle in the summer of 1970 and appeared to have spent some of his new found wealth on a better set of wheels than the 1100. Geraint's Mum and Dad bought Bobby's old one. Owen's wife usually stood in the area of the Warwick just behind the boys pen. She got well into the games screaming along with the rest of us.

Bobby Owen and another new signing - Dennis Martin from West Brom - also appeared in a football sticker album I'd managed to fill. The 70 word biographies under their pictures gave me more vital information to slip into football talk. High in Keith's attic bedroom with the summer sun warming things, I could tell it like it was. 'Martin's better off with us. They've built that West Brom team around Jeff Astle, Martin roams around too much, he's on the wing and then he's cutting inside. He's got too many ideas for a team like West Brom. He's fine with us.'

I'd moved from the local village school in 1970 and by 1971 I was finishing junior school in the metropolis of Wigton. The last day in junior school included a massive fight at lunch-time. I got jumped on in the playground and, having fought my way back to my feet, ended up in a furious one to one with Edwin Sharp, a kid with a fighting reputation and a wish to leave the junior school on a high. I remember it as a full on fifteen rounder that would have put Ali and Frazier to shame. My adult self wandering into the playground would have seen two kids trading powerless punches for a few minutes. Either way, I came out on top when Sharp got tired of taking the punishment and headed home. The inquest in the headmaster's office was another lengthy affair. He'd given pretty well when we were trading punches and I'd hit him with everything I had. Okay, at eleven years old I didn't have that much, but I still hit him with all of it. I didn't ever go looking for trouble but, probably by virtue of being just about the tallest kid in the year, I'd been jumped on a few times just for the hell of it.

This had been fun of sorts but the all out humdinger that had ended the junior school had been a learning experience to top anything they'd taught me in the last term. Edwin Sharp was hard, everyone knew that, and I'd just found it out. For the first time in my life I realised that you could get hurt in a fight. This might have been obvious to the smaller kids, including the poor sap I'd thrown clean over a table within weeks of arriving at the new school, but it finally hit me why that kid got up with a mixture of hate and confusion in his eyes.

The real world was closing in that summer with the Nelson Thomlinson Comprehensive looming in September and the certainty that, biggest in the year or not, I'd be part of the smallest bunch in the big school. That prospect was daunting enough but the grimmest twist of all was the fact that the Nelson Thom had a reputation as a rugby school and that meant playing the game for the first term of the year. I didn't know it then but life was lining itself up to give me more insight into the workings of education than I could ever imagine, or want. What I had to face that summer was the usual dilemma of the sensitive middle class kid heading for the psychopathic fear factory. Okay, it wasn't that bad but you've got a few choices and a few escape routes in this situation. First off you can behave like a complete wanker, talk posh, flaunt it and line yourself up for a serious kicking on a regular basis. This way you spend the next five years of your life without having a slash during the hours of daylight between Monday and Friday. This way you get to talk about your innermost feelings on a regular basis but many of these innermost feelings come from the serious internal injuries you get after admitting you're a sensitive type.

I was never stupid enough to go down that route and the one comforting thought I could draw on coming up to that September was that there would be others who were that stupid. I was never gonna cut it when street cred involved a full-blown Cumbrian accent and helping your Dad up the road on Friday night because he wasn't fit to walk. There was a survivable alternative that involved keeping my head down a bit, trying like hell in games lessons even when I knew I was crap and knowing enough of what mattered to get by. I could just about survive on this score and I didn't have to fake anything in the area of Carlisle United. Where others could remember names I'd seen them and I bloody cared enough to have taken on board loads in the way of useful knowledge. The boys' pen was small which meant that I knew by sight the handful of other kids from our school who bothered to go.

This was just about enough and I managed to enjoy the asylum more than I dared expect. I wouldn't say I ever liked school but there were some decent surprises along the way. Managing to enjoy some of the work was one surprise. I had mates, a halfway decent brain and a better life in terms of material comforts than most of the kids I knew. Okay, I was a lippy git who could give back more than I was supposed to to the teachers and there were times when I didn't much care who I was hacking off but, that's why you're there at the age of twelve, right? For all that, it still came as a surprise that one or two people around the place seemed to have a serious down on me.

This made more sense after a stilted conversation with one of the hard crowd. Fuck knows how it started, we may have been talking Carlisle United for all I know. He threw a few insults my way suggesting I spoke like something off the BBC News and I threw a few back that linked his family bloodline to stuff you'd find in a zoo. In boxing terms I was storming round after round. He was wading in with the predictable 'bastard' and 'twat' jabs and I was giving it the old Ali shuffle, dazzling the crowd - well, two or three bystanders - with inventive cutting remarks about what was on top of his old lady the night he got started and the long metal trough that saw service as the family dinner table. I was on a winner because it was all going predictably to form until - like Mike Tyson wading in with the only good punch he had left - he dropped a line linking his out and out hatred of me to my Dad's Jag. This kid had a down on me bordering on outright hatred because my Dad drove a Jag! We're talking prejudice and it dawned on me in a few seconds that drew themselves out into hours that he meant it. This stunned me as much as getting hurt in that fight at the end of the junior school.

It had all been clear enough to me before. You got your crowd, slagged off everyone else's and got by like that, more or less. It hadn't really occurred to me that people really did hate each other. Sure, I knew there'd been wars and there were pitched battles at football games and the rest but none of that had actually touched me. On that day in my second year, the kid had a serious down on me and I wasn't winning the slanging match at all. Every insult I could dream up only gave him more reason to hate. In the face of this hatred my suggestion that his little sister was up for shearing was putting my life in danger. This was scary, first off because I didn't understand where this hate came from and second because that much aggro seething into an oncoming insult suggests your head is gonna come off your shoulders soon. So what if he was smaller than me. He meant it. I was just taking the piss.

I learned this lesson around the time I encountered prejudice on a wider scale at Brunton Park. Two incidents stand out. One October day I remember Geraint and I heading off to see United take on Burnley with his Mum cheerfully predicting a 3-2 Carlisle win. A tense first half struggle with some impressive goal keeping at either end saw us hitting the Bovril and crisps after 45 minutes with 0-0 on the board. We debated the chances of sneaking a winner but within an hour we were stumbling, stunned, out towards Warwick Road having seen United crumble to three second half goals without reply. We did our best to reply but Peter Mellor, an opposing goalie who would come back to haunt us in a truly significant match for United, maintained his form. In the absence of local league rivals Burnley are as close to anyone as 'the enemy' at Brunton Park. This may need a little explaining to those of you brought up on genuine local rivalry.

The real local rivals were the only other league team from Cumbria, Workington. Carlisle v Workington 'friendlies' were a pre-season feature. These games pushed the envelope on animosity and qualified as classic battles in the annals of the Cumbria police and far from classic battles on the pitch. We might have last played them 'in anger' in the sixties but the friendlies were 'in anger' on the terraces. 'Unfriendlies' might be a better name. In one famous instance at Borough Park, Alan Ross was heard to bawl out a mob who had spilled into his penalty area by telling them he just wanted to get the game over so he could go home and watch the boxing on telly! A quarter of a century later, we sometimes play Workington in the Cumberland Cup. This is a low-key local competition in which Carlisle traditionally field the reserve team. I once saw a youthful Matt Jansen in one of these games. But the excitement at this level never boils over on the terraces.

Geographically speaking the nearest senior team to Carlisle is Queen of the

South, based in Dumfries, Scotland. Willing takers of a few United cast offs over the years but, in terms of gates and tradition, not considered 'local' rivals. The only senior English team within sixty miles is Newcastle United who have traditionally fought out well attended and passionate battles with us. As our paths have diverged over the years only a long shot cup draw has threatened to put the fashionable Premier League outfit on the same pitch. But we still need someone to hate.

Burnley, Preston, Wigan and a handful of other Lancashire teams have formed a regular revolving hate list for United fans. Trips to these grounds won't leave you with much change out of two hundred miles. The close concentration of teams in Lancashire also means that these teams all have genuine local rivals and don't need to hate Carlisle the way we hate them. The reasons we hate them, or say we do, revolve around their ability to outstrip our achievements. Burnley and Preston in particular have a longer and more celebrated past than ours with more major achievements, international players and regular fans than Carlisle. The traditional hatred reflects a mixture of jealousy and frustration on our part.

The Warwick went mental with Burnley pissing on us that day in 1971. They had a good reason. The differences on the pitch didn't merit the gap in the scores. Peter Mellor looked like something from the Hitler youth with his improbably blond locks and a level of agility that foiled the pace and vision of Dennis Martin, the bizarre inventions of Stan Webb and the ever dependable Bobby Owen. Mellor's presence in front of the Carlisle fans was bait for the worst insults that could be dredged from three thousand reeling brains. The usual chants of 'You'll never take the Warwick,' and 'You're gonna get your fucking heads kicked in,' gave way to some free flowing insults directed at Mellor and the Burnley crowd in the Scratching Shed. With certain defeat staring us in the face a few missiles started to fly and the police took an interest. There was some trouble outside the ground, a few flying bricks and some general attitude stuff, although Geraint and I passed well away from it. In the end, the 'local' enemy had done us over impressively and given us one more beating to avenge.

I don't know when the following incident took place. At some point around this period a visiting team fielded a black player. Geraint went. The game in question is best remembered for an incident in which the black player had his shorts ripped and had to change them on the pitch. In this era black players were a genuine novelty. My football sticker album featured 440 cards and, I think, only one black player, West Ham's Clyde Best. When the black player ripped his shorts at Brunton Park the old pair were removed to reveal a dazzling white pair of underpants that would have put a Persil ad to shame. Throw into this incident the mentality of the section of the crowd that would make monkey noises and you've got a recipe for one liners that pass as witty or illegal depending on your view point.

Out and out hatred, the 'us' and 'them' mentality of football, is central to the game. Without the wish for our lot to 'do' the opposition there really isn't that much point. You could argue that the beautiful game is a celebration of athleticism and the combined skill of a team of men playing at the very peak of their abilities. You could argue that, but how the hell you could use this argument to explain the stuff that took place on the pitch in Workington's final league seasons beats me. Deep down we go for the tribal stuff and when all else has gone we still have the tribal instinct, and we still keep going. Workington's fans in the seventies paid good money because they wanted, against all the odds, to see their boys turn over the opposition. Carlisle would eventually force me into the same grim mind-set in which I was throwing my money over the turnstiles out of nothing more than hope and habit. I'm supposed to be smarter now than I was when Burnley stuffed us and that black player ripped his shorts. The truth is I'm older and wiser only when I'm away from a game. Three days before I started work on this chapter we won away 1-0, sneaking a result we hardly deserved. I realised somewhere on the way out of that game that I'd almost lost my voice. The same thing happened when I was eleven.

In those days I grew up and learned about the differences between people in the traditional areas for such education, the hidden corners of my school and the terraces of Brunton Park. Political correctness these days would say I should condemn anyone who hurled abuse at that black player and threw a stone at the Burnley crowd. That's an easy line to take and, to my mind at least, as much complete bollocks as the kind of narrow minded thinking that passes the same stuff off as harmless fun. The racist 'fun' back then was so harmless that the first black players to risk the main stage were known to advise their families to stay at home. There wasn't much joy in it for them sitting and listening to ten thousand ape grunts every time their man got the ball.

That kid who hated my middle class life right down to the Jag in the driveway probably taught me the most important lesson of the entire year in school. He taught me that deep down we can all hate and when we do hate no amount of clever reasoning is going to change things. I didn't feel too happy with it at the time because I just couldn't understand the hate. It makes more sense to me now because I've seen more of life and yet sorting out the problem of who we hate and why we hate has beaten the best minds of every generation.

On one level the simple is important in football. The us against them bit. Without that there is no competition and without the competition the passion is gone. It's this need to keep the passion that makes the whole hate mentality so hard to remove from football. However you try and change things the main problem with the crowd violence, racist chants and the rest is that football lends itself to the whole affair so well. I've seen changes over the years but it's easy to fool yourself that these changes have meant a lot. Black players faced abuse against Northern crowds in the days when virtually every other player was white. Years later our black striker Keith Walwyn muscled his way into opposing defences and the Blue Army chanted, 'We've got Pele.' It might be tempting to think we were celebrating a hard working black player in our front row but look at that chant from another angle and all it really says is that black players look alike. That's racism. Think about it, we didn't consider chanting, 'We've got George Best' every time Frank Barton got the ball.

Football violence didn't reach its heyday until after the early seventies. It was simply more visible then because you got it on the terraces and occasionally this could even spill over into *Match of the Day* where the whole country would see it. Carlisle got its fair share of aggro at that time because we were in our prime as a high profile club and the numbers we could muster gave us confidence. Our worst excesses in the violence department are a lot more recent and thankfully most of them take place away from the pitch these days. The matches of the seventies matter to me more because I was there at a time when the whole business of hating the opposition made a lot less sense to me. For the most part I'd put down the abuse as harmless but it's too easy to dismiss the whole thing that way. Anyway, flying bricks don't come into the harmless category. Despite this, I came away from the Burnley match well able to hold a conversation with anyone about why we hated Burnley. Hell, I'd got reason enough having seen ten lucky bastards and one inspired goalie stuff us with three goals at home. Street cred in the school meant knowing about football and being involved in it. The stuff I heard shouted at the Burnley mob that afternoon, and the stuffing they gave us, could be trotted out later.

So, in those few years spanning the end of junior school and the start of the real deal in the comprehensive life taught me a little and confused me a lot. Every seemingly simple thing had a darker side that was never going to make sense. A hate list of 'local' teams that could be re-jigged every time one of them gave us a serious stuffing, and the discovery that the line between taking the piss and hating enough to do damage was just about invisible when what you really needed was a set of warning lights. Somehow the increasing confusion made sense at a football match. It wasn't so much that I could stand back and compare life to football but more that, the more complicated life got, the more football simply felt great.

Almost everything I remember about the games in this chapter is good. The crowds were big enough to feel like crowds and in the safety of the boys' pen you could just about get swept off your feet, crunch into the perimeter wall and shout and cry along with the old hands pushing against the fence behind you. Okay, the freedom from adult company, the junk food and the presence on the pitch of a team that were famously hard to beat were pretty important. But my adult self says it felt good for other reasons. If life was confusing, then football had a way of letting you feel good about being confused. You could hate a guy playing for his club and love him the second he scored for England. You could swear you'd kill someone from a town you'd never visited and then shut up if you found them waiting to cross the road beside you on the way out of the ground. Above all you could argue the toss with anybody who said it was just a game. But, when you think about it, football manages to mean so much because at the core it remains, just a game. The competition, the uncertainty, the rules that allow everyone to use the same skills and tactics, are all part of a game. The second it loses the passion and competition all the other meanings - from tribal to appreciating the whole thing as art - are out of the window too.

It never felt better than when we'd put one over on the opposition, totally fooling them into the bargain and the best experience of the lot was that day at the end of the 70/71 season when we hammered Sheffield Wednesday. We stuck it to a big city club, finished within sight of Division One and played out a match we knew didn't matter with passion and skill. Up front Stan Webb pulled the moves that only he seemed capable of pulling and we celebrated his goals and his unique talent by crashing into each other, the wall and the fences. At the heart of this there was a real contradiction. It was hard to tell whether we were celebrating or patronising this most unique of strikers. Putting the 'get the vet' chant down on paper makes it all the more obvious that Webb was supported and abused in the same breath. And yet it felt so damn good. It felt good because every one liner, every chant and every blissful moment celebrating a goal brought a sense that you could belong to the whole thing. There were things to share and things to know and in Stan Webb there was a football phenomenon to behold. Mere words can't do the guy justice. You had to be there.

Like the boy said that day, 'Stan Webb, might be a reet mongul features but he gets goals.'

3 Joe Laidlaw

Mentioned for the first time in this chapter:

These are my opinions not facts. Others - especially those mentioned below - are likely to disagree.

Alan Ashman - Arguably the best manager we ever had and beyond dispute as the most successful. Ashman started his second spell in charge of team affairs in the late summer of 1972.
Stanley Bowles - Stylish, long-haired mid-fielder with a blinding first touch. Spent almost a year at Brunton Park, headed south, never heard of again!
Frank Clark - Deceptively effective goal machine signed from Ipswich in August 1973, brother of Alan and no relation to more famous Frank Clark, hang-dog faced full back and manager.
Kevin Hegarty - Seldom seen outfield player. 'Utility' player for sure given that six of his seven senior appearances took place in the number 12 shirt. Best remembered as a bloke with an uncanny resemblance to Alan Ross when the light caught him in the right way.
Joe Laidlaw - Flying blond tresses, droopy moustache and just a hint of a gut. The legendary 'Flying Pig' of the mid-seventies strike force and a Brunton Park legend.
Ian MacFarlane - 'The Big Man' and manager who took us to fourth place in Division Two in 1971. Carlisle United gave him his managerial break and also left him - and plenty of us on the terraces - stunned when they sacked him to almost universal surprise.
Hughie McIlmoyle - Firm favourite, a striker who spent three terms at Brunton Park including a return to the club in his mid thirties for one last hurrah in the top flight.
Jean-Claud Pagal - Former Cameroon international. Played half a game at Gillingham in 97-98 campaign, sporting dread-locked pig tails.
Ray Train - Comically named, diminutive, fresh faced midfielder signed from Walsall in 1971. Hard-working, tricky opponent sometimes upended by frustrated opposing players.

Alongside Stan Webb another enigma trod the Brunton Park turf between 1971 and 1972. He briefly added a new dimension to our lives. The two Stans - Webb and Bowles - might have been on the same pitch but they offered different visions of the game and appealed to die-hard supporters in totally different ways. So different in fact that this chapter will overlap seasons with the previous one. I'm not trying to confuse things, far from it. These guys taught me different things and appear to this day in different parts of my life. I'll swap Webb stories with long time supporters and Bowles stories with people who dismiss Carlisle as a team who've never produced a decent player.

History records that Stan Bowles hit the very top in football terms, playing for England and scoring a goal for his country whilst also on the books of a QPR team that challenged for the league title. Bowles opened his account with us in a perfunctory 2-1 defeat of Oxford at the end of October 1971. The most significant thing about that encounter was the sight of Stan Bowles in the blue number 10 shirt. That shirt mattered more to me than young Stan - a £13,000 capture from Crewe - could have known. Since I'd become an active member of the Blue Army the 10 shirt had been the on-field property of Chris Balderstone, Bobby Owen and... Bob Hatton. I knew well enough that, just before my arrival on the terraces, the legendary goal-getter Hughie McIlmoyle had made that shirt his own.

Now this long haired-bargain basement hopeful from the kind of team that everyone had heard of and nobody I knew had ever seen, was out there with '10' on his back. He did just enough before his substitution to suggest that his skills could add a new dimension to our hard-fighting, fast running and solid performances. Bowles' whole presence on the pitch - slight, long-haired and positively alien by Cumbrian standards - spoke volumes about the changes he would briefly bring. Like most debuts Bowles' performance had lacked understanding, included some well placed but hopeless off the ball runs and presented the spectacle of a man with some idea and a long way to go. I've seen others start in a similar way. In 1998 former Cameroon international Jean-Claude Pagal combined moments of inspiration with the sorry spectacle of a bloke whose understanding of the game had its own logic which failed to connect with the other 21 players on the pitch. Pagal had Bowles touches but, in his early thirties, he was on the way down when we signed him. Bowles was 22 the first time he stepped out at Brunton Park. He ghosted, glided and mis-read the game in equal amounts but when the cheerful chunk of mindless, meandering mirth that was Stanley Webb slapped hands with Bowles and trotted on to make his contribution we knew Bowles had arrived. Bowles, like Webb, offered an experience - as with Webb, you had to be there to see it. For someone my age, a bare twelve when Bowles started, being there meant a pile of contradictions and a lot of uncertainty. We've done the contradictions with Stan Webb, so let's do the uncertainty.

In my mind, shaped by the tales I'd heard before I went, and the achievements of being ninety minutes from Wembley in 1969 and two places from Division One in 1971, we were a formidable team. From the vantage point of the boys' pen we were battling in the 70-71 season and not always getting the best of it. We fought Oxford and gave it some serious grunt in the second half. Two-goal Bobby Owen who had commitment even when the first touch deserted him was the difference on the day.

Bob Hatton had also been a stalwart but he wanted more than that. He left to join Birmingham City in October 1971. Birmingham, who finished below us the previous season, took second place and promotion behind Norwich City the following summer. Hatton's departure from the number 10 shirt was a blow. Worse was to come.

One miserable December Saturday; a team struggling for form and looking shapeless; some touches that looked purposeful until the self-assured players of QPR pounced on our errors and stuffed us for three by half-time. I've had that sinking feeling at half-time many times since. I've even had it when we were four goals down at the same stage of a game. But the first time lingers. That sinking feeling, that trapped, purposeless - 'I've spent my money and I'm stuck with it' - feeling. At twelve years old and not exactly wealthy, even the cheapest corner of the terraces, comes expensive. Throw in shit weather and the recent departure of Hatton the Goal Machine and you've got a sick, miserable half time drag to the 'refreshments.' They didn't refresh much. In those circumstances parting with money for anything seemed to make the situation worse. Stuck in a queue for crisps at half time I thought better of it and read my programme. I didn't want to part with any more cash that day at Brunton Park. QPR could have refreshed their half time with a fag, a pint and a legendary Brunton Park scotch pie, we still wouldn't have got back into that game.

I knew enough by then to have heard the clichés that football's great thinkers could trot out: 'Eleven men against eleven, game of two halves,' etc. A fat lot of bloody good on 11 December 1971. Our eleven men trotted out for the second half and managed marginally more shape, but that was about it. Incidentally, this game is also notable for another small slip in the definitive record. According to *The Lads In Blue* Kevin Hegarty ran on as substitute but nobody is indicated on the team list with an asterisk, suggesting that nobody went off. That might just explain the confusion we produced on the pitch. Frankly, I don't remember and I don't much care to remember. We drew the second half 1-1 giving us an overall aggregate score of 1-4 on the ninety minutes and me a sinking feeling as I dragged myself out. So finally I knew that standing and watching a defeat could thump you right in the guts. We're talking, gutted, cold, miserable, lonely and scared. Like I said... character building. Thank fuck for Stan Bowles. If you want an image of that season it is Bowles running, spraying sweeping passes and turning with his hair flowing behind him. He typified that season, not in his play, which was amongst the best in a blue shirt, but in the varied numbers 6-10-11 he carried. This says something about the search for a tactical plan that went on in the face of injuries, squad changes and determined opposition from the likes of QPR, Birmingham, Norwich, Blackpool and Burnley. Clubs who thought themselves better than us and - I was starting to realise - probably had a point.

1971-72 was a turning point for me. The romance was gone for long expanses of the games and my own interests were broadening. By Christmas 1971 I owned records. Carlisle United had to battle Deep Purple and T. Rex for my attention and money. Then there were girls, although they didn't go to football matches as far as I could see, apart from Bobby Owen's wife who was still a vocal presence behind us in the Warwick Road end.

There was never any real chance that I was going to quit on Carlisle, despite their middling league form, but my life was slowly becoming more complicated and most of my idle moments in school were spent thinking about girls. Kathleen Graham walked into my life in that first year at school. We soon progressed to action of a sort, the kind of thing that early teenagers do well, kidding on they don't care but still sticking around in each other's lives and within sight and earshot at school. Within a year we'd be cosying up at parties, falling apart over nothing in particular and making up at the next party. By the second year of school we'd even managed to find ourselves in the same class which allowed her to pass notes to me. I'd kid on they didn't matter much but I'm writing this years later and I can still remember what was in them. Kate - as she was from the second year onwards - is the strongest memory I have of those first two years at school. We were in and out of each other's lives for the next ten years and I'm still in touch with her. The last time I saw Mrs Harding, as she is now, she was 40 and still gorgeous. She definitely did more of the chasing at the start but I had a choice and I also had a vague awareness that this was a new part of life. Choice wise I deserve some credit. You'll remember your first serious kiss for life and they don't come any better than Kate's. The rest doesn't matter that much in a book about Carlisle United but most of it was great, in that teenage confused way. Which means that, looking back, I remember brilliant moments.

Having just about perfected the rituals of being a football fan I was struggling with the all-together more complicated business of getting to know Kate and girls in general. But, in reality there was only one who really mattered. Giving yourself totally in this area wasn't a goer, mainly because keeping up the appearance of not being too bothered seemed to be a big part of the deal. Unlike football I didn't have a bunch of old timers and those in the know standing behind me and barking out one liners that I could use to build my understanding.

Oh yeah, football. Carlisle United and I were still at it and Stanley Bowles' appearances were doing something to keep me interested. Our tenth place in 1972 owed a lot to Stan. The inconsistent form suggested we deserved the mid-table mediocrity of tenth place. In mid-season we went seven games without defeat. This run immediately followed the annihilation at Brunton Park at the hands of QPR. True to our inconsistent form the great run started with a comprehensive destruction of Norwich City in which we'd stung the stylish side with two goals by half time and then hung on before striking with clinical accuracy one more time in the second half. Norwich might have been champions in May but they were a sorry sight at ten to five on the Saturday before Christmas

Day. Stanley Bowles netted a hat trick that day for the one and only time in a Carlisle shirt. He kept on eluding defenders and scoring goals for most of the season.

Geraint and I were there when Tottenham came to Fortress Brunton in the third round of the cup after a hard fought 1-1 draw at White Hart Lane. I'd been excited at the prospect of watching two legendary players that day. Martin Peters and Pat Jennings, as I recall, both played. They were simply outclassed by Stan Bowles and Alan Ross, despite Spurs beating us 1-3 on the day. In another passionate United performance, Bowles was drawing comparisons with George Best - at least from our end of the crowd.

Bowles made one of his confusing appearances in the number six shirt. The varying shirt numbers added to the exotic mystery along with Bowles' ability to ghost and glide past opposing players. The George Best comparisons were not made lightly. Hell, we thought we had our answer to George Best in the form of Frank Barton. The difference between Barton and Bowles is significant in considering Carlisle United during that era.

Barton was ever present that season, eventually leaving us in the summer of 1972 to cut through the middle of the park and make the play at Blackpool. Barton was your average George Best impersonator. The droopy moustache and abundant crop of hair hinted at a wish to hit the fashion heights. But there was a thinning beneath the thatch, a working class honesty about the way he rolled his sleeves up in the thick of the action and a plodding quality behind the shimmies that marked the man out as a grafter with a good touch. George Best was all touch and class, like Stanley Bowles. Up against the top flight in the form of Spurs, Barton had to sweat, and got caught in possession if he didn't go like hell. Bowles, young and still looking slightly dazzled in the floodlights, glided and passed and drew a few comments from the old timers about his short-term status at Carlisle. Our £13,000 was going to turn into someone else's big price tag.

We slogged out the 71/72 season on the strength of the seven match unbeaten run in the middle. The last seven matches, by comparison, saw only two wins and one draw. Not a classic season. But the Blue Army could still manage shock at the sudden departure of Ian MacFarlane, the 'Big Man' who'd managed us to fourth and tenth places in Division Two in successive seasons. His departure ranks as one of the most unsavoury in our history and only the welcome return of Alan Ashman to the helm could have made up for it. The official histories suggest that MacFarlane had a straight talking style that didn't impress those further up the chain of command. My own very unofficial history would like to record that this guy bought Stan Bowles and Ray Train - a diminutive midfielder who looked like a cheery twelve year old and wiped the mocking smiles off defenders as he ran past them with no respect. Anyone who saw the potential in these two and got change from twenty grand had to have management skill. He also bought Stan Webb, so we've got to give him credit as a crowd pleaser. And finally, it was his team and their high finish that got me onto the pitch for the first time. Top man - The Big Man.

Just a few weeks after MacFarlane's departure I was back at school for the start of the second year. A member of the memorable form, 2.14. I remember that day well enough. Kate was in my form and the timetable they gave us was unbelievable. One by one a who's who of teachers not exactly famed for their capabilities in the area of riot control was read out as our timetable was dictated to an increasingly disbelieving and surprisingly small number of people. The only unknown quantities were the new arrivals, one of whom, Mr Godfrey, was the form tutor. Glances were exchanged, fists clenched in triumph and heads were sent spinning at the dizzying prospects that lay before us. One teacher wasn't even there to start the year because he was still recovering from a nervous breakdown.

I can't prove any of the following, most of which came second hand from tame teachers and/or others likely to know. I'm not claiming any of this as fact. But... the 'genius' thinking that created 2.14 may have been linked to two problems both of which had their roots in the recent combining of grammar and secondary schools to make the comprehensive. Some of the grammar school teachers did not relish the prospect of the new lunatic asylum and the nervous breakdown that had reputedly seen off Mr Leaky - the English teacher who was due to join 2.14 that year - was only the start. Throughout the school, grammar school traditions and Neanderthal students collided.

The oral English and public speaking competitions of the old grammar were still around. I could string a sentence together and as the token posh bastard in the house group I got landed with standing up in front of the whole lower school. Well, fuck it, advancing short sight was rapidly ending my footballing career so I had to be good at something that earned house points! Within two years I'd taken on and trashed all comers. The competitions gave me a privileged view from the stage that suggested I was pitching my winning performance in the first year oral English competition into a crowd in the terminal stages of bum ache, boredom and total incomprehension. In the old grammar school, the idea of reading poems aloud might have a place, in the new company it was a loser. The following year, roped into the public speaking competition, I spent ten minutes talking complete bollocks about holes. I'd pitched this one right on the nail, going for the popular vote and heading straight for stand up comedy to blow the bum ache and boredom into touch. I sat down and everyone around me told me we'd won. We did too.

The new comprehensive crowd was straining the abilities of some of the old grammar school teachers. As I understand it, the 'genius' solution of 2.14 involved finding a smallish number of self-starters who might work more cooperatively with the teachers. These teachers could then be picked from the ranks who were dodging missiles, as the meaning of the word 'comprehensive' dawned on them. My abiding memories of that year involve Kate passing me notes and physically ejecting her mate Lorraine from the chair in front of me; me getting caught fixing a metal dustbin to land on a teacher's head as he entered the room; the detailed knowledge of music I gained on the back of reading *Disc* in classes whilst the teachers tried their best and the way I shamelessly buried myself in English literature with a passion. Hell, you'd be passionate if you'd just discovered *The Sex and Savagery of the Hell's Angels*, *Angels From Hell* and... well, great books the lot of them. What the hell the poor saps up the front were trying to teach us beats me. I can remember quite a lot of what I learned before and after, but 72/73 went by in my mind in a blur that starts with Marc Bolan strutting *Children of the Revolution* on *Top of the Pops* and comes to a grinding halt the following summer with me stretched out on my bed reading *The Exorcist.* My strongest memory of the class is of getting hit on the back of the head by a misdirected missile, as Mr Leaky tried to maintain order. Years later I found myself working in a factory job over the summer with Mr Leakey's son. 'He doesn't work in state schools anymore,' said Richard Leakey. Smart move if you ask me.

By this point I was avoiding the likes of Smiths and Woolies where possible in favour of the independent, more sussed and altogether cooler Pink Panther record shop in Rosemary Lane. There were school discos to add to the parties I was throwing and, as the owner of more records than most of my mates, I got to slap a lot of vinyl on in the background. I got into close proximity with Kate and tried to figure out what else I should be doing. So there was competition to football in my life.

Jeremy Higham had the misfortune to be the son of two teachers at the Nelson Thom, not the easiest gig on the planet. His thirteenth birthday fell not long after mine and his dad took him to his first football match, mob handed. Mr Higham, a history teacher who would eventually take me to one of the most improbable 'A' level pass grades ever seen, stumped up the cash to take a handful of Jeremy's mates to the Brunton Park clash with high flying Blackpool. Blackpool had promotion pretensions and current internationals in their ranks. OK we're talking Welshmen, but international is international, right? This was an event. For starters we got into the stands, proper seats and a panoramic view of the pitch. We also got there early enough to collect autographs as the Blackpool players went in. The autograph bit had obviously mattered to Jeremy because I remember him idly talking about wandering on the pitch to get the players' autographs before the start. Like I said, I think it was his first time at a real match! We played hard, gave it the stalwart come headless chicken treatment and ran out 2-3 losers. As a regular of more years standing than the rest of the party, I remember blaming it on the absence of Ian MacFarlane from the manager's office and the recent sales of Stan Webb and Stanley Bowles. The implication being that Alan Ashman hadn't got the tactics right and the recently acquired Joe Laidlaw, who had scored that day, was no match for Stan Webb. Like the ten minute rant about holes I was talking complete shite, a speciality in which I was virtually unbeatable at the time.

Another event was the visit of Arsenal in the cup. *Match of the Day* came to that one and saw us fight like hell from our lowly league position only to go out of the competition by the odd goal in three, a gift of a goal at that. Joe Laidlaw, who had missed the 2-1 humbling of Sheffield United which put us into the fifth round had a mixed game and the defence let in Frank McLintock to score the Arsenal winner. Frank Bloody McLintock! A centre half! We'd done well and the highlights on *Match of the Day* suggested an even game. Arsenal stood on top of the league that day and they only beat us because we slipped up. All that and I saw myself on television into the bargain.

Our eventual 18th place and my increasing interest in other bits of life saw me drifting from Carlisle United, although I stayed in touch well enough to get to a few games and notice the improvement in 1973-74. With a third promotion place on offer into the First Division, Geraint and I speculated early on that United might yet see top flight action. Our optimism generated loud howls of laughter from others at school. But we had arguments to throw back. If that third place had been on offer in 1967 - after all - we'd have made it. Come the middle of September with one point from the first six games and an away defeat at Luton on the record, we were 0-6 down by half time! Things didn't look so bright.

In the odd way that Carlisle seemed to mirror my own life, I was also up against it. Years three and four at school meant the middle school, a windswept stalag with all the architectural appeal of downtown Berlin in May 1945. With its long corridors, flaking white paint job and the deep black floors that rendered the congealed blood invisible, the place needed a make over to qualify as depressing. The mile long corridors magnified every sound from the stair-wells. Most days you could hear the blood curdling screams of another poor sap being ripped limb from limb over the banisters. The sounds echoed down the corridors and visitors to the school would often find green midgets ferreting around in the cloakrooms. On closer inspection these creatures turned out to be amongst the brainy elements of the new third years. Resplendent in their bottle green blazers, their lack of height was due to walking on their hands, pushing the top half their bodies along and leaving trails of blood from the ragged stumps that hung from their waists. I remember heading into my Civics class one day. This was held in the hidden room next to the cloakroom. I found one poor specimen lying flat on his back, pale from the lack of blood and almost ready to expire. With the feeble strength left in the top half of his body he bent one skinned knuckle and beckoned me over. I had to crouch low to his face to hear his last dying words. As his eyes dimmed and shut that kid whispered... 'Where in shitting crikey are my legs?' I hadn't the heart to tell him that I'd seen the 'progress' class toasting them on a bonfire.

Teachers experienced in the softer climes of the grammar school, kids positively allergic to education, and a building fit only to be an SAS training ground. What could you expect?

TEACHER - For the last time, will one of you cretins explain to me why this boy bled to death in the cloakroom?

BORED LAD IN CLASS - His aunt gave him a Toblerone and he wouldn't share it.

Well, it made sense at the time.

The generations before us might have had a scrap or two with the Germans but I'm tellin' ya, in Wigton, 1973, we had it rough.

My league form had slipped in the second year and I'd hit a relegation position that rendered me Set 2 material for the start of the middle school. In plain English that means saveable but lazy. My own pre-season training for the demands of the middle school psychopath championships involved some tactical thinking. The ambush central architecture was a known danger and - in this environment - it was permanent open season on mouthy posh gits. Fair enough I suppose, it was too far to walk to the chip shop at lunchtime, the weather was usually crap and you needed some indoor entertainment. My tactical master plan involved shutting the fuck up, watching my back and trying to talk my dad into buying a rusty Ford Transit for the odd occasions when he ran us to school. Results wise, two out of three ain't bad.

After a low key and under-confident start I got the tactics sorted and started to feel comfortable. I saw some real relegation candidates turn in worse performances than me. The third year allowed for new faces to join us from Aspatria and Silloth, legendary outposts on the very fringes of civilisation. Silloth once achieved national fame when it was celebrated as the worst holiday resort in the whole country by BBC *Nationwide*. These new faces had been sent to Wigton to allow them to take O' levels in vast numbers whilst their less fortunate companions stayed behind at the infamous institutions at Beacon Hill, Aspatria and Silloth and sewed mail bags until their fingers bled. I saw one or two new faces being rearranged before things settled down.

By the end of the third year I remained untouched, my work was improving, I'd got Kate Graham's phone number and she'd been round to my house. That summer I started heading into school in a scruffy blue jacket that just about matched one of the stripes in the school tie. Mr James, a history teacher with a stiff upper lip and a reputation as a fighter ace in the Second World War, cornered me in the dinner queue and made it clear he was unimpressed. The gist of his rant was that standards had fallen badly enough amongst the rest of the school without the saveable types falling to their scruffy depths. He didn't know it but he'd just paid me the greatest compliment I'd ever had from a teacher. I'd pulled it off, I was keeping up the work well enough to be a contender and looking dozy enough to count as a real person. Thanks Sir!

It was a stalwart performance on my part built on consistency. Carlisle United had also responded to the blood-chilling nightmare of one point from their first twelve. Remember, we're still talking two points for a win at this stage. The dogged consistency of Frank Clark, striker brother of 'Sniffer' Alan and a £35,000 buy at the start of the season, was providing regular goals. Joe Laidlaw, the striker I'd run down on my first sighting of him against Blackpool was also proving his worth. This guy was a crowd pleaser with real character and a worthy successor to the mighty Stan Webb.

I was still getting to the odd game but it was the games I missed that really put the fire back into my love of the whole thing. We beat Orient 3-0 in February, with both teams chasing promotion. *Match of the Day* deemed it worth a 600 mile round trip to cover the events. They got their money's worth with a diving header from Joe Laidlaw cannoning into the Orient goal. With his flowing blond hair, the all important aerodynamic rounded front with the hint of a beer gut, and an approach to the game that combined equal amounts of bravery and skill, Laidlaw was always likely to connect with a ball in a crowded goal mouth. The results, although unpredictable, could often be spectacular. They didn't come any better than that goal and I only saw it on TV. I was missing out and reduced to the same state I'd been in at the age of nine. In my absence that February afternoon 'The Flying Pig' had dived into Brunton Park legend. Laidlaw was a grafter in the great Carlisle tradition and his performances, along with the rest of the team had been blended into an outfit every bit as formidable as the great teams of the past. A hard working outfit for sure, but winners - 5-1 winners over Swindon, a game I missed, 2-1 winners over Nottingham Forest another game I missed and 1-0 winners over promotion chasing Sunderland, another game I missed. Sunderland was the last straw.

The report on Border Television described a hard-fought encounter with Chris Balderstone keeping his cool from the penalty spot to score the only goal whilst Alan Ross performed heroics in the other goal mouth. Balderstone was another stalwart, like Laidlaw, who'd come through. His Carlisle team place had been threatened at the start of the season when he'd seen out the cricket season with Leicestershire and been fined by Alan Ashman on his return to Brunton Park. That report on Border TV did it. I could hear the roars as the penalty went in, feel the tension of the last minutes ticking away and it wasn't really so different to my nine year old self hanging on to Gavin Bell's stories of the legends who wore the blue shirt. Hell, some of the players were still the same and in that Sunderland game Balderstone and Ross - players I'd idolised from the start - had made all the difference.

I was watching television on Friday 3 May, missing out on another match but this game was in London. Border Television carried the news. The previous Saturday we had beaten Aston Villa to finish our season standing in third place, Orient were two points behind with Villa to face in their final game. An Orient win could take them past us and into the top flight. Despite their lowly position Villa had made us sweat for the 2-0 victory and on 3 May they held Orient to a 1-1 draw. That result with Orient said everything about Villa's fighting spirit. That game secured fourteenth place for Aston Villa, condemned Orient to fourth, and left us safe in third and secure in the knowledge that we were a Division One outfit. It also sent me tearing around the house on a lap of honour. Being a posh git we're talking a sizeable house here, so this was a gesture!

With my parents out at the folk club in Ireby and my sister unimpressed, it was a lonely and pathetic celebration for the greatest moment in my club's history but at that moment it felt good. It felt totally bloody improbable and more than anything else it put the love of the whole thing back into my life. I didn't deserve them, I'd wandered away and missed some of the games that would now be legendary but the feeling I got was a small dose of guilt to a huge explosion of love for the team and what they'd done.

I may have wandered but I was going back. I wanted everything else in my life and, frankly, I couldn't help myself wandering in the direction of Kate but I'd neglected Carlisle. I knew better now. Carlisle got to the First Division the only way they could ever have made it. They played solid, well organised football with a manager who knew the flow of a game and the strengths of his players. Stanley Bowles may have dazzled us but we knew we couldn't hang on to him. Joe Laidlaw and Frank Clark headed, booted and scrambled us up. Alan Ross threw himself at net bursting shots and the mid-field blend of youth and experience that pitted the little ferret-faced Ray Train and the sophisticated Chris Balderstone into the same area of the park kept the play moving and the opposition chasing shadows. Grafters first and stars when the moves came together, United were a stalwart team in the great tradition. If you needed someone to sum it up then, I guess, Joe Laidlaw was your man. He'd looked pretty damn ordinary in a hard-working but defeated team the first time I'd seen him from the stands in that 2-3 defeat by Blackpool. Against Aston Villa in April 1974 he was a goal hungry strike machine who'd hit home before half time to settle the United nerves. 'The Flying Pig' was a stalwart who'd needed service and luck but he worked hard to get on the end of anything that flew goalwards and he'd scatter defenders to make the touch.

Like me, he'd started the season poorly and left serious doubts about his ability to cope in the thick of it. He didn't miss a game but he'd left it till mid-October to score his first goal. By the end of the season he'd got the blend right. As far as the goal tally went, he was getting the results that suggested he was a real contender but he still looked dozy enough to count as a real person. I recognised that combination well enough. I'd found myself another hero, a role model for sure and he'd done it so deceptively that I had to give him real credit for the way he'd crept into my affections. Hell, on a good day, Laidlaw could teach Stan Webb something about crowd pleasing. He'd already taught me something about writing off footballers, and football teams, too soon.

4 Les O'Neill

Mentioned for the first time in this chapter:

These are my opinions not facts. Others - especially those mentioned below - are likely to disagree.

Peter Carr - Fair-haired moustachioed defender. Athletic, handy with a swift punt up-field and usually reliable in his understanding with Alan Ross... usually reliable!
Bill Green - Tall centre back and captain. Disciplined, not known to respect the feelings or bodies of highly rated opposing forwards.
Les O' Neill - Diminutive playmaker with distribution, vision and a surprising amount of class for an ungainly little feller.
Bobby Parker - Defender with good positional sense and good commitment. A real team-player. One of three ever-present players 74-75 and a great servant to the club. Leaving eventually in 1984 to local football with almost 400 Carlisle United games to his credit.
Eddie Prudham - Forward signed from Sheffield Wednesday with a view to strengthening the First Division squad. So injury prone 'Weakness' could have been his middle name. Less than twenty appearances in three seasons.
Stan Ternant - No nonsense diminutive defender. Good reader of the game, hard worker and not known for respecting reputations. Went on to forge a tough management career based on teaching smaller clubs - like Bury and Burnley - to stop respecting the reputations of bigger clubs.

'Reaney, you second hand slimy bastard!'

Late November 1974 and - following a dream start - we were falling quickly down the league. On that day in November our effort based game came up against a great side who were themselves on a downward slope. Leeds United came to Brunton Park. We lined up, ran around and gave a debut to young Eddie Prudham, a capture from Sheffield Wednesday, drafted in to strengthen the creaking forward line. We needed more pace and movement. We got it until Eddie's slight frame collided with one too many Leeds defenders and he left the field. That game was the first real inclination I had that things were not going to work out. In response, I was letting rip.

The swearing was one of the best things about that First Division season. I'd got a few corkers revved up and ready to go. Many of these had started life at school years before. The 'Second hand slimy bastard' one for sure. I owed these one liners to Peter Scillicone, 'Skilly' to his mates, which didn't include me. When I was in the second year Skilly had been a fifth former with an attitude a mile wide. As we all trooped up to the bus stop it appeared to me that Skilly's entire purpose in life was to make the life of a boy nicknamed Joe 90 a complete and utter misery. Joe's spotty complexion was - probably - misery enough. Add a pair of plastic framed glasses and you have enough angst to trouble your average sixteen year old. Put Skilly on his back every night as he trooped up to the bus stop and you've got a teenage torment of wrist-slashing dimensions.

Hindsight and a bit of *Guardian* reading over the years tells me that abuse on this scale is a life changing trauma from which some never recover. My memory tells me that Skilly was the best entertainment on offer at ten to four in the drizzle. His ability to create a free-form stream of non-stop swearing bordered on full-blown Tourettes Syndrome. I could only marvel from a distance at the volume, timing and invention that kept the act alive for an entire year before I moved to the middle school. Years later as a comedy writer, being paid well to push the envelope on attitude I would spend long evening hours in search of the same linguistic invention that made Skilly a giant amongst fifth formers. My sick humour over the years owes something to the man.

It also owes something to Leeds United. They were the first team to make it obvious that we were going to struggle. Man for man, pass for pass, we were a match for them. We fell short in the fouling department. I'd had higher expectations of Leeds, a team still packed with the players who'd brought a league championship, an FA cup and European glory to Elland Road. These were dashed in a performance that saw crunching tackles breaking our rhythm and convincing Eddie Prudham that enough was enough.

The First Division dream had started so well. What I mean is it started well for the team and several thousand supporters. I missed the start of the whole adventure, like I'd missed the Watney cup and a brief European excursion in the Anglo-Italian Cup in 1972 on account of being on holiday with the family. The usual pattern involved a long caravette trip across Europe. I missed Carlisle United's only foray into Europe because I'd gone to Scotland in 1972. In 1974 we landed back in the UK on 25 August. First priority for me was a look at the Sunday papers and an inspection of the league position and the match reports. With no reference point I started scanning at the bottom of the First Division, couldn't find Carlisle, started moving up and up and... WHAT!!!!!

If you're a Cumbrian you know the rest, if not, I could take you for a few quid in a bet. Because, on 25 August 1974, after three winning games in Division One, Carlisle stood on top of the entire Football League. Remember there was no Premiership. We were first, there were 91 clubs below us and three of those clubs - Chelsea, Middlesborough and Tottenham Hotspur - were already regretting the day they met us. Alan Ross had kept three clean sheets and Les O' Neill had three of our five goals to his credit. What a week, what a team, what a midfield dynamo, what a shit time to be wandering round a French camp site.

Let's hear it for Les O' Neill. Alongside the class and experience of Chris

Balderstone and the endless darting energy of Ray Train, the touch and vision of Les O' Neill got us to the top of the heap. Not tall or athletic, Les O' Neill had the kind of deceptive class that makes the likes of Paddy Crerand and Ray Parlour into star players. His class was an understated blend of hard-work, accuracy and anticipation. Throughout most of that season it was the journeymen with a sense of their own self-worth who gave Carlisle United a pride and a shape on the pitch. Defenders Bill Green and Bobby Parker and little Ray Train in the middle of the field didn't miss a single game between them, cup-ties included. They all displayed that understated class but Les O' Neill held a hell of a lot together. His inheritance of the number four shirt also cast him in a tradition established by Stan Ternant. Ternant remains a name known to hard-core football aficionados to this day. He is now a manager who forges teams on a shoe-string budget, teaching them tenacity in the face of classy opposition. In 1974 Ternant was a name known to Carlisle fans for displaying the same qualities on the pitch. Tough little Stan had departed for Sunderland at the end of the 73/74 season, it was going to take a talent to impose his personality on the team. O' Neill played a slightly different game, was similarly useful on the left side and made the step up to the top flight with confidence. He was never better than in the First Division season 74/75 and the rest of the team were rarely better than Les O' Neill. Maybe if he'd played in every game...

O' Neill missed almost all of October and by the time he returned, our slips - which started with a home loss to 'Boro in the fourth game - were worrying. For me this worrying slide could be seen from two angles. We knew there weren't many pundits who fancied us to stay up. So we could just sit back and enjoy the ride. On the other hand we were already in unreal territory and, given the start to the season, anything seemed possible.

Hell, I was passing a few personal milestones, at parties, close up with some female company, in the things I was getting up to and getting away with. Life held opportunities and the Neil who returned that season to Brunton Park to howl at skilful international players on opposing teams was a boy old enough to know what life could offer and too young to be scared of some of the consequences. Given all of this I could manage an optimistic slant to the pre-match conversations with Geraint, who went off and on by the name of 'Geg' from this point. Geg, our mate Phil, and me were also making reasonable fist of playing music together. We thought we were okay. Tapes I last heard years ago suggest otherwise. But, life seemed full of possibilities.

It was possible we could have beaten West Ham, Chelsea, Leeds and Newcastle but they all turned us over. At least I had my growing habit of grabbing life's opportunities to sustain me. Geg and I saw out the West Ham match in the Scratching Shed, surrounded by Hammers and chatting cheerfully away to the members of some Scottish rock band who were killing the afternoon before gigging in town that night. I swigged away at their wine and discussed

Les O' Neill. We lost but there was hope at that stage and I was still new enough to alcohol to leave the game feeling heady, and satisfied having chatted away about music and football with blokes old enough to know their stuff.

We never quit on the top flight and on our day we had it, ask Arsenal, or more importantly Everton. They finished fourth that season, four points away from being champions. We took four points out of them with home and away wins. We've never played them since, giving us a 100% league record against them. We took three points off eventual champions Derby County. But, in the way that these things work, we lost twice to Luton who looked relegation candidates from day one and eventually took the dive back down. Luton had come up with us the previous season and their form was a good guide to our own progress. Their 1-2 destruction of us in mid-March was one game in which my positive attitude failed me big time. Despite his heroics, including our goal, I think Joe Laidlaw came in for some of the flack. Geg and I stood on the Waterworks end for that one. I remember walking up and heading for the exit as the game still raged. I didn't leave but it was as close as I've come to heading out of the gate whilst the action was still going on. When all is said and done, my middle class background hides the spirit of a true tight Northern bastard. Then and now, when I pay for football I stay for football, however fucking grim.

This game - I think - is notable as the encounter in which my own eyes watered as Hughie McIlmoyle took a thump right between the legs and collapsed in front of us. Even the one liners from the crowd were desperate. I felt pains right where it hurts as the trainer ran on and applied the freezing sponge. McIlmoyle had been drafted in to strengthen the squad. He was 34 at the start of the season. He scored twice and never played again after that Luton game.

I was hitching to games on a regular basis from this point. Geg did the same. We'd hitch apart and meet up in town. Lucky git, he got the real nutters including a transit load of head cases from West Cumbria who were prepared to punch each others' lights out in a row about the letters on Smartie tops. Saving bus fairs meant money for food and twice in this season my love of a decent snack put me as close to a genuine football ruck as I'd been up to that point. I got my scarf ripped off heading into a Carlisle supermarket and, on another occasion Geg and I got hassled heading for a city centre chip shop. Kids stuff that one, we pushed past and that was the end of it.

I missed our stuffing of Burnley and the home annihilation of Everton as I was bobbing along the Caledonian Canal with the rest of the family doing the old exploring the world and expanding my mind bit. Hell we scored seven goals in my absence as we staged a very late rally. Liverpool, with their eyes on the championship put it beyond doubt when they beat us at Anfield in front of the biggest crowd we'd see that season, over 46,000.

We were 22nd by this point anyway and my foul-mouthed rants had done little to turn back the tide of tricky opposing forwards who'd swarmed on the edge of the United penalty box all season. With only pride at stake and spaces visible all round the ground the team lined up in the centre of the pitch before the kick off against Wolves in mid-April. They waved to the crowd and turned round to target every part of the ground. Belligerent, stroppy and headstrong I might have been, but I almost choked on what I felt watching them in that unexpected moment. They were still my team and Alan Ross and Chris Balderstone were both in the line up. It was the last time I'd see Chris Balderstone play. In that moment I felt an honest, almost painful pride. This team had nothing to be ashamed of, they couldn't have tried harder. At times that season it was just painful. Hughie McIlmoyle might have been a legend but against Newcastle he'd looked short of pace; willing but out of his depth. Chris Balderstone could size up situations and spray out passes but there were teams in that league with the pace to make him look ordinary.

So in our final home game of that campaign we beat Wolves 1-0. Like my first wander into Brunton Park, it was a pointless encounter between two teams with nothing to play for. Officially the crowd numbered 9707. I'd give Wolves a good four or five hundred of that, add a few of the curious who had come for a last look at the top flight and our die-hard support that season was around 9000 - the people who still cared when there was no hope. And I, for one, am proud to have been one of them.

There was pride in the team and what we'd achieved. The pundits who had had us down as relegation certs couldn't take that much credit. Many of the same pundits had stated we would never make it in the first place. I coped with relegation, despite caring more than I had for years about that team. I was having good moments in my life and I'd stood munching my way through the sharp crusty round tops of legendary Brunton Scotch pies as I watched the very best the English game had to offer. When I think of that season now I remember moments which seemed to define it all.

We beat Ipswich 2-1 in a display of passion which took on and trashed a well organised outfit under the direction of Bobby Robson. We lined up and missed a penalty. The ref decided the goalie had moved and ordered a re-take. Having gone into explosions of curses at the first miss I was screaming my heart out about the referee being a Cumbrian. We lined up the penalty again and missed the fucker a second time! The result meant nothing to us in the long run but Ipswich finished third, two points behind the champions Derby with a superior goal difference! But for that game they could have been champions, a situation that might have given Bobby Robson an earlier shot at England management and our national team a shot at qualification for the 1978 World Cup. Well, it's a thought eh?

Joe Laidlaw scored the goal that secured both points that day. These days 'The Flying Pig' can be encountered still indulging his love for adventure off the ground as he plies his trade as a roofer around Portsmouth. I wonder if it has ever occurred to him that he delayed the appointment of an obvious England manager and ensured the gloom of a country as Italy dumped Don Revie and his troubled team out of the tournament. Worth turning over in your mind as you tile a roof.

The slide out of Division One was slow, steady and scattered with 2-1 victories over Ipswich and other hope building events. I cared about Carlisle United and I would happily argue my case with anyone and everyone, along with the arguments about favourite rock bands, the genius of the Monty Python team etc. That summer there were foreign exchange students, parties, more drink than a fifteen year old had a right to expect and many other good things in life. For the most part I was back as a regular supporter and Carlisle were back in my life. I'd got through a losing season relatively unscathed and I could justifiably have pride in my team. In answer to the usual taunts about United being useless I could always fire back that I'd been there, Revie's Leeds were psychos and we'd fought our corner in a tough division.

Well, I could almost always argue that. If you were there that season you've probably spotted the obvious missing game from this account. The hell ride from which we staggered bloodied, disheartened and unable to excuse the result. I know I've got to mention it so let's go: 8 March 1975, our first - and still our only - excursion into the quarter finals of the FA Cup, Carlisle United 0 Fulham 1. Fulham, Second Division Fulham. Bobby Moore and Alan Mullery in defence and Peter-Fucking-Mellor in goal. The self-same Mellor who'd denied us as we leaked three second half goals against Burnley in 1971. The baby-faced, improbably-blond stopper who bore a resemblance to something from the Hitler Youth.

The cup mattered to us. The move up to the top flight had simply confirmed our 'as good as those bastards' mentality for a season. Our presence in the sixth round of the cup with Wembley almost in sight and some good teams already out of the running was a real boost in a tough season. Fulham were a division below us, not likely to get promoted. Londoners as well.

This was a time for the casual and regular support to get together. Statistically speaking the difference between the two at Carlisle is awesome. We're moving a little ahead of the game here but Michael Knighton's 'genius' in taking over the frankly pathetic remnants of the once great Carlisle in the early nineties and attempting to harness the club's potential rested squarely on a few ideas. The acreage of land owned by the club, close to the main motorway link, is one feature that a guy with a background in property development could appreciate. So is the army of latent support out there.

If Bury have a good cup run they could put bodies on the gate at Gigg Lane, but those same bodies have Old Trafford, the City of Manchester Stadium, the Reebok Stadium and Ewood Park within striking distance. Then there's rugby league, a decent motor racing track at Oulton Park, clubs, cinemas and... yeah, well Carlisle isn't quite that well off. When he took over, Knighton compared us to Norwich City. Two clubs marooned in a large rural area. Get them performing and the people will come. Give them a cup run and the people will come in numbers, and they'll talk about their undying loyalty.

In the 73-74 season Geg and I had gone along to watch the eventual winners, Liverpool, dump us out of the cup. The following Monday at school I got a graphic lesson in the loyalty and pride that the casual support of Carlisle United could muster. Jeremy Higham, son of two teachers and the kid whose birthday party had put me in the stands for the first time, pledged loyalty to Liverpool. Okay so far, most of us had grown up saying we supported some flash club as well as Carlisle. What Jeremy did that stepped out of the unwritten rules was to turn up at the cup-tie in Liverpool gear walking in with the Liverpool fans. He got a kicking the following Monday at school. I knew the kids dishing out the punishment and I also knew that I didn't see them regularly at Brunton Park. They sure as hell weren't around the following season when I went to most of the home games.

The Liverpool crowd had been huge - over 21,000. A year later against Fulham the crowd was around the same size. The week after the Fulham game we played out that dire encounter with Luton in front of less than nine thousand. I'm wandering around the point, hell I don't want to go back to that place. This hurts, really bad. Geg and I were once again in the Waterworks end and close up to the action. This put Peter Mellor in front of us in the first half and allowed for discussions that this was the same guy who'd done it for Burnley in front of us a few years back. We already knew that the FA Cup was our only hope of glory that season. From the start we set about reminding Fulham that they had no place standing in our way. The stuff we threw at them would have humbled anyone. Hell, we'd worked less to stuff Ipswich and they were championship material. I read reports after the game and I've read books since. They will tell you that Mellor denied Les O' Neill, Bobby Owen and Joe Laidlaw. That doesn't begin to describe it. The mid-field of Ray Train, O' Neill and Balderstone spent most of the game pumping balls forward, running into space, twisting to make passes and letting in Owen and Laidlaw. Forget the ones that nearly hit the back, the whole game was alive with moves and chances. We penned them back in the first half which put Fulham and their fear-eyed defence within easy sight and abuse hurling range of the Waterworks end. Trust me here, they knew they had a game on! Every move, every pass to a running blue, every corner was greeted with roars of approval. The only things that didn't go down well were the leaps, twists and suicidal dives into crowds of players that left the ball in Peter Mellor's hands. Forget the bloody score for a minute, we were brilliant, worthy of Wembley, worthy of anything. I know cos I was bloody well there.

The half time scores were an opportunity to discuss the next round, the possibility of drawing West Ham who hadn't been that far above us in class in the league game and agree that Fulham just couldn't bloody manage another forty five minutes like the last one. To give Fulham their due, the old heads at the back were keeping things calm but there must have been white shirted defenders cradled in Bobby Moore's arms in that dressing room at half time. 'Please Bobby, please, don't make me go out there again!'

Alec Stock, a bloke who'd always struck me as an unlikely manager given his schoolmasterly aura and seeming lack of emotional involvement, was in charge of Fulham. He must have said enough to get their shattered nerves back in shape because they emerged for the second half. They got more of the same. To put this in context, this was the opening of *Saving Private Ryan,* those white shirted Londoners were storming the beach and our gunners were picking them off at will. Shots, headers, corners, all now at the far end from Geg and I, were raining in.

Then they got a break... I don't want to go there... please don't make me write this. Peter Carr's defensive skills were never the equal of an Emlyn Hughes but he was usually sharp, fast on his feet and capable of clearing a dangerous ball into the midfield. Carr and Alan Ross misread each other with a dangerous but containable ball heading in on the Waterworks goal. The misunderstanding left Ross stranded and stretching to hold it at the last minute. He didn't smother it, he pushed it out into the path of...

I remember seeing it hit the back of the net, I was probably too stunned to look away. It took months in my mind, but the television replay on ITV the following day confirmed that ball moving pretty damn quick. I don't think any goal conceded has ever gutted me as much. Honestly, Cheltenham's equaliser was easier to take. I'm old enough to know better these days and like waking up the following morning with someone you hate, like the stunts I've pulled drunk and regretted sober, like all my worst moments - trust me on this I was the only bloke on the planet who didn't know she was a lesbian and I asked her out!!!! That goal lives on in my mind as strong, sickening and downright bloody undeserved as it was that day in March 1975. Carlisle United 0 Fulham 1, and it was our cup that year. The same team that we humbled for 89 minutes that year made it to Wembley where, in one of the dullest finals of the seventies they were deservedly beaten by West Ham 2-0. West Ham were mid-table mediocrity on legs that season, even if they did do the double over us. If they were good enough for Wembley and Europe, so were we.

I think Geg's mum was still driving the 1100 at that time. I have a vague recollection of heading home, full of chips, still feeling empty inside and listening to the round up on the radio. The bit I remember is 'Diddy' David Hamilton, Radio 1 DJ, 'celebrity' Fulham fan and gloating southern git talking about the result and how it had been well worth his while hiring a plane with a few mates to come all the way to Brunton Park. The obvious follow up story, the one about how the staff at Carlisle airport had covered the runway in butter and given their fire brigade the rest of the day off, never came.

Alan Ross was the master of understatement. Speaking to *The Big Match* the following day he simply said 'I let the lads down.'

Ross made one slip, Peter Mellor was outstanding to a lucky/unbelievable/cold sweat nightmare degree. Somewhere along the line things got seriously screwed up and having not wanted to write about it at all I now can't stop going on about that game and what should've been.

So, that First Division excursion was a season of slow sliding torment with added agony and injustice but it had good moments. I was back in the fold, I cared about this team and I belonged on those terraces, every one of them. I stood on every part of the ground at some point of that season. I was growing up and the First Division adventure went hand in hand with adventures into unexplored territory in other areas of my life. In football and life there was plenty of effort and when these efforts delivered results they were brilliant. I saw so many games that season but it is the moments in this chapter that stick with me. Most of all it is the well of emotion I can still touch from watching that team stand in the centre circle and salute the nine thousand odd die hards who'd come to see them beat Wolves when there was nothing but pride to play for.

Somewhere along the line I'd found a way of belonging to that team that would see me through the rest of my life. Older now and not so romantic I still cared enough to hurt over the results. But I was also realistic enough to know what was going on. On balance we deserved that relegation. Not as much as some pundits would suggest but we'd made our own mistakes and the lack of a squad big enough to sustain a reserve team really told on us.

So this was an older, more realistic love at a pretty unrealistic time of my life. I could accept the faults, work on the good bits and keep on reminding myself why it mattered. By contrast the only thing that my approach to relations with the opposite sex taught me was that the world was surprisingly full of girls who were as desperate as me.

5 Mike Barry

Mentioned for the first time in this chapter:

These are my opinions not facts. Others - especially those mentioned below - are likely to disagree.

Mike Barry - Mid-fielder with fierce shot, some positional sense and an occasional lust for glory.
Phil Bonnyman - Scots born midfield/defensive minded player. Acquired during shapeless 75/76 campaign, went on to become regular in later seasons. Scored a few, including one at Arsenal.
Martin Burleigh - Capable goalie, but not Alan Ross.
Martin Harvey - Manager, welcomed on arrival. Despatched with little sympathy at very short notice.
Mick McCartney - Short on finesse, strong on being strong. Midfield/forward thinking player with ability to score goals.
Ian McDonald - Lanky centre-half, willing and sometimes able.
Bobby Moncur - Formerly famous as captain of Newcastle United. He had a contract with us that required him to manage.
Billy Rafferty - Big centre forward, good at the skilful stuff and handy in a goalmouth bundle. Some of the best news in a generally poor period at Brunton Park.
Trevor Swinburne - A goalie. Shared the number 1 shirt with Alan Ross from this point on.

'Fookin 'ell.'

Wuzzell had spoken. It was somewhere in early August 1978 in the changing cabin that stood on the edge of the main fitting shop in the British Sidac factory in Wigton. I'd been working at Sidac since mid-July. A summer job to stock-pile cash before continuing my education in the hope of finally learning to read and write. Well, a Cumbrian is nowt without ambition, right?

'Fookin 'ell, what's with that then?'

I wasn't ignoring him, I just didn't realise he was talking about me. I knew I'd dropped my cheque book and once I'd got my boiler suit piled onto the bench I was going to pick up the cheque book, stuff it in my denim jacket, go to town and get some cash. This is Wigton, 1978. Rumour has it that *Tomorrow's World's* feature on the cash dispenser was edited from the edition of the programme shown in Cumbria in case it provoked a mass panic. Imagine it, getting cash out of a wall with no hope of stopping to chat with the person doling it out. When automatic cash machines were introduced to my part of the world there were several incidents of people breaking bones in their hand after they cuffed the machines for failing to answer back when asked, 'What fettle?'

Cumbrians - big on human contact, prone to confusion.

'Fookin' 'ell,' so back to Wuzzel. I can't honestly remember where he came from. I'd been to school with a lot of the lads in the factory but I don't remember Wuzzel. This would put him - probably - in school around Silloth or Aspatria. Whatever, it finally dawned on me that he was interested in my cheque book. The thing that interested him wasn't the obvious bit about it hitting the floor. It was the pictures on the cheques. A door-mouse, badger, woodpecker and some other animal I can't recall. I'd requested a pictorial cheque-book because each time the bank issued such a book a fraction of a penny was donated to an animal charity. Something like that anyway. With lining myself up for college my poncey posh-git liberal tendencies were starting to show. On the other hand this cheque book was different and that made it fair play for a laugh. By the end of the afternoon the joke had developed and everyone was getting in on the act.

'You can get a cheque book for owt now, Shirtlifters have their own, l'al chequebook with a fookin' great lump of lead stuck to it. You're bent over so long with your arse stuck out trying to pick it up that...'

Hilarious eh?

How we've moved from the shuffle out of the First Division in 1975 to my first stint in the factory will take some explaining. My life, and the part of it I devoted to Carlisle United, appears to exist in moments over these three years. We're talking teenage years, wilful depravity, sex, drugs and rock 'n' roll and Carlisle United somewhere at hand most of the time. But we're talking moments. Key moments that seem to define my life at this time. One of them put me in the fitting shop, slopping grease out of the cracks in my hand with Swarfeager and heading up into town for a lunch-time pint. I was never likely to work my entire life in a factory. Mouthy posh gits are in short supply in fitting shops. By the time I stepped into the shop I'd completed my A' levels, put in an application for university and read some books written by Frenchmen with no mates. I'd pulled off this and the ability to survive the knock about, hammer wielding, humour of the factory because I'd thrown myself into other things apart from football. In a fitting shop a posh student can easily go over the line of being different. You know, like insisting on having little badgers drawn in your cheque book. Too far over this line and the playful ribbing turns into grease down your underpants. I avoided that and made it through the first of a handful of factory stints the same way I'd made it through school. Knowing a bit about what mattered and being funny when the alternative was getting my head kicked in.

If Carlisle United helped me grow into the ass-whupping psychopathic jungle of the Nelson Thomlinson School then by the start of the 5th year there were experiences I needed to get some other way. But I still went to see them and - while girlfriends came and went - the love of the club never left me.

Now let's talk about moments, and Carlisle United. Moments wise those difficult teenage years were packed. It wasn't all sex, drugs and rock 'n' roll but I remember those things better than I remember the geography lessons on the climate of East Anglia. The sex was the usual predictable stuff, discovering that there were girls who liked me and who weren't drunk and desperate when they said it. Figuring I could handle something approaching a relationship and getting into the usual head on collision of sincerity and out and out lies that it involves in those years.

Of course, it wasn't all sex, drugs and rock 'n' roll. Sex wise it was happening, less than I thought about it, but it was happening. Rock 'n' roll wise I went to my first proper gig - The Sutherland Brothers and Quiver - in Carlisle in December 1975. Within a year I was a gig regular, there to see anyone who dared play in the city. By the time I left school and entered into discussions of animal cheque-books at British Sidac my album collection was getting pretty varied and well into three figures. Drugs wise the opportunity would have been a decent thing. Hell, I was sixteen before I saw anything passing around the school and I was in the lower sixth before I saw any gear worth buying!

Life's rich tapestry was spreading before me in West Cumbrian pubs, clubs and the occasional bedroom... and Brunton Park was still standing. It took less time than I thought to change things. Carlisle's fall into the old Second Division coincided with my own fall back to the main school building. Here there was some semblance of law and order. You could read books in the library and rumour had it that some kids did their work! Carlisle and myself had both returned to familiar territory. We both proceeded to have our moments. My first sighting of the new squad - pretty much the old squad - was on *Match of the Day.* Away at Chelsea they took a 3-1 pasting in a game that marked the halfway point of a four match losing streak that left us with one point from five games and, I think, twenty one teams above us in the league. Chris Balderstone had left and the mid-field was missing his calming influence. We lacked shape and passion but there were moments. In the Chelsea game Mike Barry picked up the ball in the middle of their half, lined up, took aim and proceeded to unleash a thunderbolt of a shot that would see action for months in the opening sequence of ITV's *The Big Match,* win their goal of the month competition and figure highly in their goal of the season consideration. What a moment! Shame about the result.

As I write this I would say that the best goal I ever paid to see a Carlisle player score came in October 1994. The best goal I've ever seen a Carlisle player score anytime, anywhere, left Mike Barry's boot and screamed into the back of the Chelsea net on 23 August 1975. In October Alan Ashman left Carlisle and Dick Young took charge. Anoraks time: Dick Young had never managed a senior side before and he was 58 years old when he took charge. This - if I'm correct - makes him the oldest management debutant in football league history and gives Carlisle the curious distinction of having the oldest and youngest first time managers in the league at various times in their history. Ivor Broadis became the youngest ever football league manager when he moved to Carlisle in August 1946 at the age of 23. He also became the first manager to officially transfer himself when he moved to Sunderland as a player in 1949. Not that I gave a toss about Ivor in the growing gloom of the autumn of 1975.

Results on the park weren't shaping up. On some Saturdays my loyalties were seriously divided between Bruton Park, Pink Panther Records and the four-screen cinema at the bottom of Botchergate. Life in Carlisle eh, so much action, so few hours on a Saturday afternoon!

I never seriously thought we'd go down, even when the league table screamed 'relegation' at anyone who'd got eyes to read. Dick Young had been there or thereabouts at Carlisle for as long as I'd been going. He'd been the trainer before taking over the team and although he couldn't produce much magic on the pitch, he changed things around enough to get some fight out of some of the players. This was still the same team that had matched the best in the country stride for stride twelve months before. Curiously, it wasn't the Flying Pig, Ray Train or Les O' Neill who really got stuck in. O' Neill would finish his professional career in his early thirties at the end of that season. Gradually some of the First Division stars moved out. To their eternal credit Alan Ross, Dennis Martin and Bobby Owen stuck it out. One way and another Ross had a nightmare start to the new season. Out of condition and favour, he didn't play until the winter had well and truly set in.

We struggled as teams as lowly as York took advantage of our mistakes. Gifting spaces and possession that were never made available to the likes of Everton and Arsenal. In the face of this it was the unlikely lads in our squad who stood out. Eddie Prudham chased everything and bundled the ball into the back of the Portsmouth net the day after my sixteenth birthday. Six games into the season it marked our first win. Mike Barry's screamer of a goal ranks as another sublime moment from a player who'd existed on the fringes of the First Division squad. If you'd blinked in the First Division you could have missed Mick McCartney's contribution to the campaign, but Dick Young drafted him in to add some bite to the front end of midfield the following season. He managed a few goals and by the end of that season the shaggy main and odd shaped body of young Phil Bonnyman was also on show.

Maybe it was my life, maybe what I remember is true, but that team stand out in my mind as an outfit that put in a serious amount of running, passing, shouting and sweat to almost no useful purpose. Stand on the terraces and follow John Gorman, Alan Ross or Bobby Owen with your eyes and you'd see a decent player, working hard and doing the right things. Watch the shape of the game and you'd see us being humbled by lesser mortals with more sense of purpose and organisation.

I've forgotten the boring Friday nights stuck in front of *Starsky and Hutch* waiting for my life to start but I can still remember the odd events, like the Saturday lunchtime in March when I staggered out of Carlisle station and found myself amongst a mob of Midland accents. The Carlisle scarf was well enough out of sight to keep these Nottingham Forest supporters off my back but I wasn't prepared for the odd experience of bumping into a bunch of suits standing on the pavement. The strange thing was the presence of the odd black face amongst the well-dressed young blokes. On this evidence alone I knew they weren't Cumbrians and then I spotted Cloughie. I kid you not. Right there, within easy bricking distance of his own supporters, stood Cloughie surrounded by his team. It was the first week of March 1976. What they were doing there I don't know. Perhaps train travel with the fans was a necessary economy given the cost of keeping Larry Lloyd in beer. Perhaps their coach had broken down, maybe Brian fancied a swig of best quality British Rail whisky on his way to the date with destiny in Carlisle. Whatever, it is one of those moments that stands out in my mind. It was also one of our better performances that season. Not exactly classy but certainly committed, we held the future European champions 1-1 at Fortress Brunton. Then again, the whole idea of Fortress Brunton was starting to look pathetic. Beaten at home by Notts County and Leyton Bloody Orient, come on.

If you want a measure of how far we fell in terms of fighting spirit that year it is worth looking at the knock out competitions. Dumped out of the FA Cup at the first hurdle and staggering into the second round of the League Cup mainly on the strength of a pathetic own goal that killed off the impressive fighting spirit of Gillingham. 0-1 and they were still up for a fight. Everton - over whom we'd done the double the previous season - put paid to the League Cup hopes. Add the FA Cup and League cup 'runs' together and we scored three goals in three games. Look a bit harder at these figures and the only one of those three goals credited to a Carlisle player was Joe Laidlaw's opening strike against hard working Gillingham.

I still found some things to cheer but the real rushes of excitement were coming outside of Brunton Park. Puffing away on the odd Malboro, swilling a few cans of bitter here and there and discovering that the dog eared copy of *The Joy of Sex* I'd bought in a second hand shop was indeed anatomically correct; I'd hit that teenage alchemy stage. The stage when you realise that all of this stuff works but - on the odd occasion it works for you - you're not sure how exactly you made it happen!

Football wise, the rushes of excitement often bore a similarity to a bad case of premature ejaculation. Picture the scene. A few hard passes out of defence. John Gorman teeth bared, running away down the left and laying it off to Dennis Martin. Martin looking for space. The confidence and shape of Division One wasn't there but you'd still cheer the speed and the attempt. With Frank Clark running for space up front, Martin would see the oncoming defender, lay it off to Mike Barry and... 'Shit no, he's gonna shoot again!'

Somewhere nearby an Iraqi, freezing and miserable in Carlisle as he completed his pilot training at our friendly local 'airport' would be grasping the wheel of a light aircraft. Flying over the city he would see the oncoming projectile, register inside a split second that it was a football and fill his newly acquired Marks and Spencer's thermal underwear as the spinning hunk of leather and wind rattled his windscreen and put grey hairs in his lovingly combed moustache. Whiter than he would ever believe possible he would turn to his instructor and say... 'Please, how does it happen?'

'It happens because Mike Barry can't forget the screaming thunderbolt he netted against Chelsea.'

'Please, what is Mike Barry?'

'Never you mind, Son. Just fly the fuckin' plane, there's a good lad.'

Mike Barry and me had more in common during those days than I'd care to admit. A history of memorable moments, spectacular success in small amounts and a habit of trying to repeat the greatest moments and coming off looking like total tossers. Apart from the totally unexpected sight of Cloughie and the lads at the Citadel, my clearest memories of that season are Dick Young urging the team forward in the final minutes regardless of the score. That and Mike Barry missing the target time and again in fruitless attempts to stage another *Big Match* moment. The number of good moves wrecked by his attempts at an encore doesn't bear thinking about. Then again, it was one hell of a goal.

Over ninety minutes we often looked useful. We never lost by more than a single goal at home. Over a month we were worse because of the consistent habit of letting points slip away. Luton, Nottingham Forest and West Brom partied at our expense during some pathetic away games. It added up to a poor season. Nineteenth place might have been safe from relegation but the presence of Hull, Orient and Plymouth above us said it all.

Mike Barry's attempts to rekindle his greatest moments provided one link between my life and the team. However, like Carlisle United twelve months after the top flight adventure, the main change in my life was the company I kept. I don't know exactly when it happened. It was somewhere between the hard fought and well-attended home draw with Sunderland [in which Mike Barry managed another goal, but one that would never make goal of the season], and the acres of space on the terraces for the 4-2 hammering dished out to the shapeless Bristol Rovers. Geraint stopped speaking to me. I've got to get this one into context.

Since our early adventures to games we'd changed a little but - by and large - we'd stayed together. We were in the same 'band,' a motley assortment who'd meet at my place gather round the piano and/or bash away on our cheap and cherished guitars and dish out ritual murder to country rock standards before plumbing the real depths by performing our own compositions. The last time I tried to play the reel to reel tape of these attempts the drive belt on my machine broke. I never got it fixed.

By 1976 Geg brewed his own lager, sat next to me in the generally saveable set who were destined for O' levels, owned a passable Yamaha acoustic, expressed a fondness for Neil Young before I'd really got it with the great man and generally hung out like one of the gang. One day in 1976 he simply quit speaking to me. I still can't tell you why.

To the best of my knowledge his girlfriend didn't howl my name at the height of their most mind-blowing physical moments. Incidentally, I went out with her off and on much later in life and the only time I heard her really howl my name out loud she was bawling me out for forgetting to tell her to turn off a main road. All other speculation here is pretty damn pointless. Geg and my other good mate Phil Nelson would often rib each other mercilessly and Phil laid off speaking to me the same day but by that afternoon he was back on side and we stayed mates until he left school later that year.

Geg just quit speaking and that was that. Years later, with a bunch of mutual friends and Geg just back from his latest covert stay in the USA, we headed out to see the blindingly brilliant *Rust Never Sleeps*, Neil Young's second movie. Geg was back in the gang and the last to be picked up. There was some discussion on the way to his house about whether he'd speak to me. We were 22 by this point and the general agreement was that he would. I think it was Chris Storey who brought it up when we arrived, Geg mumbled something that sounded like 'Yes' and I got in a reasonable one liner. 'So, Geg, how've you been for the last six years?'

So anyway, 19th place and a mate that used to be. The 75/76 season.

That summer on the strength of about one week's hard revision for my O' levels I headed into the sixth form, Geg headed to the local tech college and work as an electrician, and the football team we both loved headed for some changes. The team that had chased and closed down the best the First Division could offer no more than two years before were dismantled. Bill Green went in one direction to West Ham, Joe - Flying Pig - Laidlaw went in another to Doncaster. Ray Train had already joined Sunderland, playing his last game for Carlisle the day I collided with Cloughie. The team that took the field in early September 1976 to play Hull couldn't, in all honesty, claim to be the same team that had taken us into the First Division. We fought out a draw, looked less than impressive and - true to form - Mike Barry managed a spectacular moment of skill in the third game of the season to hammer home our only goal of the ninety minutes. Then again, *The Big Match* were never keen on dour encounters between unfashionable teams. That strike would be remembered by only 7,530, minus those in the toilet at the time.

The Neil that took to the sixth form around the same time was also a changed animal. Rock music had delivered more mind blowing thrills than Carlisle United in the previous season and the priorities were slowly shifting. The dawn of the sixth form was also the dawn of serious party time, hell I was getting served in pubs, getting somewhere with the opposite sex and getting a sense of what life had to offer. The love affair with Carlisle United was a comfortable constant in a changing world.

A comfortable constant that took me to a smattering of games over two seasons in which we plodded our way through the Second Division.

Those next two seasons and years at school were real flurries of moments. The way it makes sense to me now is that the stuff that normally gives your life some kind of shape and direction was pretty much out of the window for me. There was this vague idea that the A' levels I was doing would lead me somewhere, I hadn't much idea where. I had my job at Stan Palmer's Filling Station and the problem of finding time to spend the wages and any other cash I could earn. But really my main concern was having a decent time. On a good day I was something of a party animal, on a bad day I was somewhere the other side of out of order. The final verdict on those years, decent parties, shame about the A' level results. The final verdict on those two seasons at Brunton Park, decent moments shame about the league positions. My performance on the terraces was patchy.

I've got to give my parents their due. One thing that happened during those decent partying years was a steady stream of my mates kept coming around to our house. 'My house' was out in the country, over half a mile from the nearest village, over four miles from anything you'd call a town and more than seven miles from Wigton where I went to school. It would have been easier for me to go to them. My folks were brilliant. That is brilliant as in tolerant, generally non-interfering and a stable influence. Years later, in the same position myself I'd come to appreciate just how good they were. More than anything they cared about me and my sister and we never doubted that. As bad as it got was my Dad once saying to me he thought I might have 'grown out' of getting up early to be in The Pink Panther shop the second their summer sale opened in 1977. I think he was really hacked off that this involved him in giving me a lift as far as Wigton. Me and my sister threw some decent parties and had people round all the time. The worst of the damage done was to people. The house is still standing today.

Peter 'Croc' Crossman was one of those people, drunk to the point of complete insensibility he left one of our parties in the back of a car and stayed comatose with a few mumbles thrown in for effect. The poor saps trying to return him to his loving home scoured Wigton phone boxes for a directory in the hope of locating Croc's house. They found it but their loving care ran short when it came to unloading the dead weight from the car. Croc's head smacked on the door-sill and the pavement - he ended up with a headache to remember. Years later I'd encounter him ordering a pint for a jelly baby which stuck out of his overcoat. Predictably, he ended up working as a psychiatric nurse and tackling punishing endurance athletic events. I can remember getting close to a girlfriend upstairs at one party and hearing a massive ruck starting outside. A gang ran Croc to ground as he screamed, 'You'll never take me alive.' Great days, even better nights.

I could still rouse myself to go to Brunton Park although working many Saturdays in the filling station left me pumping petrol into cars trailing blue scarves from the windows. In the season to May 1977 I spent as much time talking to Carlisle fans as I filled up their cars as I did standing with them on the terraces. The following year I probably managed more time talking at the filling station than I did at Brunton Park. Whilst I was getting up to speed in other areas of enjoyment I was falling behind in terms of football. I had few friends who gave a shit about Carlisle United.

When I did get there I had to listen in to others to catch up on the new signings. One new signing needed no introduction. George McVitie had been a favourite in the first team I'd seen before heading off to West Brom. In 1976 he was back. The mantle of Hughie McIlmoyle, Bob Hatton and Joe Laidlaw had now fallen on Billy Rafferty a summer of 1976 signing from Plymouth Argyle. He was big, effective and clinical in close; he could score, even if he couldn't always chase back and rob the opposition in mid-field.

He was on target when we stuffed it to Sheffield United in February. A 4-1 win by our lowly placed team. Bobby Parker netted the second, the only time I ever saw him score. He hit the net half a dozen times in a decade at Brunton Park. His longest goal famine lasted over five years, so that day was a treat for the few who saw it. On the evidence of the acres of concrete visible at the Sheffield United match there were more people than me staying away. There were days I was glad to be away from it. The 0-6 home defeat to mid-table Southampton was one such occasion. Martin Burleigh had replaced Alan Ross in goal for the middle part of the season, leaking twelve in January. I wanted to think that my return along with Alan Ross for the 4-1 stuffing of Sheffield United marked a new start in that miserable season. It didn't.

The early March visit of Nottingham Forest brought the same game at the same time of the year as the previous season. Predictably, the same result 1-1 and the same scorer, Dennis Martin. Not a great day out but better than the crunch match I missed through work in May when Bristol Rovers, whom we'd seen humbled in a season saving performance at the end of the previous campaign, turned up for the last home game. Both of us were in the same relegation mire we'd faced the season before. I got the half-time score on the radio, we were 2-0 up. An hour and a bit later I filled cars for some miserable people and heard the rest. We'd let in three in the second half and Rovers' winger Jimmy

Hamilton had engineered the lot. The people to whom I spoke reckoned we should have closed them down, penned them back and/or broken Jimmy Hamilton's legs. Based on a handful of games and a lot of talk over the pumping of petrol I reckoned it was mainly a defensive problem. My target for major blame was lanky centre back Ian McDonald who committed the unforgivable crime of not being Bill Green. Bobby Moncur's management, which had started in the winter of 1976 didn't much impress me either.

'It can't get any worse than this,' I told the few who'd still listen when I talked football. This was 1977, I knew nowt! We were deservedly relegated on goals with the two teams above us also fronting a pathetic 34 points. Billy Rafferty, and George McVitie had found the net often enough. We'd leaked like a sieve at the back despite the presence of John Gorman and Bobby Parker. Mike Barry was amongst the departures in the close season.

The next fixture list promised Chester City, Walsall, Exeter and Lincoln City. My limited funds also had to stretch to alcohol, girlfriends and any illegal stimulants I could get. I'll pull a few punches to protect the guilty. I ended up getting booted out of school twice, one such incident being a pretty serious suspension which lasted five weeks and resulted from a lunch-time excursion to a local offie followed by some decent drinking. The mistake we'd made was to take somebody who didn't swill the same quantities as the rest of the gang. Those of us with an income fit to sustain a drink habit had been regulars in this department for ages and finally getting rumbled at the start of the upper sixth was a shock mainly because we'd got used to the whole thing.

And there were drugs. The whole caper started when a mate of mine had totalled a borrowed motorbike. In the convoluted logic that followed this event the rightful owner of the said bike had been obliged to play innocent, leaving my mate copping the responsibility for taking the machine without the owner's permission. The said owner then made it all up to my mate by way of off-loading a lump of dope fit to stone a regiment. Spread over many sunny afternoons that lump regularly did the business. As the high summer of punk roared into top gear I could be found stoned, smiling and loving every living thing to the sounds of Pink Floyd, John Martyn and pixie-era T.Rex. Who needed Mike Barry with this lot on offer?

The rest is pretty predictable. I was banned from one pub before I was legally old enough to drink. I was lucky to get off so lightly, I deserved a trip to casualty. Another time that sticks in my mind is a party, the only all-lads party I ever went to, in which my drug buddy and myself ate our way through a decent size plug of gear. Stoned senseless on half the plug, we swallowed the rest and lost touch with reality. Later on, I'd hear snatches of conversation, close my eyes and marvel as my mind flew off in a thousand directions at warp speed. Every half-baked, pretentious sixth form philosophy exploded into hundreds of possibilities, each of which I could see in total clarity. Cosmic consciousness was on me, big time. Every time I tried to open my eyes and join in I couldn't put my mouth in gear beyond a dull mumble. It took me ten minutes of pathetic slobbering to tell everyone else that I was - cosmically speaking - several light years ahead of them. The others thought this hilarious. Things turned nasty later on when the second plug hit the top of my head and scrambled my brain to death-trip levels of paranoia. The speeding thought that I'd got so much poison inside me that I might not get out alive was a real bummer. It took a few days to get my head straight again. And that gear was classified as a 'soft' drug. The hard stuff - smack, acid and that - turned up later. Been there, done it, worth a look, but sticking around in that company is for tossers. And I'm not gonna talk about it here.

I will talk about one hysterical afternoon when, after some decent drugs during the previous days, I flogged myself through a hot games session, before dogging off in the afternoon for a bout of bonking in the woods. Late in the proceedings she was preparing to ask me how it had been when I got killer cramp up the back of one leg. I was lying there groaning and desperately digging my toe into the dirt to stop the cramp. She thought I was in ecstasy and couldn't come down. Bet she was disappointed the first time she shagged someone who turned right over and fell asleep.

Sex, drugs and rock 'n' roll kept happening. Meanwhile football had a steady familiarity. Like eating a sherbert dip, it was a happy throwback to a different time but not the place that was gonna change my life anymore. I saw Carlisle score one goal that season and it was good old George McVitie who struck home against Colchester. Shame about the three goals we conceded. On another occasion, well into the mind expanding period I watched Peterboro and Carlisle bore each other stupid into a 0-0 draw over ninety minutes. I'd challenge any member of the Blue Army present that day to recall anything that would qualify as a highlight. Between these two games Alan Ross managed a fifteen match spell in the goal but Trevor Swinburne was the latest in a long line of the great man's understudies trying his best to get regular action. I was tuned in enough to credit his performances as workmanlike and lacking the class of the great Scotsman. Ross was highly visible on the two occasions when we played stunning football that season.

We'd managed to avoid Manchester United throughout our entire history. No cup ties and never in the same league. If this sounds confusing to you younger readers then the story of how we avoided them is worth chasing up. Six years after they won the European Cup the mighty Manchester United were humbled to the point that their last game of the season represented a ninety minute battle against relegation. To make matters worse the opposition that day were Manchester City. In a scenario a film producer would reject on the grounds of improbability, the bitter local rivals dumped the once proud European champions out of the top flight. The killer blow came when a veteran striker, who had a golden end to his career with City, struck home with the United defence beaten. That striker was Dennis Law, a former United legend and the one notable absentee from the side which had won Europe's highest football honour at Wembley in 1968. His goal condemned United to the final relegation place. And what a goal it was, an instinctive strike with his back to goal. Law's reaction to this was a mixture of shock and dejection, he was substituted immediately. So when we went up, Manchester United came down. A season later, we swapped back.

The first meeting of the two clubs in competition came in the third round of the FA Cup in 1978. I reasoned - rightly - that the tie would be televised. Nobody had reckoned on the complications that reduced *Match of the Day* to coverage of one half of the game. Still the 1-1 result guaranteed a replay and *Sportsnight* managed coverage of all six goals. 0-2 down at half time we played United to a hard fought 4-2 win, in other words we took them on goal for goal in the second half and looked for all the world like a team that enjoyed the prospect of turning over highly rated opposition. This Man Utd side had finished FA Cup runners up in 1976 and gone on to win the same trophy in 1977 with a classic fluke of a goal. It isn't too surprising that they opened their account the following season by dumping us out. The surprise was that it took a replay. Those televised matchs got the old adrenaline pumping more than any visit to Brunton Park that season.

So much for the edited highlights of the sixth form. Just trust me here, the truly outrageous bits are better off in my mind than on this page. The whole predictable point here is that the years from sixteen to nineteen taught me that football is a constant in a changing world. They also left me somewhere in the Premier League of party animals and turning in a steady Conference performance at school. Meanwhile Carlisle were mediocre to the point of being invisible. Tenth in the old Third Division is about as uninteresting as football can get. Without the Man Utd cup tie that season we were in danger of dying of apathy.

At the end of this time my highest intellectual achievement was two sorry A' levels one of which was General Studies - an unseen exam on a range of topics that was manna from heaven to mouthy posh gits everywhere. I have a theory about this A' level. I reckon a few education minded types with studies full of books and houses full of dope smoking waster kids once got together and tried to figure a way of saving the academic futures of their offspring. Figuring that the only things their kids could do well was ponce on about life, the universe and everything they invented A' level General Studies - an exam stuffed full of essay questions about life the universe and everything - and sat back to reap the rewards of their kids who would clean up their lives somewhere after university and go on to be a credit to the family. Hell, it worked for me!

The only proper subject I managed was an E grade in history and both myself and my mate Jonty counted ourselves lucky to have pulled this off. Two days after the results came out we headed off for our usual pint or twelve at Wigton

Rugby Club. Dave Everett, history teacher, all round good bloke and one teacher I'd always rated, despite bunking off his lessons for sex and cramp in the woods, was also cradling a pint of bitter in the bar. He clocked me and Jonty, and we clocked him. He knew the score well enough. He'd had us sussed as a couple of pint swilling borderline cases from the start. Let's give Dave Everett his due, he was an excellent judge of character. 'You lucky bastards,' he said.

Within weeks I was at the factory stashing the cash that would keep me in beer, gear and college books. The conversation about the animals in the cheque book which opened this chapter said a lot about how far things had gone in a few years.

I still cared about Carlisle United, but life was more crowded and the things I was chasing hardest were the new experiences. What was wrong with football was the way you had to stand back and watch. You could get right inside the sex, drugs and rock 'n' roll. I was never stupid enough to think I'd find the meaning of life this way. But it was worth a look.

6 Paul Bannon

Mentioned for the first time in this chapter:

These are my opinions not facts. Others - especially those mentioned below - are likely to disagree.

Paul Bannon - Occasional goal getter, all round character. Started 78/79, established the following year and holder of permanent place in my heart.
Peter Beardsley - Okay, we've mentioned him already. But, his stint as a Carlisle player starts here.
Paul Haigh - Pricey, unflashy and ultimately dependable defender. Signed in the dark days of Third Division struggle, stuck around long enough to see a few highs and lows.
Jim Hamilton - Lanky forward-playing journeyman who netted a few in the Beardsley era team.
Bryan 'Pop' Robson - Chunky, ageing, goal-getter drafted in during grim survival campaign of 80-81.
Gordon Staniforth - Perm, tache, tight tight shorts, fashion guru and sometime scorer in late 70s/early 80s teams. Record signing - £120,000 - from York City.
Bob Stokoe - Next to Alan Ashman, the only other contender for best manager at Brunton Park, ever! Gritty, realistic and capable of working with a little to achieve a lot.

I first encountered Sunderland Polytechnic in a newspaper ad concerning their Communication Studies degree. Slapping in a late application, I got a late interview and found myself confronted by a handful of confused looking lecturer types all hell bent on having a coffee break and none of them especially keen to grill me on anything academic. We waffled for a few seconds about my A' levels, got onto talk about climbing mountains and skirted round films, the meaning of life and the quality of the common room coffee. I knew deep down I'd found some kindred spirits. Rumour had it that there was at least one researcher around the place who could spell 'academic rigour' but you shouldn't trust rumours. In the first year I was there, the college book shop put ring-binders on sale that spelled polytechnic as 'polytecnic' and by the time I'd got there the stocks had been hastily returned. The folders in question had passed through enough hands to suggest there should have been some kind of quality control but the thing that had alerted everyone to the embarrassing mistake was their popularity amongst the students. Never before had the college's own brand sold on this scale. The truth of the matter is there were dozens of students happy to attend the college that couldn't spell its own name and every one of those ring-binders stood a sporting chance of becoming a treasured souvenir.

As for my admission, we could have saved ourselves some time. All they had to do was take my pulse. The ability to stand up, breathe and say you actually wanted to come to Sunderland seemed fairly high on the admissions criteria. I should stress at this point that my opinion is not the opinion of my publishers. It should also be noted that we have already established that my main concerns involved getting off my face so it's not as if I was the best judge anyway. A Sunderland Rag Mag joke, 1979.

TUTOR - How many A' levels have you got?

COMMUNICATION STUDIES STUDENT - 27

TUTOR - You're taking the piss.

COMMUNICATION STUDIES STUDENT - You started it.

How those of us on the Communication Studies course laughed at that joke, once someone from the Science Department had explained it to us.

Sunderland was a shock. Never more so than on the first Saturday when I went out mob handed with a bunch of virtual strangers and headed for a few pubs. Semi-sozzled and considering a disco to finish the evening, I staggered out of a town centre pub around half ten and found myself standing between two fights. I passed a few more scraps on the way back home. Shit, this town was rough. I'd seen this kind of stuff before, I once found myself in the thick of a fight in a Keswick disco and ended up leaning against a door alongside a bouncer as we listened to the morons on the other side beating the shit out of each other. Stuck together in this hilarious and scary situation, me and the bouncer had briefly discussed Carlisle's impending relegation from Division Two, the way you do when there is a skull thumping the other side of the door a couple of inches away from your own head. As a football fan I'd also seen some serious rucks going down inside and outside the grounds. What hit me about Sunderland was the scale of the whole thing.

Within a few weeks I'd got a handle on it. If they didn't know you, you were okay, most of the time. A lot of the aggro was people settling scores from the week. You know, close knit community stuff. Two blokes meet, one gives the other a gentle talking to in the form of a serious kicking, an ambulance ride and a limp that lasts the best part of a month. A fortnight later they're in the same pub and the one who can walk without a limp casually says, 'You fixing to shag my sister again?'

The limping one cradles his pint, makes as if he's weighing up the matter deeply and grunts, 'Well... mebbeze not eh?' Everyone is happy again and the talk turns round to Sunderland's trip to Anfield. I miss those old earthy values, don't you?

Some places were off limits, The Royalty pub for one. There were odd skirmishes with the locals but as often as not these involved instances of suicidal stupidity, like a student in a shipbuilders' pub ordering a gin and tonic. I knew the form quite well, and survived three years without incident. As bad as it got was some guy giving me serious lip in a chip shop. I got out of that one discussing football. This was pretty rich really because my presence in Sunderland, Carlisle's presence in the old Third Division, and my presence in the student financial bracket, left me little chance of seeing United in the flesh. It wasn't exactly the end of an era but the sixth form tradition of indulging other interests at the expense of football really took hold whilst I was at college.

Carlisle got along well enough without me. In my first year at college they topped out sixth in the Third Division, a feat they repeated the following year before plummeting to nineteenth in 1981. I wasn't a total absentee but I was reduced to occasional matches on the weekends I was home. Holidays were a different matter and four goals in two home games in March 1980 went down well enough. The opposition were Blackpool and Plymouth, both of whom we beat with confidence. Given the complete break I'd had from Cumbria let alone Brunton Park there were a few changes. Unfamiliar faces on the park and everything seemed to have shrunk, especially the crowds.

Life had taken a few strange turns by this point. I'd moved in with the lovely Dawn and broken up with her and I'd taken a couple of trips back to Cumbria to 'get my head together.' The whole romance had started out somewhere near *Nine and a Half Weeks* and ended up around the final scenes of *Fatal Attraction.* Dawn was born to privilege and the story of how she ended up in Sunderland would make a decent book on its own. For a brief period we lived for each other. Dawn was more devoted, caring and loving than anyone I'd met, or dared imagine I could meet. It was intense, and the ins and outs of the whole thing don't matter much in the history of my longer lasting love affair with Carlisle United. When I ended it all in the early part of 1980 the fall out showed up your average TV drama for the shallow, half-baked bilge it is. To leave it quite like this really isn't fair to Dawn. I'd discovered more in the previous nine months about building your life around someone and thinking about that person all the time than I'd believed possible. 'Significant' doesn't do it justice and both of our lives took different turns as a result. Nobody talked about post-traumatic anything in 1980, we suffered from it though.

This matters in the great history of my lifelong love of Carlisle because it changed me and that, in turn, changed what I was doing watching my team. Having already noted that Carlisle United were there in the manner of many other familiar things, there was a time around Easter 1980 when those comfortable and familiar things started looking more attractive than they had for a hell of a long time. I'd pushed the envelope to the point of coming up hard against the real limits of sanity and survival. Given the way I was feeling, the comforting sight of Brunton Park was a welcome relief and the matches around March and April 1980 were all the better for the fact that this was a team with some hope of achieving things. What I needed most in my life was a sense of hope and the idea that there was something - anything! - in the future.

I'd always had some oddball tastes, a fact that had left me checking out some events on my own. Around Easter of 1980 I took this solitary behaviour into another dimension. I started heading off on my own to football matches. Given the intimate atmosphere generated by three and half thousand fans I soon got chatting away to the other blues around but in the social atmosphere of a football match this was still an odd move and it felt strange turning up alone. Regular reading of the *Sunday Sun* and other sports coverage available in Sunderland had kept me in touch with team changes. Familiarity wise Ian McDonald, Trever Swinburne, Phil Bonnyman and George McVitie were still around. Given the Third Division opposition McDonald was well able to cope. He was as effective as Bill Green had been an entire division above this level. The strength at the back was improved by a familiar looking figure in an unfamiliar beard. Ageing and a little slower on the ground he might have been but 'Tot' Winstanley was back with some experience and a greater readiness to upend anyone quick enough to try and run around him. Tot's imposing presence and McDonald's deceptive speed were a useful combination. I have to admit it, Trever Swinburne was pretty good. Just as well since Alan Ross had retired at the end of the previous season.

The team were just about managing to cut it as a credible footballing side. Fortress Brunton was almost worth the name, but this fearsome reputation had something to do with the less than fearsome opposition. Hell, I'm not saying that the Third Division was weak that season but that jumped up bunch of nobody's from London - Wimbledon - the rank amateurs who'd taken the league place of Workington in 1977, had fought their way into Division Three. They fought us to two draws that year and finished bottom of the division. It was obvious Wimbledon would never amount to anything!

There were some new faces to me in that Carlisle squad. I'd missed Jim Hamilton the season before and his height up front had its uses. The buzz, such as it was amongst so few people, concerned the little youngster up front Peter Beardsley. I've got to admit, on first sight I didn't really get it. Sure, he was fast and he had the skill to get round defenders. But the guy was so bloody short he could be overturned by any decent size lump of blubber in the opposing defence. Then again, Beardsley's flashing strike in the first half against Plymouth which set us up for our second win in four days was a moment of lightning reaction class and I was airborne in response. Don't get me wrong, I didn't have anything against him I just saw solid journeyman goal getters all over the pitch at Brunton Park and I wasn't sure that this youngster was completely out of their league.

What was great about Paul Bannon, on the other hand, was his mournful look. He looked like some world-weary police constable jogging around his beat in the total certainty that life's darker side would present itself at any second. A natural athlete only up to a point, Bannon oozed character in a subtle way. I'd managed to miss him the previous season - not hard given his lack of action. He came on as a substitute for the new wonder boy Gordon Staniforth. Staniforth had the Keegan perm, the obligatory tache and a sense that the cameras were on him all the time. Bannon had the tache, the long hair and a totally different aura - he was the anti-Gordon Staniforth. It all came clear for me, still trying to get up to speed with the new faces, when Bannon jogged on as sub and somebody close by shouted out, 'Smile you miserable twat, you've got a game.'

He didn't smile. I'm not sure he managed much of a smirk when he scored. But I'd found another crowd-pleaser, even if he had to convince the rest of the crowd. Thinking back on this, it probably had something to do with the shout as he came on. It may even have had something to do with the time I'd spent at college. Academically I was still in the lower leagues. I'd do what I had to and head off to the pub, record shop or wherever once I'd got the basics delivered. Despite this, I was also in the student mentality of looking for meanings, messages and the rest wherever I could find them. Give me a few like minded pals, something stimulating to help the evening pass and I'd lead the conversation into undreamed of interpretations of anything and everything. Paul Bannon with his combination of seething miserable undercurrent and the positive role of a goal hunting forward player had the same, hard to fathom, combination of opposites as the soft spoken clinical killers played by Clint Eastwood. At least, that was the way I told it back at college. More to the point, I went to two games to get grounded in old familiar surroundings and Paul Bannon scored in both. He sure as hell had something. He bagged another brace, with concrete still visible on the Warwick in mid-April. All this and you could still catch sight of him walking back from an attack or wandering into position from a set piece with his head down. Bannon had sunken cheeks and an expression that suggested he read miserable French novels for kicks.

Maybe I just needed Bannon. 'Cool' as a student often revolves around contemplating the messages for us all cooked up by miserable writers with a history of not being held enough as babies. I got Sartre, Camus and the rest but they didn't grab me. Paul Bannon - by contrast - was a revelation. For starters, he embodied existentialism in a way anyone could understand. Just relax here, I'm not going to start poncing on about all that self-centred crap. I did enough of that at college. But it goes with football, sometimes. Albert Camus, who could write about alienation, the human condition and futility saw it all first hand from between the goalposts. He played once as an international. Paul Bannon's football had the world-weary quality of Camus' writing. Peter Beardsley, by contrast, existed somewhere between the philosophical schools of depth fronted by Emlyn Hughes and Bonnie Langford. If we contrast their two styles we could say that Bannon's head down, sunken cheek expression says to us, 'The goal is merely a fleeting moment in a journey of abject and unavoidable pointlessness.'

Beardsley's scurrying, fast flowing passing and lay-off game of the time also has a message to the world: 'Hey I'm enjoying my football and I can't wait for my beans on toast afterwards.'

Beardsley and Bannon got totally different treatment from the crowd. Bannon was never a favourite and, despite almost five years at Brunton Park, he took frequent stick. For my money he combined the same qualities as some favourites, like Billy Rafferty. Not a touch player, but effective. His strike record wasn't that bad. He scored regularly and achieved under the 'management' of Bobby Moncur. Moncur was never a manager to think laterally when dour predictability would do. Even if I'm half right about Bannon those team talks at the end of the Moncur era must have been a riot.

MONCUR - The scouting is pretty solid. They're weak in the left side of defence. Georgie I'm looking to you to carry the ball into their back left. Beardo, every time George is running forward with the ball you cut in right from wherever you are. When George delivers the ball turn your man and flash it over the box. Stanny and Paul should be running on and if we move fast enough there will be space in the middle because they'll have to pull men out of position to cover the weakness on the left. Any questions?

BANNON - Why?

MONCUR - Cos they're weak there. There's no mobility on the left side of their defence.

BANNON - But why?

MONCUR - Cos they've got injury problems. We can exploit their...

BANNON - Why boss, why?

MONCUR - Eh?

BANNON - Why are we here, what is it all for?

MONCUR - Cos you're getting decent money to play football.

BANNON - But what does it all mean?

MONCUR - Mean?

BANNON - Yeah, life and that. What does it mean?

MONCUR - There's something wrong wi' you Bannon, I dunno what it is but I'm gonna get to the bottom of it if it's the last thing I do.

BANNON - It's all bottom, there's no such thing as 'top,' in the end everything is futile.

SQUAD - Fucking shut up etc etc.

Bannon and Beardsley first played together under the functional and frequently ineffective management of Bobby Moncur. Bobby Moncur, to the best of my knowledge, never did fathom the enigma that was Paul Bannon. The last thing Moncur did at Carlisle was part-company with the club around the time Dawn and I split. He went on to manage Hearts and take them to a similar level of stumbling mediocrity as the Carlisle team he left behind him. Who or what he is managing now, I don't know. If your local supermarket opens an area of listless displays it might be worth looking at the pictures of the managers they like to display out front. You never know...

Martin Harvey was in charge by March 1980. Harvey's main weapon in the new tactical armoury appeared to have been to turn up the speed control. Where Moncur's 'tactics' seemed to involve people holding positions, running into predictable gaps and generally shouting through a megaphone to tell the opposition what was coming, Harvey had gone for the revolutionary idea that you could enjoy your football. Tactically we weren't that different but the added speed, the odd bit of invention and the extra yard of pace that comes from having a good time was a welcome change. Carlisle and myself both pulled ourselves out of the depths as the cold wet winter of 1980 turned into the cold wet spring before taking a headlong Joe Laidlaw style dive into a wet summer.

One week after Easter we bagged five goals in two home games, Bannon got three of them and took stick from the terraces in both games. Promotion was a mathematical possibility. Still the crowds didn't come. There were bigger clubs likely to grab the promotion places, and mid-table position for most of the season hadn't done much to inspire confidence, but my faith was returning. Harvey's team took crowd pleasing seriously, and in the second half against fellow promotion outsiders Reading we ran hard and fast in search of both points. Behind for a good part of the game, an unremarkable but highly effective Bannon strike finally secured a point. I didn't see any of the final three games. Shame when there was a Bannon brace in the final home game against Colchester. Still, I'd rekindled the faith, despite apathy from my fellow students. I'd manage the odd conversation about England or top flight teams but Carlisle didn't rate with anyone. One smart-arse once labelled the Third Division the 'Turd' Division.

I met a lot of people from Sunderland but even more from 'SUNNERLAND.' That is Sunnerland as shouted fast and loud with a sharp stop at the end of it. I once had something going with a girl who lived just off Roker Avenue, in the shadow of Roker Park. My whole idea of football crowds was changed the day I tried to get to my girlfriend's place and found myself walking against Sunderland's home support. Carlisle were playing out the late season in front of three and half thousand fans on a good day. Sunderland were fighting for top flight survival in front of ten times that number. Sunderland, with a population of 300,000, was - in 1980 - Britain's biggest town. The entire population of Cumbria was less than half a million.

These people, their power and the sheer scale of the whole thing came home to me one day. Crammed together in the bedroom a few streets away from the ground it was still - just about - possible to follow the game on the back of the shouts that carried a few hundred yards. The odd sense of being involved but also being totally distant from the game put the dwindling crowds and the futile last minute scramble for a Third Division promotion miracle into perspective.

Despite this, the season ended on a positive feeling for me because Carlisle had been there for me at a time when I needed them, and the familiarity of the ground, the shirts, the crowd and the rest had been part of that healing process.

The season of 1980/81 dawned with me alone at home. It's twenty to five on 16 August, I'm facing the prospect of a long bus ride with a walk on the end only to be savaged by a neglected dog. Was it worth it? Carlisle United 0 - Sheffield United 3. I'm not saying we were complete shapeless shit with a death wish thrown in, but two weeks later the crowd for a league game on a Saturday afternoon in bloody August was down below three thousand. That day - our fourth match without a win - we were complete shapeless shit and the 1-4 hammering we suffered at home to the matchless Newport County was verging on a let off. Hell, earlier that year me and Carlisle had both hauled ourselves from unaccustomed deep holes. I thought we'd turned a corner together. Newport! I mean, Newport bloody County, come on. They put four past us. A month later I'd turned twenty one and headed off for my final year at college. There was a complete lack of Third Division teams within striking distance of Sunderland. The closest games were in Carlisle and in one of them the week after I went back to college a Carlisle team containing Peter Beardsley and a couple of old-timers who'd seen much better days - Bobby Parker and George McVitie - took an almighty stuffing at Fortress Brunton. Chesterfield ran out 2-6 winners sticking three goals without reply in the Carlisle net in the last forty five minutes. I could still talk up Paul Bannon to the handful of my fellow students who gave a shit. There was a grim security in all of this but Carlisle's position as a punch bag for the high flying likes of Chesterfield and Newport bloody County rendered them invisible to most football fans. I could talk bollocks about any obscure band and find a soulmate but my lower league fixation was a lonely passion at college. Still, I was happier than I'd been for the best part of a year. The main reason for this was another serious revelation that hit me in that memorable year. I wasn't thick after all.

Up to that point, I'd never been so sure. Thinking about my situation as part of the intellectual elite of the country I reasoned it a bit like this. My O'levels had been conjuring tricks of a sort. Slap in a week's hard revision and even the maths started to make sense. My sixth form party time had been saved by some decent blagging in the history exam and the ray of hope offered to all bullshitters in the form of A' level general studies. With around seven months of the degree course remaining, I knew that I'd have to learn something if I was going to make it out with a qualification. Having opted for a Conference level course, I'd finished my second season as a student staring relegation into the Unibond Premier League full in the face. One tutor, tearing apart an essay that had involved a whole hour's effort on my part, informed me that he'd left the mark where it was because another one per cent off would have left me failing a module. Frankly, he couldn't be arsed wading through more of the same shit if I was forced to re-submit for his part of the course.

Somehow or other I had to turn this around or fail. The only person who'd managed to get me into the library on a regular basis had been Dawn. At the end of 1980 I started hauling myself down there on my own. I started building a collection of hardbacked, thick and serious books in my room. Where the previous use of a hard-backed book might have been as a surface for skinning up I was now reading them. My friends started to fear for me. The first signs that something was seriously wrong came that Christmas. I took home essay titles, due in weeks ahead, and spent entire afternoons writing. I'd been able to gauge the time I was taking on essays before by the number of albums I got through. I wasn't kidding about the sixty minutes for the shite essay that reduced my tutor to insults. If I remember that one correctly it took both sides of the second Clash album and around one side of the first Undertones album. Now, I left essays unfinished after an entire afternoon, went back for more in the evening and even took more than one day over getting them right.

Given the way our lives kept shadowing each other, Carlisle United duly responded by beating Burnley 3-2 at home on Boxing Day. Shit season so far, scrappy game, decent Beardsley goal to seal the points and a new recruit at the back. For £100,000 Paul Haigh should've been decent. This was 1980 and we were at the arse end of the Third Division facing relegation into the bottom flight. Even today teams in that position fill their trousers in the face of six figure transfer fees. With Haigh and Staniforth together we had almost a quarter of a million pounds of 'talent' in two bodies. Haigh's addition to the defence was down to Bob Stokoe, restored to the dugout following the early season stuffings suffered by Martin Harvey's team. Carlisle United had reacted by telling Martin Harvey to get stuffed and calling in the dependable and experienced ex-manager. Stokoe duly saw his team humbled 2-6 at home to Chesterfield but he slowly got a grip on the results.

I had a soft spot for Martin Harvey, mainly because he wasn't Bobby Moncur. I also valued the boost his team had given me earlier that year. Harvey had been offered a coaching position beside Bob Stokoe and he told United where to stuff it. He was certainly better than the league position in September 1980 suggested, but it's a hell of a lot easier to argue that from the safe distance of history than it was then to watch a once great team teetering on the edge of the lowest league. In the face of a panic situation the one guy you would want on your side is Bob Stokoe. After leaving Carlisle for Blackpool he'd seen higher highs and lower lows than Carlisle had managed in over fifty years. He'd taken Sunderland to a cup victory that defied belief, and a season later he'd been sacked by the same club when the Second Division narrowly failed to crumble before the cup winners.

There were some suggestions that Stokoe could do an Alan Ashman and produce miracles. He didn't. The Boxing Day scramble to victory was pretty much par for the course of a season in which we fought for survival and ended up - survivably - in nineteenth place. The lowest league position 'enjoyed' by any Carlisle team since my blooding as a supporter. More typical performances than Boxing Day took place in two home games over Easter. Two draws, one goal, plenty of kick and rush football and my first sighting - in a blue shirt - of Bryan 'Pop' Robson.

With his comb-over strand flapping above his balding head and his shirt sleeves rolled up, Robson looked like a down-market Bobby Charlton. He was thirty five, packing a body that could never be described as athletic and signed - in all probability - as a result of Stokoe's Sunderland connections. Having played out his highest profile years at Newcastle United and West Ham Pop had moved on to star in Sunderland's Second Division years. With Sunderland just clinging on to top flight action, he wasn't figuring in the plans.

Like a prize-fighter at the end of his career Pop had the moves - in a rusty sense - and he had retained the one thing that had always seen him through, his punch. Pop was an out and out striker and the down-market Charlton idea isn't too wide of the mark. Where Charlton was deadly with a run and shot starting forty yards out, Robson could do the same from eighteen yards. We needed goals, we lacked shape and we could scramble attacks in an unpredictable fashion. If the tactical master plan showed the failings of a team built on two expensive signings and a bunch of journeymen and grafters, at least we had Pop. There was no sense of dominance on the pitch that season. We could still put the odd ball deep into opposition territory and muster a charging wall of blue shirts to chase it. So long as the rotund form of Pop Robson was thereabouts, there was a chance of a goal. Like Ian Rush, the guy could score goals as if his life depended on it. And, like Rushy, you'd be struggling to argue the merits of many of them as classics. The nineteenth place we'd managed was survival, just. To put Robson's impact into perspective it is worth looking at the final positions.

Four clubs finished that season on 41 points. We were third in that list of four. Our goal scoring performance was poor, Walsall, below us were only one goal worse. Forty points or less and you were in the shit. Remember, these were still the days of two points for a win, so the totals that year were slightly higher than average in the Third Division drop zone. We were one point from disaster. Proof that it could happen to us and we could find ourselves in the bottom flight was staring us in the face. As we stumbled through three straight league defeats in our final games we were faced with the worrying sight of bigger clubs with bigger histories shambling along below us. I saw nothing after Easter when Pop Robson hammered home an unmemorable and vital strike to gain one point against Exeter. We finished the season in nineteenth, two places below us Sheffield United finished with forty points and a goal difference that would have done credit to a mid-table side. Remember, they'd run in three of those goals in

August stuffing a Carlisle side that bordered on complete shapeless shit with a death wish! We scrambled a point away in Sheffield when the deep, indescribable enigma that was Paul Bannon scored our second goal in the second half. I wasn't there but I'll bet he didn't smile.

So let's give Pop his due. He played nine games, scored six goals and managed in that total to net two winning goals and two that sealed 1-1 draws. Take any one of those goals away and we were dead meat. Paul Bannon only managed the same goal tally and he played all season. Pop Robson wasn't classy. He was on target, decisive, and not known to shirk a tackle.

I'd teetered into the 'dead meat' area myself, academically speaking. Having bordered on academic oblivion before turning it round I finished the college season with a better string of results than three straight defeats. In reality I was only going to scrape a passable degree. Some of the final grade of the course depended on second year work, and I'd done sod all during my second year. I got stuck into the coursework with a vengeance and discovered that my brain worked better than I'd dared expect. The transformation was - roughly speaking - the difference between riding a bike without gears and changing onto a Harley. I hit speeds and levels of performance I'd only dared dream about and all I'd done was start treating the course as if it mattered. Submitting essays ahead of time, doing the reading that the lecturers suggested and actually planning something before I put it on paper. I'd also bought a typewriter to help with my fledgling sideline as a music journalist. Given the handicap I'd given myself by way of missed second year marks, there wasn't a hope in hell I'd catch up all the way, but I was getting marks that dragged my previous relegation performance comfortably into the level of mid-table. At the end of the course I was coming up fast in the current form league, an earlier start at the same level of performance and I'd have been challenging for a place in Europe. You get the general idea. I'd scrambled out of trouble and finally learned something worth knowing, I was capable of hard work!

I had one final summer in the factory. I'd had a fairly easy ride for a student during the successive summer shutdowns. That summer they finally got me! I was working with Dog. His birth certificate said Dennis Osborne Graham. Saddle someone with the initials D.O.G. and that deep-thinking Cumbrian approach to original nicknames will do the rest. Dog was great, he could pace a job to perfection, he'd talk away and share jokes all day and, once or twice, he'd put me up on a Friday night when I was planning to meet Geg's former lady friend, Lorraine, in Wigton. One afternoon Dog started working like he'd swallowed a serious hit of speed for lunch. This should have warned me. He was cutting lengths of pipe, the cheery crack was gone and he looked stressed. In the middle of the panic he blurted out a request.

'Hey Vitas,' [The year I'd started at the factory Vitas Gerilitus had made the semi-finals at Wimbledon. His long fluffy blond hair looked slightly like mine.

I'd been 'Vitas' at the factory ever since.]

'Hey Vitas, I've got a rush job on. Can you gan' oot and ask Lindsay if his sister is dancing on Border News tonight.'

Lindsay Thwaites was also working at the factory. He'd had a reputation as the hardest kid in the year above me at school, but Lindsay was no thug. Lindsay was an intelligent bloke, easily as bright as anyone I'd met at college and a guy who could see both sides of a problem well enough. I'd got on reasonably well with him that final summer. Dog's request struck me as odd but I went with it because I'd been around these lads long enough to trust them. Idiot!

It struck me that I didn't remember Lindsay's sister at school. I'd got about this far when I asked if she was dancing on television that night. Lindsay went quiet, threatening sort of psycho quiet. Then he growled, 'You bastard! My sister is a cripple.' He was moving, slowly, in my direction and I knew I'd had it. I was going home in an ambulance, if I got lucky. Since I was gonna die anyway, I was slowly edging backwards because I'd spotted a lead hammer lying on a bench. He was going to do me. Despite me giving it the predictable 'I didn't know, honest,' flannel, he was still coming. I would go down fighting back with a lead hammer. Me and a lead hammer versus Lindsay's bare hands was still like putting in a gerbil to fight a lion. A few seconds dragged like hours and then Lindsay laughed out loud.

I was right, he never had a sister. What a laugh eh?

The screaming nightmares ceased sometime in early 1983, eighteen months after that I came off the medication.

I was registered for tax now, in need of regular income and weighing up the career options whilst I waited for someone to offer me shitloads of cash for my writing.

I was going to have to do something about doing something and, after the factory, the real world was closing fast. Fifteen miles down the road from my country home Bob Stokoe was thinking about doing something to keep a once proud football team out of Division Four.

7 Jack Ashurst

Mentioned for the first time in this chapter:

These are my opinions not facts. Others - especially those mentioned below - are likely to disagree.

Jack Ashurst - Mr No Nonsense, dependable defender. A stalwart worthy of selection in any era at Brunton Park.
Tommy Craig - Been around, seen it all, so he decided on Brunton Park. Arguably the best manager we never had!
Ian - AKA Ian Teasdale, a good mate from Aspatria. Not a noted football fan.
Bob Lee - He looked like a centre forward, sometimes displayed the mobility of a hot air balloon marooned in quicksand, and still put it about well enough to score a dozen goals in two seasons.
Lesley - my little sister. Has never been to Brunton Park, does watch Newcastle United.
Thomas Ritchie - Another Scot in the ranks, loaned from Sunderland to add some decent passing to a team blended in battle since August 1981. Stayed a few months in 1982.
Dave Rushbury - Not as fast as his name would suggest. Thin, angular, occasionally clattering, defender.

So, at last, it was time for the real world. The world in which results mattered and you had to work to make yourself a winner. The Football League responded to my new found position as a person in search of results with a system in which every win was worth three points. Looking at the previous season's 'results' suggested there would be little change in Carlisle's league position but the points total might go up by a dozen or so. However, whilst I was edging towards the lead hammer at British Sidac, Carlisle had been busy in the transfer market. Given the lowly league position of the previous season our pulling power was reduced. Then again we had Stokoe, a man who had already proven his worth as a signer of talent on a tight budget.

At the back, during the previous season, we'd leaked like a bucket full of holes. In search of composure we'd run around in circles and shouted at each other. In August 1981 we acquired Jack Ashurst and Dave Rushbury. Ashurst from the tragic Blackpool, a team so desperate they'd finished below us in the Third Division the previous year. Rushbury from Swansea. Dave had the same strange angular features as Paul Bannon, while Ashurst looked like Beardsley's more sensible big brother. Given the strange angular features of goalie Trevor Swinburne I wouldn't have been surprised to hear rumours of inbreeding linked to the team. Imagine a gaggle of Greg Rusedski faces and you've got the general idea. The limited movement and dinosaur quick reactions of the zombiesque Bob Lee - a summer signing from the hopelessly free-falling Bristol Rovers - were less of a bonus.

As August rolled into September I was stumbling towards job applications, the odd visit to my mate Ian starting his PhD in Liverpool, and the strange realisation that the traditional disastrous start to the season hadn't materialised. Pop Robson popped one home in each of the opening games which left us with a truly middling position and record of W-1, D-1, L-1 goals for 6, goals against 6. Hell, at least we weren't bottom. On my 22nd birthday Carlisle, and I, celebrated the first win, 3-2 over Southend. The short, stocky and decidedly human presence of Beardsley, Robson and Ashurst on the same pitch gave the team an odd look. Their physical similarity combined with the angular wonders mentioned earlier, meant that there were two groups of three people in the team who looked like close relatives to each other. The truly individual Paul Bannon was missing, in fact he didn't get a run out until the end of November.

I stumbled around in search of work, knocked out some writing and a few job applications on my typewriter and wandered into everything from an unpaid stint in local radio to some semi-regular kick arounds with a few old school mates. My luck changed when my good luck charm appeared to predictable jeers. Bannon bagged three goals in his first two games as November turned into December. Around the same time I'd hit lucky, if you'd call it that, with some job applications.

The advert in the local paper said 'Lecturer in Communications' at Carlisle Technical College, my degree was in Communication Studies and I slapped in an application. Around the same time, my Dad's mate Mike, who worked at West Cumbria College in Workington and Whitehaven, mentioned they were short of staff and desperately short of a lecturer to teach Body Systems. I was doing nothing and felt up for it once I discovered that the hourly rates put most other casual employment to shame. The idea of teaching Body Systems was a riot. I'd taken A' level biology and failed it. So had my little sister. The one thing Lesley had over me was a neat set of notes, still lying around the house. A week after Mike mentioned they were looking for someone, I jogged onto the turf to face a packed house of social care students in Workington. The crowd was well into double figures, putting it on a par with anything at Borough Park that season. By this point I was also on the books at Carlisle where they'd dropped me into mid-field for their team who were teaching Communications and General Studies.

The Communication Studies soon expanded to work in Workington teaching a cracker of a subject, 'Social and Life Skills.' I was teaching kids on the new YTS scheme.

You have to question the wisdom of putting a former mouthy posh git with a newly acquired degree in front of a bunch of hardened Cumbrian kids. Once I was well into a visit to the threadbare excitement of the old Tullie House museum I was spinning out the stuffed birds to add another twenty minutes to the riveting 'lesson' when one of the YTS kids launched into a discussion on several unsolved local crimes and the likely culprits. Remember, I was there to teach him Social and Life Skills!

These 'kids' were more streetwise than I could ever hope to be and more informed on survival than the people who put together programmes on Communication Studies and Social and Life Skills. Some of them also knew Carlisle United and one route to respect in Carlisle was to discuss the players and high flying First Division team I'd seen. Whilst I'd been on the terraces these kids were still drawing matchstick pictures of their mums. In Workington I had to survive more on my wits but, once we'd exhausted the meagre local attractions, there was - at least - a roller disco.

I was working hard to grind out results but there was a developing shape to my play and I came away with something in most of the encounters. I'd been thrown in with a group of Carlisle welders on a Friday evening. These guys were third years and they'd seen off a steady stream of part-time staff in their time. By the ninth week I'd struggled through most of the obvious stuff. I hadn't a hope in hell of talking about the services in the local Post Office. We were plumbing the depths of depravity in discussions and running our way through the handful of worthy and outdated films in the college when one of the students pointed out to me that nobody had lasted as long in their company as I had. Given the stunts they were famous for pulling, including walking from room to room above the ground floor and outside the building, I wasn't totally convinced of this fact. Later on, one of their tutors confirmed that it was true. Hell, if I could survive this, maybe I had a future in this game.

If I was grinding out results and improving my game plans, so were Carlisle. By Christmas we were well established as front runners with an ability to slog it out rather than impress with our class. Stokoe's fighting spirit and sublime ability to blend a tactical plan with limited resources was showing the others in that limited division the way home. Peter Beardsley was sometimes great but also wildly inconsistent. I'd realised some time before that he was genuine class but that is a mixed blessing in the lower divisions where ageing, limited and frustrated defenders assault nippy young hopefuls. Beardsley's lack of height always put him in the firing line for such attention but probably the worst challenge he faced that season came from a young defender by the name of Steve Bruce. As the fierce December weather set in with a vengeance, Bruce left Beardsley pole-axed on the Brunton Park turf with a challenge that would have been ruled out of order in a Bruce Lee movie. Both players would become household names, that day their careers could have come to grief.

The weather went from bad to newsworthy. On 19 December the only game in the division was at Bristol Rovers. We won with a Bob Lee goal. I wasn't there, I can only assume it was a mud-bath because fast moving runs which glided past defenders were not exactly a Bob Lee speciality. Furious flailing mud-spattered surges at goal on the other hand... Yeah, it must have been a heavy pitch and shit home defence at Bristol because Bob Lee scored. Against his old team as well. Maybe they just stood back and laughed as he ran at them with his usual mixture of bluster and incompetence. Mechanical Bob Lee's strike mattered because those points put us on top of the table. The first time we'd been top of a table since August 1974 when we'd been top of bloody everything.

I was there on 30 January for the top of the table clash with Lincoln City. I was one of about four thousand who saw Paul Bannon bury the winner. He looked oddly depressed after scoring the only goal in a game that kept us top. But, that's the wacky, manic-depressive, world of Paul Bannon for you. Then again, maybe he had a point. He is credited with the goal. In truth he collided with a clearance and the ball hit the back of the net. All he had to do was to be, to exist, to fill that space at that time. It was a Paul Bannon sort of moment, doubtless he pondered it with his usual abject misery.

BANNON - What is man, what does he do but fill a certain space at a certain time in the generally futile hope that he might achieve something by accident?

THE REST OF THE DRESSING ROOM - Shut up man, we're top of the league.

As an aside here, it's worth noting that my treatment of Bannon was the subject of more e-mails than anything else after the first edition of this book. He'd been a cult hero and I was surprised to discover my take on the Bannon enigma was shared by a few who'd loved him for exactly the same reasons. Somebody else also explained to me why he always looked so miserable. It's not funny and we're not going there, ever.

And so it went. Carlisle grinding out results with a team built from a range of misfits and hopefuls. There was promising young talent - the most promising of which, Peter Beardsley, generated a club record fee of £275,000 on his way to Vancouver Whitecaps. He'd be back on loan but he'd never be ours again. He'd cause us nightmares in 1998 but we've got a few adventures to share before that game.

Amongst the journeymen we had Jack Ashurst. Solid defender, club captain and taker of shit from no man. Paul Haigh, the man whose six figure transfer fee had put several pins in the Martin Harvey voodoo doll, came good under the watchful eye of Jack Ashurst. Pop Robson kept popping and Bannon plied his world-weary trade scoring goals which looked like they were dying of apathy even as they crossed the line. Bobby Parker - the only link with the First Division - had his best season since the top flight and Trevor Swinburne's athletic impersonations of Alan Ross looked convincing.

Never pretty, barely athletic in some quarters, this was a team built to sweat.

In an average season, surrounded by average opposition, Stokoe's tactical plans began to tell. The veteran Scots campaigner Tommy Craig joined the mid-field for the later half of the season and Thomas Ritchie - another Scot - arrived, allegedly as interpreter for Craig. In all probability Ritchie was there to add to the percentage of passes that hit the target. Five draws in six games over February and March took the edge off the manic surge to the top but we kept scoring as Ashurst ran the defence like his own personal protection squad. Physically, philosophically and in terms of hairstyles Bannon and Pop didn't exist in the same universe. Somehow they managed to forge a partnership on the pitch that rattled in goals in the face of last-ditch defensive tackles. The lanky and deep one with the 'tache and the jovial, baldy little side-kick picking up the crumbs and mimicking the behavior of the other. It had proven itself a killer combination once before but let's not drag up Hitler and Mussolini this late in the day eh?

Speaking of dragging up history and horror, the 81/82 season brought another twist in the on-going fortunes of Carlisle and Workington. A futile attempt to play out an FA Cup tie with the mighty Bishop Auckland ended in a swamp at Brunton Park and with a serious winter setting in and fixture congestion piling up, somebody looked at the map, realised Sellafield was close by and reckoned on the radioactive warmth of the Solway solving the problem. And so it was that Borough Park, Workington, heaved under the crush of four and half thousand bodies and saw a professional team in the shape of Carlisle fight out a hurricane blasted encounter with non-league minnows. Heavy pitch, furious encounter and - naturally enough - a Bob Lee deciding goal. It could have been, should have been, a mad head-down charge on the Bishop Auckland goal with elbows flailing, mud flying and defenders taking flight and landing amongst the tightly huddled supporters. Instead it was a header in enough space to allow the slow wits of the god of gormless goal-getting to get a gormless goal, in a god-like way. Trust me, Bob Lee and Borough Park were made for each other. Following the league slow-down we came to grief at promotion chasing Fulham when we leaked three in the first half and ended up 1-4 losers.

Around this time I was also slowing down. The repeating of the same old stuff in class left me thinking seriously about the game plans. I could do it. The real question was whether I wanted it. There were changes going on in my life. One of them had created some suspicion. The previous November I'd been out with the gang I'd joined after coming home from college. Hitting the Sunset Inn at Silloth we'd done the usual few pints, few dances and unwinding after a hard week. I was meeting the same people on Sundays to play football and this would soon develop into scratch matches against other hopeless local outfits.

I can recall one moment quite well. I was sitting alone at a table with a pint in front of me, once I'd downed this one I'd got almost a gallon on board and I was near enough stone cold sober. I remember my Dad once telling me about 'celebrating' his 21st birthday in the Royal Artillery. Marooned somewhere on the far side of nowhere he and a couple of others downed a bottle of whisky - each! There was, supposedly, a peculiar biological quirk in the clan which allowed us to build a tolerance for alcohol that was almost unreal. Let's get this in perspective. I've been drunk in my life. On several celebrated nights this has been spectacular. But, slow the rate down to manageable proportions and I could knock the stuff back all night and still read a book before I fell asleep.

I was sat at the Sunset Inn that night watching a gorgeous girl on the dance floor who bore more than a passing resemblance to Angie Dodd on my degree course. It struck me that I was clear headed enough to drive her home although I'd got enough beer on board to give a blood sample with a head on top. I started mentally replaying classic Carlisle goals and generally searching out the stuff that needed concentration. Anything I wanted from any part of my brain was still there and I was well into my seventh pint. It started with a decision to stop drinking for a month. The purpose of this was to lose some of the tolerance and allow myself to get lashed again. Honest, I never intended it to last over twenty years when I started. It's just that I never really missed it. In terms of satisfying, mind-bending experiences drink was always a poor second to sex and drugs, allegedly.

I've been quietly asked if I was an alchy, whether I was taking powerful medication for some serious and life threatening condition, and more than one person has simply asked me what was wrong. I quit drinking, okay? I also started seeing Kate Graham again, sometimes at the Sunset and, since she knew the DJ I often ended up in the booth with her and Barry, the said DJ. This allowed me to slip in the odd record at the bottom of Barry's stack as he lined the singles up for the turntables. My tastes had headed in every bizarre musical direction I could find over the previous few years but the Sunset crowd wouldn't shift to anything but the familiar. The best I managed was a regular play for Pigbag's *Papa's Got A Brand New Pigbag*. This crowd liked it straight, uncomplicated and heavily smattered with chart fodder.

A few months after I'd stopped frequenting The Sunset the mighty John Peel did a gig there and found himself squeezing his chubby frame through a toilet window before the end of the night's festivities. This undignified escape owed everything to the fact that the chart sounds crowd were attempting to kill him for the crime of playing unpopular, mysterious and intelligent records. Peel was working on his autobiography when he died. In 2003 he'd heard through some mutual contacts that I knew something about the Sunset gig and rang me one afternoon for the story. Since his version may never see publication, this is what I understand:

In the Summer of 1982 the Sunset asked its members questions about what they wanted to see in the place. Some of our gang voted for Peel. The management of The Sunset spotted the trend in their market research and booked

Peel, but by the night in question several of the gang, myself included, were employed many miles away. Most of the Peel listeners I knew in Cumbria were not Sunset members and only heard about the gig after the near riot made local news. The Sunset - by contrast - thought they'd cracked it simply by booking a Radio 1 DJ. The crowd that night included a crowd from Cheri-Foam and a hen party. To the end of his life Peel rated it the worst gig of his career. The real choker is that enough people to have filled the place twice over found out about the gig after the riot and wondered why the hell they hadn't known it was happening.

My new healthy lifestyle included a reasonable amount of time in Kate's company and close attention to Carlisle United. Bob Lee's regular selection was an insight into the true quality of the side. Any side relying on his levels of invention in the box was going to be short of class. But this was a Stokoe team! Eleven men of varying abilities blended into a fighting machine because the great man could make it happen. When we'd gone top he'd stated we weren't that good. Stokoe, wasn't easily fooled.

There were moments - Bobby Parker had two against Millwall. One of them he put through our net and the other splattered a Millwall defender's scrotum over eighteen square yards of pitch. With the poor sod practically into an out of body experience of agony, Tommy Craig netted the rebounding ball and the home crowd celebrated whilst a few of us couldn't help clutching our own nuts in sympathy. Having been reminded of the frailty of all human flesh the only person fit to score a winner was Paul Bannon. He duly delivered. Spring broke over Cumbria and life was changing. The impossible was happening, I was teetotal and the home crowd were right behind my man Bannon!

Wimbledon, the southern gits who'd replaced Workington were summarily stuffed at the start of May. We were - potentially - one win away from automatic promotion with five games still to play. Wimbledon had even managed to score our winning goal themselves. This lot from the London suburbs were a complete disgrace, they'd never amount to anything and their place in the Third Division was rightfully under threat.

This far from the end of the season near certain promotion was a cheering thought as the war escalated in the South Atlantic and a predictable England squad warmed up for the World Cup finals. Three away games generated one point at Reading and the jitters really struck home when we faced the southern scum at Wimbledon. They'd committed suicide at Brunton Park but they stuffed us in London. The opposition were closing, we were running out of games.

Boring Bob Lee was dropped for the last home game, with Bristol Rovers, his old club. We had a perfect warm May day. Three points would ensure promotion. One more point - away at Chester - would make us champions. I managed to rekindle some of the old feeling, more so because the team ran to the centre of the pitch and staged the same wave to the crowd that had ended the First

Division season. The division that year had been dire all round which was why such a mediocre Carlisle side could stride out with promotion in sight.

We were shit. So bad that Bob Lee would have improved things. Solid and gormless as he was, he could have been useful. The rest of the team could have picked him up and used him as a battering ram to clear a path to the Bristol goal. It took £120,000 of Staniforth striking talent to score our only goal. A penalty. Bristol Rovers scored two. 1-2 at half time, we came out fighting. There were fast desperate moves on the Bristol goal. The only fluid movements were filling the trousers of disbelieving Cumbrians as chance after chance went begging. We put pressure on their defence, made the spaces and shot at low flying aircraft. The spirit of Mike Barry was alive and well just when we needed it least.

I didn't go to Chester. We won, with another unremarkable looking goal from the one player old and experienced enough to have seen many bigger games. Thanks Pop, you made all the difference. Twelve months before he'd earned us survival in the Third Division, this time you got us out of it. Given the end of season nerves, I for one wouldn't have been surprised to see the team that crumbled in front of Bristol Rovers facing the same lowly opposition for another season.

So it was the summer of 1982 and Carlisle United faced big changes and a step up in the class of their work. I was bunging in the odd job application myself.

Blue Nightmare

Once upon a time a man was in London. On a station platform he spied a poster. The poster said, 'ENJOY CARLISLE.'

'Oh that looks a lovely place,' said the man studying the picture of a castle on the poster, 'I must go there.'

So, the man bought a ticket to Carlisle. As he was walking along the platform at Carlisle the man saw a poster. The poster said, 'LONDON IS LOVELY.'

'Oh yes,' thought the man, 'I would really enjoy a visit to London,' so he bought himself a ticket and got back on the train.

But when he got to London he saw the first poster again with its lovely castle. Once more he headed straight for the ticket office and waited his turn before saying, 'A single to Carlisle.'

The man's odd behaviour continued for several days. Although he was reasonably well off, his bank account soon began to run down because the journey between the two cities isn't exactly cheap. This story unfolded in the distant days of British Rail. Their services may have been more punctual than Virgin on this route, but they were not known for offering cheap fares.

On his thirteenth visit to Carlisle station the man got a nasty surprise when the ticket man said to him, 'I'm not taking another bloody cheque, the one you gave me yesterday bounced. Oh, by the way, they've just put a stop on your credit card as well.'

'Oh dear,' thought the man, 'And I so wanted to go to London. It looks exciting on the poster.'

A few hours later the man was rudely awoken by a British Rail guard who discovered him stowing away in the guard's van of a Carlisle to London express.

'Right Pal, you're out on yer arse at the next station,' said the guard showing no respect for the fact that this man was the best private customer that BR had ever seen over a seven day period. When they got to Crewe he kept his promise and flung the man out.

Dusting himself down on the platform the man headed for the gents to wash up. As he did so he passed a poster. It had a picture of the rough end of Crewe on it and some words. They read, 'DON'T COME TO CREWE, IT'S CRAP. IF YOU'VE ANY SENSE YOU'LL GO TO LONDON OR CARLISLE.'

8 Don O'Riordan

Mentioned for the first time in this chapter:

These are my opinions not facts. Others - especially those mentioned below - are likely to disagree.

Kevin Carr - Goalkeeping's answer to the chocolate teapot.
Russell Coughlin - Welsh mid-field wizard. Ninety nine parts graft to one part magic.
Scott Endersby - So impressive when playing against us for Swindon that Stokoe signed him. A welcome sight after Kevin Carr.
Gary Fulbrook - Six, little remembered, games 87/88. Our first black player.
Tony Fyfe - The kind of 'star' striker to which we were reduced by the late eighties. The guy has been known to command an opposition penalty area and score goals, but he was playing for Penrith at the time.
Harry Gregg - A manager with heart, no money and a patchy squad. We needed a miracle worker, Harry was a grafter. Maybe in better times...
John Halpin - Fast, skilful and passionate about the game. The best news of the 84/85 season. Just about the only good news after that.
Brent Hetherington - Skilfully challenged, forward playing scorer of a handful of goals. Signed from Workington, managed to cope with the step up in class. Then again, by the late eighties there wasn't much of a step up in class from Workington to Carlisle.
Dean Holdsworth - Yes, he played for us. It was over pretty quickly.
Garry MacDonald - Striker, so unspeakably crap he proved that even Stokoe's astute buying had its failures.
Dave McKellar - Despite being signed from unemployment, the best goalie we'd seen since Alan Ross and an impressive servant to the club for years.
Clive Middlemas - Yup, things were getting desperate in late '87. So desperate we needed a manager who'd seen similar depths. Middlemass had played for Workington. He knew how to cope with desperation.
Eric Nixon - Same name as my Dad, quality keeper signed on loan who made sixteen appearances for Carlisle.
Malcolm Poskett - He came, he scored forty goals, he went. He came back, he scored twenty goals, he went.
Jason Prins - Look, just don't ask! Don't even go there, alright? His fifteen minutes of fame are coming up much later, he gets a name check in this chapter.
Don O' Riordan - Another in the great crowd-pleasing tradition. The man may be a certifiable schizophrenic. Listed as a defender but, in truth, much given to leading everyone on the pitch through the most positive of examples and then

punctuating his performances with shameless attempts to kick opposing strikers over the main stand.
Rich - AKA Richard Philip, initially my mate, later my sister's boyfriend and - from 1990 - my brother-in-law.
Wesley Saunders - Solid and unfussy. Sadly, he wasn't another Don O' Riordan.
Alan Shoulder - Former Newcastle striker, famously signed for the Geordies from non-league soccer and gave up his coal mining job for professional football.
Rod Thomas - Another one making a premature appearance in this chapter. Light years ahead of Jason Prins and worthy of more than fifteen minutes of fame.
Jim Tolmie - ARGHHHHHHH!!!!!!!!!!!!!!

So we were stepping up a gear. I'd attempted as much myself by putting applications around in response to job adverts. Predictable stuff like lecturing and a few pots at a media job. Media wise, you couldn't get a job without experience. So you needed a mate on the inside or the ability to work for free for long enough to earn a break. In Cumbria the chances were limited. I'd put in some time at Radio Carlisle where - amongst other things - I'd got pissed on with rain as a farmer tried to string a sentence together about the price of lambs. As a student, I'd worked with a few others at BBC Radio Newcastle. This was a decent station, I'd been let loose with portable recording equipment to do my own features. I'd had journalism published and in 1982 I placed my first piece of rabid fiction in a magazine. None of this was bringing in decent money.

I got stuck into some adventures. I dropped in on a few communes, mainly hoping to find some sex and drugs. Less than an hour after meeting a girl at one place down south I was on top of her. Afterwards I finally learned her second name. A few days later we were at her London flat, around the start of the new football season. Carlisle were stepping up a gear, I was surrounded by... well, every kind of gear there was. When she wasn't shagging strangers, she was dealing. I made a couple more visits to her place!

On one of these I got an urgent message about an interview at a college in Essex. I knew that I would get a train fare back to Cumbria for simply turning up, I hadn't a clue where Thurrock was and I had a load of scruffy gear packed into my rucksack. Just before Carlisle opened their account with a convincing stuffing of Derby at the Baseball Ground I threw my rucksack into an office in a college that served some scruffy industrial wasteland within sight of the Thames, and waited my turn to talk to a bunch of blokes in suits. The main thing I took to that interview was the ability to start work the following week. My boss - Tony Mulvihill - would later say that the thing he remembered most was that rucksack.

They were talking to me, obviously they were desperate. There were six of us there in all and the first thing they told us was that there were two jobs on offer. We divided ourselves into two groups and I was up against a couple of blokes one of whom wore a loud check suit and couldn't seem to talk about anything but athletics. Hell, I knew I was in with a chance and I left there that afternoon with the offer of a job to go back to. A week later - along with Carlisle United - I was stepping up a level. I had a full-time job and a range of opposition some of which was likely to give me a stiff test.

Carlisle started the season with a similar set of contradictions to the previous year. Three games in they'd been all over the place, humbling a Derby County side who had been awesome within the recent past, losing out to the odd goal in five at home to Grimsby and falling to a 1-4 defeat at Burnley. Given the hurried return, the packing of bags and the long journey to the north bank of the Thames, there wasn't much time to take on board the new team or the new star striker. Malcolm Poskett looked like the sweaty, skinny one hanging in the background in some low-budget American movie just before the red necks in the bar kill a stranger. In ordinary times Watford would have hung on to him. But, with Elton John's money shaping a winning outfit Poskett was surplus stock. Alan Shoulder joined the strike force from Newcastle continuing the great Pop tradition of North Eastern players slumming their final years at Brunton Park. Shoulder and Poskett scored all the goals in the 3-0 demolition of Derby that opened the account.

I was dropped in at the deep end for sure. I had everything from 'ESN' [you were still allowed to say 'Educationally sub-normal' in those days'] to mature engineers who needed demanding Communications work. With wall-to-wall YTS making up most of the other hours I was really thrown in to the job. Almost everything was new and the location took some figuring out. Grays Thurrock is basically nowhere. Its current claim to fame - the proximity of the Lakeside shopping complex - was nowhere in sight in 1982. There was simply an almighty hole in the ground.

Watching Carlisle in this new location meant locating and visiting 'away' grounds. Then again I was close to London and we shared the division with Crystal Palace, Charlton, QPR, Fulham and Chelsea. Palace visited Carlisle in mid-September. I'd been at the hard end of the job a week and I combined getting ready for the next gruelling five days with a short exploration of the delights of Grays Thurrock. 350 miles up the road from Grays, we won 4-1 with Poskett scoring the lot. Hell, I'd have loved to be at Brunton Park for that one. Careers eh? They fuck up your life!

The hard working world was on me with a vengeance. The party time a few months before was well and truly in the past. I had one odd experience that summer that might just have suggested it was time to calm down. We'll keep the names out of this since the others involved went on to responsible jobs.

Basically I was tripping on drugs near the sea. Spaced out and loving the sunset colours and dark clouds. I saw a huge flash. I turned to my mate - who'd done no gear and was keeping me out of trouble. I was after telling him that this was magic gear, there were flashes going off in my head. He was staring wide eyed into the space above us. 'Did you see that?' he said, going on to say lightning had hit an electric wire over our heads and run a sheet of flame across the street. Typical eh, the best moment of a trip and he gets a better hit than me, when he's taken nothing. The rest - like what would have happened if the lightning had hit us - only occurred to me when I'd come down. Maybe, just maybe, there's a message for us all in that little experience.

The 4-1 win over Palace suggested Carlisle would survive when dropped in at the deep end. The fact that I was getting laughs, getting people to write things down and getting out of classrooms alive suggested I was up to the new job as well. I'd been given three and four hour sessions to fill. This, at least, allowed for trips into town, visits to anywhere local that would have us and the odd venture further afield in a mini bus. As to whether any of this would benefit the lives of the Essex YTS further down the line I was dubious. We did get to talk football though. The general verdict on Carlisle was that the inhabitants of Grays knew them like they knew Stenhousmuir, a name on the football results. West Ham, Arsenal and Spurs all drew fans from this crowd and those with an active interest talked in detail about the ICF and West Ham's travelling army. Since our dizzy heights in the recent past had only included lining up against the might of Chesterfield and Grimsby I could only respond with stories of the last time I'd seen West Ham in action, all those years ago when I'd shared wine, chat and an appreciation of Les O' Neill with that travelling rock band at Brunton Park. Still, the students preferred this story to the stuff I covered about the exciting range of services in the Grays Post Office.

Within a month it struck me I could cope with this for a living. I hadn't a fucking clue if I was doing the right thing. I've managed to avoid most of the usual confused phases - mid-life crisis and that - by spending my whole adult life confused about pretty much everything. Then again, there were some positives. I had to knock out page after page of stuff to help me cope and that ended any doubts about whether I'd got the discipline to crack it as a writer.

My boss, Tony Mulvihill, was a real enigma. There was a fair amount of distrust and rumour where he was concerned. He didn't share a lot on a personal basis but to this day I'm still learning from the examples he used to lead us. When our paths finally went in different ways I thanked Tony for teaching me that looking after number one was sometimes the best policy for everyone. It got a laugh from the people we'd worked with but I meant it and it does hold true in many situations. The one thing I learned in the first weeks in that job was that I'm a survivor.

At 22 I was the baby of the team. In fact, I've never worked with anyone in education since who was that young. Further education colleges include some of the best and some of the worst things you're ever likely to see in education. Where I'd landed there were people committed to making the whole thing work. Some because they genuinely cared, some because they cared what they could get out of it. The one common thing about most people working in the area is that they never intended to do it when they left school. I'd fallen into an Essex college. Many on the staff had themselves a little earner on the side so my writing wasn't a problem.

As in Cumbria, some of the old timers were suspicious of the YTS. From one perspective it was a scheme to help those in most need. From another viewpoint it put slave labour back on the agenda and clean buses on the streets. One student I taught on a 'Motor Vehicle' programme complained because they wouldn't let him fix buses in his workplace. Instead, they turned off the bus wash, leaving him to wash double deckers with a hosepipe. Not a lot of laughs in January.

I spent half of my first full-time year trying to put the lives of the YTS into some shape. Results wise I came away with a score draw. Like the YTS in Carlisle, these lads - and they were all lads in my groups - could teach me everything about local crime, tellies available in pub car parks and using three cushions to pot an impossible black on a pool table. I had the edge on basic literacy and how to cope when you have to send that telegram. Somewhere in the middle we all managed to negotiate a pace of work and a survivable pattern to the week.

I'd soon got on top of things to the point that the Second Division fixture list offered some reasonable options for the weekends. Reasonable that was until twenty to five in the afternoon. Heading off to Brunton Park on my own was one thing. Negotiating London with an A-Z in search of the less fashionable grounds was different. The biggest change was the number of supporters travelling through the main stations and the absence of Carlisle supporters in these crowds. I played it close to home when confronted by the trip to Loftus Road in November or Charlton in February. There were Carlisle fans at both games, both involved convoluted train journeys for me and both ended up as disappointing results. Queens Park Rangers who finished top of the division that season were barely worth their 1-0 win over us. Crap game, end of story. We were - by now - struggling at the lower end of the division. I was in over my head and still surviving; I expected to see Carlisle doing the same. There was some of this in evidence at Charlton. Charlton were in the same situation as us - short on skill, short on fans. That one ended without a goal. In the Charlton game Russell Coughlin's beefy frame fought off enough challenges to impress a bunch of cold and apathetic supporters. Where Mally Poskett had a killer instinct and a deceptive level of invention - hell the guy threw in a creative back-heel the day we hammered Palace for 4 - Coughlin simply ran, passed, sweated and collided with the opposition.

I was in unfamiliar territory but I was the same lovable mass of confusion, sick humour, inconsideration and crass stupidity I had always been. Carlisle United had changed. It wasn't just the new faces. The McEwan-Younger logo on the strips was a new departure. I was tee-total, the sponsors were wasting their money on me. I was also getting herded into the crappy away enclosures. Nowhere I went was familiar or friendly territory anymore. The odd lot of an away supporter came home to me in a legendary story which - I think - relates to this season. I didn't make the trip to Stamford Bridge in March 1983. Chris Storey did. Chris had been a couple of years above me at school, started off at art college and shared with me a love of Carlisle, Neil Young and stories about the paranormal. Probably because we tended to finish each other's sentences or repeat the same arguments, we'd managed friendship but didn't exactly hang out together the whole time. On a famous occasion Chris went to a Chelsea/Carlisle game on his own and got set upon by Carlisle supporters at the tube station. The story I heard came third hand and had grown in the telling:

We'd gone down in a six goal encounter because Chelsea - despite their own pathetic position within sight of the drop zone - had put two past us in each half. Chris, alone on the platform, was set upon by a mob of Carlisle supporters who had him figured for a Londoner. When the jostling got to knocking him off his feet he started shouting up about his history as a Carlisle fan. This made things worse since - to the Cumbrians about to land him in casualty - he'd announced himself as a soft southern shite. However, once he'd recited a few legendary Carlisle names they realised he was genuine. This put the pummelling into a different light. Laying off and helping Chris sort himself out they shuffled about a bit, mumbled, 'Sorry, Lad' and - according to one report - insisted Chris came out for the longest and least enjoyable pint of his life. Actually, it was less of an event, Chris e-mailed the real story a few years ago.

By May of 1983 we'd ensured survival in the form of mid-table mediocrity and I was investigating the whereabouts of Craven Cottage for the first time in my life. With two games to go in the league we faced our last away encounter against a team that could, mathematically at least, make it to promotion. In front of a heaving crowd we got a lesson in finishing. Shoulder and Poskett didn't get a look in as they put one past us in each half. The absence of Jack Ashurst and the mighty Paul Bannon would have given me the basis of an excuse if anyone at my work had cared to bring up the subject of the game, but they didn't.

By this point I'd mapped out a life in and around London to go with my work on the fringes of the city. I'd got together with Tricia, a Scot from Kirkaldy who'd been down in the capital long enough to work her way through a succession of jobs. We could get out most weekends and see something in the city although her interest in football extended only to knowing that Raith Rovers were her local club. As Carlisle survived a season back in the Second Division

I finished the academic season somewhere above mid-table mediocrity. I'd performed well enough against the opposition to earn support from the manager and a lengthy discussion of skills and tactical plans for the following year. Like Carlisle, these tactical options had to be drawn from a limited choice. Three hundred and fifty miles up the road Bob Stokoe was also making decisions based on limited options. He drafted in an unemployed recruit - Dave McKellar - as the new first choice goalie. Trevor Swinburne headed for Brentford. No doubt his first days in the new club were a riot as the backroom staff and team members all asked him the same thing.

'What kind of creature is Stan Webb?'

McKellar's 'unemployment' became a legend. In fact, McKellar had faced retirement from the game due to a back injury. Swinburne had gone to Brentford and it was Brentford who were prepared to place McKellar on the scrap heap. Bob Stokoe knew form and players with a depth few others could understand. If Hollywood can make millions with Robert Redford starring in *The Horse Whisperer* what fortune awaits the screenplay and ageing 'name' actor who plays the title role in Bob: The Football Whisperer. It would cost more on catering for that movie than Stokoe had to spend on players that close season. So McKellar was an inspired signing. He would come and go twice from Brunton Park. Years after being consigned to the soccer scrap heap he would sign for Rangers. He might have been cover in Glasgow but when the reserve matches included runs out against Celtic the crowds were respectable. In one reserve game - vs Celtic - McKellar played in front of over 10,000. Bad back or not, he played in every Carlisle game bar two for the next two seasons.

I weighed up a few options that summer. I had a full-time job and I knew I was up to it. I had the chance of one day a week off over two years to get the teaching qualification I lacked. Once you were on top of the job you could make time for other things. There were marathon runners in the same college clocking up mileage during the daylight hours, there were other people running businesses on the side and the main job of educating people was getting done well enough to keep the students coming. I weighed up my own position. I had a few things going for me and several stacked against me. I wasn't going to get a massive advance from a publisher overnight, in fact I'd be lucky to get one at all. I didn't know anyone in the writing business apart from Tricia.

On a personal level I had some shortcomings to consider. Mainly the fact that I'd partied my way through an education that had left me qualified for nowt much. I'd drifted into a job that was starting to look like a long-term prospect. That was fairly normal in my college and some people coped by staggering on doing nothing much for years because - short of shooting a student in front of witnesses - they were un-sackable. That felt wrong to me. The 'star player' potential was there, but then it is there in most youngsters who get dropped into the deep end and survive for a while. Years later in a desperate Carlisle side, we'd look at anyone short of twenty five years old and hope they had potential... even Jason Prins.

For a dosser with seven years of 'could do better' on his school report I'd also started cracking the self-discipline in other areas. I'd started jogging around the time I quit drinking. In 1983 somebody, probably my mate Ian, suggested a crack at the suicidal 49 mile trek around the four highest peaks in Lakeland. A few weeks before the event I'd come badly unstuck, falling down Scafell. At first I thought I'd broken my ankle. I'd only sprained it but I'd done enough damage to leave me hobbling down from three thousand feet. Three weeks before the big day my chances of playing were shot - or were they?

Short of training and fitness on the day, I did it. Somewhere around thirty six miles, coming off the worst section of the lot on the mind numbing grassy slopes that make up the back of High Raise I realised it was on. Stumbling into the check-point at Steel End, with another three thousand footer to go I ran into the rest of the mob. Rich and Ian hadn't any excuse. They were fit and I'd caught them up. Three weeks before, the day after I'd almost broken my ankle, I couldn't even walk properly. We slogged our way over the last mountain and back to Keswick. The secret? Not inspiration, not natural ability, I just wanted it. If you want something badly enough you can overcome the obstacles, ask Dave McKellar and Bob Stokoe.

I was grafting my way to a reasonable level of performance. Strapped for cash, Bob Stokoe set about building a team to challenge for promotion. In addition to McKellar he brought in Don O' Riordon a defender so disciplined he put the unfussy efficiency of Jack Ashurst to shame. I wasn't to know it that summer but Paul Bannon's days in a Carlisle shirt were numbered. Just as well then that as one of my heroes departed Stokoe acquired a born crowd-pleaser. Don O' Riordan wasn't a man to let his feet do the talking when there was a team-mate within earshot. 'Inspirational' barely does the guy justice. Lob a troubling ball into the Carlisle box and it would be Don who killed it with his first touch, blustered past two opposing players and scrambled a clearance to the feet of a breaking Blue. The guy made Peter Shilton's outbursts at team mates look restrained, and could turn up anywhere on the pitch with a telling touch. Hell, he was a defender and he bagged almost twenty goals in two seasons! Telling touches out of position all of them. The man was class to his very bootlaces and yet he hid a character trait that raised his crowd-pleasing antics to the levels few will ever touch. Deep down, O' Riordan possessed a psychopathic tendency that left opposing strikers airborne and stunned and left sore throats for the Blue Army as we screamed with absolutely no conviction, 'He fucking dived.' The really entertaining part of this trait was its unpredictability. Faced with an incisive run on the Carlisle goal Don could tackle fairly for the ball, lay it off and lay into the rest of the defence with a fury that would tighten things up for a few minutes. Faced with an acre of space, a 50/50 ball and the certainty of a 2-0 lead already in the bag, O' Riordan could win the ball, slip his man and then respond to a second challenge with an all out assault that would leave the sound of cracking bones echoing around the ground. Hell, Don was a find in the great tradition of Carlisle characters. By placing O' Riordan next to Ashurst and putting David McKellar behind the pair of them, Stokoe had excelled himself. To put this in context in 82/83 we conceded 70 goals. The following season we leaked 41. Bob Stokoe, genius on a shoestring, I rest my case.

Stokoe and me, it was going to take graft for both of us. I've never grown to love the south east and even people in the south east would struggle to like Grays Thurrock. Just take it from me, it's Cleator Moor on Thames. It was an effort to face it some days and an effort to stay with Carlisle United. Sticking it out in Grays meant building part of my life around dates when we faced southern teams, the unpredictability of cup competitions and looking at the fixture list before deciding which weekends I'd head home. Add to this an inordinate interest in the promotion and relegation of teams I'd never considered in the past, and you've got the picture. Like life really, you've got to plan to get results but you're constantly reminded that the bigger picture is never under your control. In a good season I could easily make a quarter of the games. Despite this, in May I'd find myself with some curious emotion amongst the predictable reactions to Carlisle's fate. At the end of a good season, like the summer of 1984, I was sad at the relegation of Cambridge United and, therefore, the lost chance to walk into the Abbey Stadium by way of the allotments. Such is the lot of the expatriate fan.

The net result of this is that I've taken the attitude of many of the Cumbrian expats I've met down south. We're stuck in limbo, nostalgic for the sights and sounds of home and - paradoxically - more Cumbrian because of our distance from the place. It's like being a racial minority with an added twist. Because we aren't any kind of ethnic minority, the only people who'd begin to see us as different are ourselves. Put a group of Scots or Irish together in a big city bar outside their home countries and the results are predictable. Cumbrians are the same but nobody outside of Cumbria recognises us or knows what it is that makes us special. We're a minority and we're totally invisible. There aren't even enough of us to mob up in most places. In the face of this, we cling on to the things that make us special, one of which is our only professional football team.

Time and again I've chatted away to some Cumbrian at a game and, after the usual discussion of current league form, the predictable 'crap down here' slamming of wherever we are, we can get into enjoying the football. In those early eighties days I hadn't much to offer in these conversations. I'd barely made a life for myself in the south and it ached every time I headed south after a good break in Cumbria. It still does but, in the immortal words of Bob Dylan: 'I've never gotten used to it, I've just learned to turn it off.'

We're never likely to be southerners and - given our desertion of home - we're not really Cumbrians. If we're caught midway between the two that leaves us stranded in Crewe, and that really is a toilet. I was stranded in Crewe once, halfway down the motorway to the south with the big ends all but knocked out of the car. So, just maybe, my view of the place is skewed by a shit experience, a shit garage and a shit car.

Sticking it out for the job, the cash and the proximity to London, my life quickly established a pattern. The fixture list for 83/84 offered some real bonuses. Two home games in quick succession at the end of August whilst I was at home. The only goal of the two games hit the Carlisle net but we had shape, commitment and O' Riordan. The return to Charlton offered better weather, a worse crowd and a better result than the previous season. It was also the last sighting of Paul Bannon in a Carlisle shirt in the south. He only played in four games that season, one of those was as a sub. On the occasions he started he was hauled off and subbed. At Charlton, short of pace, a telling first touch and much involvement in the proceedings, his performance had finally caught up with his sullen facial features. It was all the more obvious because, elsewhere, we were giving a good account. Substituted, Bannon finally let rip with what he'd wanted to say all those years. Bursting into the directors' box he held up a banner which screamed, 'THE WAY OF ALL FLESH IS TO DECAY AND DEATH, JUST LOOK AT MY FUCKING PERFORMANCE THESE DAYS.' Luckily the stewards restrained him just before he got the gun to his temple. Had he pulled the trigger he'd definitely have been charged with bringing the game into disrepute.

We surged through the season hitting the top three after a fifteen match unbeaten run. I never saw Carlisle lose in the south in that campaign. Crystal Palace and Cambridge leaked two apiece and Chelsea and Fulham were fought to 0-0 standstills. Chelsea, were a good side in a strong Second Division. Hell, this division was so strong that Newcastle outspent half of the First Division and still scraped promotion by a whisker.

It felt good to survive a nerve shredding 90 minutes, find new grounds and get in and out alive. The absence of promotion to the First Division and our eventual seventh place was a mixed blessing. Had we kept up the top three position - we were third in the middle of March - I'd have felt I was really missing out living so far away. I'd also have feared for our safety facing the clinical midfield at Anfield or the fearsome pace at Old Trafford. Seventh in the circumstances, was creditable and probably about fair. This team were not the equal of the 73/74 side and the top flight had got harder in the decade since we'd scrambled into that level. At least, that was the way I worked it out in my own mind.

I'd finally got my life under control. Hell, I'd got time to listen to John Peel again and I'd discovered The Smiths. Busier than I'd ever been, writing and running seriously in my spare time, and still following football, I'd reduced Carlisle to something on a par with my other loves but they were still there for me and, to a Cumbrian stranded in the south, they mattered. These were pre-internet, pre-satellite TV days. Hunting down game reports on Carlisle sometimes involved scanning every paper on a Sunday. Some of the news came late. Paul Bannon's departure for Bristol Rovers at the start of 1984 was inexplicably left off the front pages. Hell, *The Daily Mirror* could have given their savaging of Margaret Thatcher a miss for a day to cover that. Bristol Rovers seemed a reasonable home for the one-man enigma. Apart from anything else this team had employed the questionable 'talents' of Bob Lee and that proved the football supporting public of that city had a taste for strikers with their own unique angle on being human. Speaking of Lee, he had also departed, his destination, Hong Kong. This left the worrying thought that Bob Lee was still - just about - on the same side of the planet. But he was well away from Brunton Park.

The summer of 1984 gave us a heatwave, me a holiday of unbelievable proportions and Bob Stokoe the same old headache on trying to build a side on a budget of loose change. Whilst the contractors toiled at Thurrock College to strip asbestos from the ceilings I sweated out hard road miles in the heat. I'd entered a race in Essex to get a feel for the whole competitive end of running and that summer I entered two up in Cumbria. The first, the annual pre-season training fun run at Brunton Park pitted me against some of the players and saw me finishing with a sprint in front of the paddock with a few blue shirts in the pack behind me. My first half marathon in Workington a few weeks later sealed it. I could handle this. I could handle it a hell of a lot better than the merciless stuffing I saw at Brunton Park when Brighton turned up to get in some target practice in the first league game of the season. They'd scored all the goals in the game - all fucking three of them - by half time. To make matters worse our new 'star' striker, Garry MacDonald, was beached out of reach of a decent pass somewhere in no man's land. The *News and Star* said he was a striker. Anyone could say they were something. Adolf Hitler said he was an artist. Garry MacDonald never scored for Carlisle and a matter of weeks after joining us from Middlesboro' he jumped ship and found his true level at Darlington. The Hitler comparison isn't so far from the truth in the case of Garry bloody MacDonald. On the evidence of his non-performance against Brighton he had something in common with great dictators like Augusto Pinochet. For starters, he seemed to think that people herded themselves into football grounds for the sole purpose of being tortured.

By the time we were taking four points in two home games at the start of September my world was changing on a major scale. Starting the second year of my lecturer training course, I was stuck in the canteen of an agricultural college as the new first year group arrived. My mates Eric and Chris were 'talent spotting' amongst the new group and all three of us noticed one of the new intake. The lack of seats obliged the new crowd to split up and, once we'd persuaded her to join us, Eric waded in with a pile of up front questions - name, age, where she lived. From where I was sitting I soon sussed that she wasn't wild about this, subtle as fist, approach. I also got her name, Jane Wilson. A few nights later we were together on the dance floor at Dukes, the nearest thing Chelmsford had to a nightspot.

Soon after that I was round at her place for the first time and meeting the rest of the outfit. Three year old Owen was sitting on the kitchen worktop, spinning the water off some lettuce and eyeing the unfamiliar man in the room. Within minutes I was messing about with him on the settee and, things went on quickly from there. Which, in a round about way, explains my limited presence at Carlisle games over the next couple of seasons. The results ground out, whilst I was starting to play happy families, took Carlisle into the top end of the table although we never got above seventh, our finishing position the previous year. The rot set in after that whilst my life just got better and better. At least I was back in the frozen north by Boxing Day. Little had changed. We still lost 0-3, we just spread the leaks out over 90 minutes as Middlesboro gave us a lesson in passion, clinical finishing and all round organisation. The Boxing Day crowd was pathetic, with good reason. Three days earlier a Carlisle supporter had taken a fatal blow to the head after being struck by a missile hurled by a Blackburn fan. The guy from Blackburn served a term for manslaughter. The incident took place in the car park behind the main stand at Brunton Park. It made national news headlines. A few weeks later, it was a talking point with the students when I got back to work. Those that cared about football had noticed the story and it got us talking about Carlisle.

Carlisle have a hard element to rival most teams. The only real difference is the lack of numbers compared to the bigger teams. But the rivalry with Wigan, Blackpool or Burnley can bring them out. Years later, a Carlisle supporter, Paul Dodd, celebrated by the tabloids as the worst hooligan in the country and banned from Brunton Park, published his own account of football violence. *England's Number One* is a page turner and it'll give you an insight into a part of the Carlisle crowd that don't appear in this book. Blackburn might have killed one Carlisle supporter at the end of 1984 but we've been involved in causing trouble ourselves on a regular basis. The death that Christmas got some of my students talking about Carlisle United.

'Can your mob fight then?' was a fairly regular question.

Yeah they can. Trouble in various forms has been there or thereabouts for most of my life as a football fan. I've seen some, usually as I was running away from it. The most involvement I've had is going over the wall on several occasions. The lower in the league you go the easier the walls are to clear and the slower the stewards are to clear you off on the other side. Wimp that I am it's never about causing trouble when I go over. End of the season, just lost our league status, that kind of thing...

I've got less against the troublemakers than many fans. One thing that doesn't get written on a regular basis is that the worst troublemakers still pose very little threat to the 'scarfers.' I guess I'd just about qualify as a 'scarfer' in that I'll usually sport colours and I've never thrown a brick. I've never knowingly met Paul Dodd and, really, there is no reason why I should. If we ever did strike up a conversation the most pressing thing I've got to tell him is that I couldn't put his book down and I finished it inside a day. He'll organise a ruck in a car park, I'll be well on my way to the station when it kicks off. If we ever rubbed shoulders in the queue for pies, he left me well alone and that is just fine. Take away everyone who ever got involved in a fight and you lose half the noise, a hell of a lot of the income and some decent one liners from every game. Take these people out of the lower leagues and you've got part-time football for certain at a couple of dozen clubs. This is not a defence of every stitched cut and thrown brick, it is simply a recognition of the fact that our national game is a rallying point for a range of emotions. The solution to the trouble problem isn't simple, and anyone who thinks it is now solved because games are more lawful than they were twenty five years ago is missing the point. The middle class 'designer' football fan can disappear as easily as he arrived and the hard element are still there. They just fight in a different place. If football prices itself out of the market or lowly teams lose their appeal to the point that financial ruin threatens an entire division, the people who are going to keep a club like Carlisle afloat will include the same people who are mobbing up in 'away' pubs ahead of the game. It may be an uncomfortable thought but, to my reckoning at least, it is the truth.

Short of giving people employment, a sense of their own self worth and some ambition, you'll never get rid of the causes of football violence. A handful of the worst offenders have all of these things, they just like the rush that goes with a good ruck. Short of a social change bigger than any of us can imagine we've got trouble on the fringes of football long into the future. It may be a curse, really it's a mixed blessing. I don't think I'm the only one who shrugs it off as part of the territory and feels relieved that the problems tend to erupt away from the grounds these days.

So, that Boxing Day we had the best policing and the worst Christmas crowd we'd seen for years. We should have put some police on the Boro attack. On the plus side this was my first sighting of John Halpin. Fast, committed to the point of danger and running hard from the moment he came on as sub to the end of the game. The league position bordered on worrying. Halpin suggested Stokoe's touch was back after the disgrace of signing Garry Fucking MacDonald.

It has to be said, from this point on my weekends belonged to Jane. By the end of that season I'd registered the 2-3 defeat at Craven Cottage, including Don O' Riordan capping a decent performance with a goal. Carlisle wise, this was about it. I'd also registered a feeling of belonging and sharing things I'd never known before. The ins and outs of this don't matter too much in the story of my unconditional love for Carlisle except that, for a time, I had to work at something else that was more important. I don't know how early on I knew this was the real thing but I'd suspected it almost from the start. I'd never thought of myself as relating to children before but Owen and I hit it off from the start. It opened up a world that I'd never imagined. Adding a new dimension to my life. Seeing things through a child's eyes shrank the time I had for other things. Owen was three years and two months old when I met him. At this stage in his life we were never going to share stories of Chris Balderstone passes or Don O' Riordan's entertaining combination of defensive mastery and attempts to murder opposing strikers. Within a few months of knowing Jane and Owen I was dreaming that I might get the chance.

When Carlisle put together a nine point bonanza coming up to Easter, a sequence that included a 6-1 smattering of the southern excuse for a team that had stolen Workington's place, I was impressed. I was struggling to talk to Jane about it, there just seemed to be more important things to talk about. Years before, I'd spent a period falling in love with Carlisle United. As a kid I'd allowed them to fill my thoughts and shape my imagination. Jane was now doing that, more than I'd thought possible. It started with simply trying to figure a few things out. Jane's husband had left to go off with someone else. I alternated between doubting his sanity and wondering who could have convinced him that his time was better spent away from Jane and Owen. Within a matter of weeks none of this mattered. Jane and I were working at making it work, it took some effort in the circumstances, but the will was there on both sides. The weeks became months and we managed a week away on Rhodes the following Easter. That sealed it, and by the following summer I was helping her to move into the first house she'd bought on her own. I thought then that the next time she moved we might be going in together on the mortgage.

As for the long-term love affair I'd had with Carlisle, things were probably falling apart more than I'd like to admit. I wasn't working at this one except when it was on a plate. The following summer I was up at home but organising the timings around families and missing out on the pre-season friendlies and the opening skirmishes.

Carlisle and I didn't part company but, in the way of a romance that is neglected, our distance from each other allowed things between us to cool badly. Then again, you can't blame the few quid of mine that they missed for sending them into a dive in the 85/86 season. Whatever could go wrong did go wrong. Tommy Craig had been an inspiration on the pitch. Even when his legs couldn't do the job you knew the other players respected him. Many closer to the club than me reckoned he should have been manager after being player-coach. Bob Stokoe moved aside in the early season of 85/86 to give Pop Robson the manager's chair. Craig went off earlier in 1985. A few shit results and Pop legged it. You'd have to struggle to get any positives from his fifteen minutes in the hot seat. Being really optimistic you could say the ninety minutes it took to beat Oldham and achieve his only victory provided a good afternoon. Being hopelessly optimistic you could say that his two-month stumble through the bog end of the division cast the managerial careers of Martin Harvey and Ian McFarlane in a better light. Being honest you'd have to say he was shit. He turned his managerial career around years later running the reserve team at Manchester United, that made us all feel really good in Carlisle.

Stokoe had earned his retirement and the undying affection of Carlisle fans. Still, he came back again. He didn't deserve the rest of that season. I saw some sights I'd sooner forget. A 3-0 hammering at Charlton for starters. We got off lightly. The goalkeeping that day was good. I never saw the accident prone Kevin Carr in goal. He'd come and gone by the time the travelling circus came to Charlton. In his place we'd hired Scott Endersby. In defence, the sublime skills of Don O' Riordan had been replaced by Wesley Saunders. At the time I was working with a former football scout, Jim Cook. Jim had taken a job in Student Services at Thurrock and he told me to look out for Saunders. Fair enough, Wes was unfussy and solid. The problem was, he was surrounded by disorganisation. Jim Cook had also worked with a youngster who had incredible strength and playmaking skills by the name of Paul Gascoigne, shame we didn't sign him!

We limped, we stumbled, we fell and on Boxing Day I persuaded my mates Bif and Ian to come along to Brunton Park, 'for old time's sake.' We'd never been to Brunton Park together before, but the sentiment was there. We scrambled a 1-0 win over Boro and failed to convince anyone we were fit to be out of the drop zone. John Halpin was great, and he scored. The result bothered me, but elsewhere things were wonderful. I was settling in with Jane to something like a regular life and the family aspect was bringing back some of the magic of childhood. Maybe this more than anything left me needing less from the familiar sights and sounds of the past, like Carlisle United.

When you are pouring your emotions into other areas of life, working them up for ninety minutes on a terrace seems futile. Carlisle and I, it seemed, were heading away from each other. We were soon back on a parallel course. Around the time I saw the most unbelievable sight I had ever seen at a Carlisle game my team and I both hit the bottom, both of us in free-fall. What happened on the pitch was painful. What happened off it still hurts me now.

It was desperate, we knew that. Two games to go and three points needed from the last home game to keep the slim hopes of Second Division survival together. The opposition that day, Charlton Athletic, needed a win to maintain their solid hopes of promotion. By now it was obvious why we'd scrambled the Boxing Day win over Boro, those losers were as good as down. Against

Charlton we were 2-0 up after forty minutes, survival in our hands. The rest... oh hell!

Like the magic strike of Jimmy Glass this is one of those moments to be remembered for centuries. Jim Tolmie was on our team. Who or what he was doesn't matter. He passed the ball back to Scott Endersby in goal. Tolmie passed back from half way. Nobody in their right mind would have expected the pass, or the height and force he attached to it. There was a wind but that isn't any fucking excuse. Endersby was a trier, not exactly Alan Ross, but he had heart. He hadn't a bloody chance. The goal is a legend. I know that because three days before I wrote these words for the first edition of the book - and now I'm talking early May 1999 - Big Mick, a photographer I know, told me so. Mick follows Charlton, he knows the story because that goal prompted a second half revival in which they ran out 3-2 winners and, near enough, secured promotion. One place behind them were that lot who'd stolen Workington's place and discovered that their yo-yo lifestyle could be stopped with long balls and hard tackles. Wimbledon made the top flight in third place. We fell into Division Three in third last place. Wimbledon got up by playing the long ball game, by now their trade mark. We committed suicide with one long ball that even they couldn't imagine.

I'd never heard my Dad say things like that before. It wasn't just that my Mum was ill. It was the way he said it and the things he'd done. She'd gone into hospital, he'd taken her some flowers from the wood. The three acre wood that we owned alongside the house. I knew it was bad from the uncertainty, the way he was clearly scared and the touching gesture with the flowers. Lesley and I went up from London together and, my Mum had changed totally from the person I'd seen a few weeks before. Frozen in part of her face, positive but so simple in her outlook that she didn't appear to be an adult anymore. There would be tests, things found out and things we didn't know, but I felt after a few minutes that this was it. The person inside her already seemed to be departing. I didn't really want to think that. Dad and Lesley seemed more hopeful and genuinely confused by what was happening. He rang Jane to ask her to tell me that the tests in Newcastle had found a brain tumour. Once I knew that, he rang me after the operation to tell me that they couldn't get it all and Mum had somewhere between three and six months to live.

I was twenty six, I already knew people, like Ian, who'd lost parents. Ian's Dad died just before Ian faced his final exams at Oxford. Knowing people who'd been through it didn't really help me then. For years we'd talked about being a close family. I knew and appreciated that I'd been blessed with parents who had never been judgemental. By the standards of their generation and the place in which I'd been raised they were inspired thinkers. They'd worked to make the lives they wanted - creative and fulfilled lives. Coming from generations of more rigid minds and life chances that were more about obligations than opportunities, they'd inflicted nothing but free spirits on my sister and I. We had our rough moments, but they were fewer than most families. Now we'd have to test the bonds we had like never before. The holidays in education were - in comparison to other jobs - criminally good. I spent almost the whole summer at home. I could say the things I needed to say. I could nurse my mother and deal with the worst that her condition could throw at me. I knew from the start of this that there was no hope for her. Despite that, it was a privilege to be there and to spend all of that time with her. As the cancer spread, her awareness of what was happening loosened and changed. She remained unconcerned and almost serene in the face of life slipping away. She'd done more than anyone to hold our family together. She'd been there for us when my Dad was working away and, in a family that had been encouraged to pursue their talents, she'd been the one who'd made the most sacrifices. She could have been a professional musician. Instead of this, people would remember her as a music teacher. Sometimes, as she slipped in and out of consciousness, her hands would move to strike invisible piano keys.

The further away she slipped the more we pulled together to look after her. She'd done more than any of us to make this possible and, at the end, she would never know how well we coped. We owed so much of our strength in this situation to her. There were other things she'd never know. I was close enough to Jane and Owen to begin to understand what she had given to her children. I'd only started to talk to her about these things because I'd only started to see them. She died without knowing if Owen would ever become, in any sense, her grandchild. She died without knowing if she'd have any grandchildren at all. In the face of her death we were, quite simply, all the things she would have wanted us to be. None of which stopped it hurting. My mother died as the winter of 1986 began to take hold. There really wasn't anything much else that mattered at the time.

Bill Shankley, great man. He might have managed Liverpool to glory but he learned management at one school that could guarantee to teach him. The school of hard knocks at Brunton Park. As a rule, people forget that bit of his career. Like I said, a great man. But that famous quote, the one about football being more important than a matter of life and death. I hope he was kidding. Because if he wasn't, that great man hadn't a clue.

I'll tell you how much football mattered then. I was at home when Carlisle opened their home account in Division Three. At three o' clock on Saturday 30 August I was pegging out the washing in the wood. After that, I went in to sit with my Mum.

As the months rolled by I headed up home, to spend time with my Dad. We went out fell walking. Slowly, we were learning the ways of a new relationship. I didn't think he'd really get over it. In all honesty, he didn't want to. But he still had things to live for. One of which were the local fells. By the following summer he was coming down to see Jane, Owen and I in Essex. Not really himself, but working at it. These things take time, a hell of a lot of time.

There are people who follow football, live around fixture lists, follow league positions and work out permutations as the matches tick away. They'd tell you they are worried. Three matches to go and you need seven points to avoid relegation. Oh yes, that's stress. But you see, if you're worrying about a football team like that, the chances are, the rest of your life is pretty stable. Stability of a sort was back with me the following summer. By May 1987 I'd seen something of Carlisle, none of it impressive. In May 1987 we were losing, we were in the drop zone, we got relegated and we bloody well deserved it. I managed to work up something of a reaction to this disaster. In the circumstances, this was a positive sign.

Another positive sign was the interest I'd got back in the ups, downs and issues of the whole football business. For sixteen games in the previous season Eric Nixon had kept goal for Carlisle. This was noticeable to me simply because the guy had the same name as my Dad. More significantly, Nixon was the kind of player we'd once attracted. Solid, confident, classy and adaptable. 'Adaptable' doesn't begin to do the guy justice. His stint at Carlisle helped him set a record that year. On the books at Manchester City he played for this club and others including Carlisle, becoming, in the process, the only person ever to have played in all four divisions of the English game in one season. We were struggling to attract any real quality players and the loan signings made for inconsistency. They also made the gulf between the current side that the squad of fifteen years before all the more obvious. The team I'd started to watch at Brunton Park had a goalie as good as Eric Nixon, by 1987 we could only get one when he was surplus to requirements at a bigger club.

At least I was back involved and planning my life around the fixture list. The current manager, Harry Gregg, had been given a small glimpse into football hell. I worked up some real sympathy and admiration for Gregg, but this was in 1998 when he gave one of the most emotional and heart-rending accounts of any event in sports history that I've ever heard. Harry had been on the Manchester United plane that failed to get off the runway in Munich and he'd pulled his team mates from the wreckage. On the fortieth anniversary of the disaster his talk to BBC Radio about what he'd seen had a few million people spellbound with a story of simple heroism in the face of almost unbelievable horror.

On a smaller scale you could say the same about his time in charge at Brunton Park. No money to build a decent squad and a mixture of quality players on the way down, promising youngsters and a few journeymen. Gregg hadn't the vision of Stokoe in his great days. But then, the Bob Stokoe who returned after Pop Robson had popped off lacked that vision as well. From our point of view the only dependable good thing about the 87/88 season was the form of Newport County. Maybe my memory has forgotten the exact figures but, I think the

Newport team had an average age of twelve and their centre half was a fifty seven year old league novice, newly signed from a pub team. It has happened since, notably at Doncaster, that a team built largely of YTS and old salts has been scrambled in the face of massive debts to fulfil a fixture list. To all intents and purposes Newport were on the way out all season. We sealed our own escape from relegation into the Conference on 2 April when we scrambled our second away win of the season at Newport, thanks to two Malcolm Poskett goals - our first away win in five months. I didn't go to Newport but I had developed a survival strategy for an exiled Cumbrian with family commitments. Anywhere two hours from the southern base was fine, any excuse to arrange a visit home to include a game or two at Brunton Park was better. With one notable change to the tactics this is the strategy that has kept me going ever since.

That year I had Cambridge, Colchester, Peterboro and London to go at. Confined mainly to away games you get snapshots of the whole season. I missed Gary Fulbrook's half dozen runs out in a blue shirt. He played a few games, put in some decent tackles and eventually returned to Bath City - historic because he was our first black player. Dean Holdsworth didn't stay much longer but he was just about the best news in our 4-1 stuffing at Leyton Orient. Away from home my snapshot was taking in some desperate form, empty grounds and rapidly changing line ups. Tony Fyfe came at the end of the season and - to me at least - looked useful in our final match at Cambridge. With nothing for either team to play for we won 2-1 and Fyfe and Brent Hetherington managed to scramble our goals. As at Colchester earlier in the season I found myself pretty much the only punter in the whole place. I think the players took a break and sat down when I went for a slash. In reality it was a meaningless game fought out in a shoebox of a ground with allotments out back. Cambridge's insistence in naming the place the Abbey 'stadium' was about as ambitious as they got in those days. I was back on track but this Carlisle 'team' were just a bunch of blokes earning a crust for putting on a blue shirt. I could dream, but Tony Fyfe's presence on the pitch wasn't remotely close to the enigma of the mighty Paul Bannon. In the case of Fyfe the enigmatic appeal revolved around whether he could react to a pass without falling flat on his face or swinging the wrong leg onto the ball. Brent Hetherington was Bob Lee firing on three cylinders and this was part of the dynamic strike force we would take into the next season.

Second bottom with another manager ousted, former Workington player Clive Middlemass at the helm, and about enough cash in the bank to buy a round of fruit gums. It looked grim. We needed characters to make sense of the quagmire of mediocrity that threatened to overwhelm us. Somebody had to help us make sense of this. Unseen by the players and backroom staff at Brunton Park, I finally did my bit for the club. I became Don O' Riordan.

Oh yeah, and Workington won the FA Cup.

Blue Nightmare

Mentioned for the first time in this chapter:

These are my opinions not facts. Others - especially those mentioned below - are likely to disagree.

Simon Davey - Promising midfielder signed from Swansea. Established himself 92/93, showed real class thereafter.
Darren Edmonson - Well fed product of the youth team. Went from Coniston to Huddersfield Town by way of an impressive stint at Brunton Park.
Paul Fitzpatrick - He tried to be inspirational in defence. On a good day he managed to tackle and clear the ball.
Ricardo Gabbiadini - Chunky and intermittent. I can confirm the rumours he had at least one good game. But he had some stinkers too.
Eric Gates - As mobile as a walrus stuck in treacle, but not quite as thin. He played for England you know.
Craig Goldsmith - A man who once earned his living as a professional footballer.
Mike Graham - 1988/90 - Willing, if predictable, defender.
Mike Graham - 1991/92 - Past his sell-by date and easily passed by any opposing striker with two good legs.
Mike Graham - 12 Feb 1992 - A blue nightmare. The worst individual performance in the worst Carlisle team I've ever seen.
Steve Harkness - A rarity, a decent and consistent performer in the 88/89 team.
John Holliday - Massive, misfiring, uncoordinated defensive enigma. To think, Bill Green once wore the same number on a blue shirt. Damn good journalist these days and a decent bloke when I spoke to him. But that's another story.
Mike Holmes - A passable member of a shit team in a shit season.
Simon Jeffels - A passable member of a shit team in a shit season II.
Michael Knighton - Fleetingly mentioned already but his era starts now. The most controversial figure in the history of the club. Chairman 1992-2002. There was seldom a dull moment, the scaling of heights and plumbing of depths came in quick succession and the man's matchless gifts for soundbites and inventive twists on the art of club ownership put United on front pages as well as the back of papers. A larger than life figure on his quietest days, more famous than any of his playing staff and a source of countless incredible tales told by fans, some of them true.
Aiden McCaffery - One time player. Remembered mainly for managing the worst team in the history of the club.
David McCreery - Former Man Utd midfielder. First player-manager of the

Knighton era.
Steve Norris - Useful striker and fan favourite. His loyalty was - allegedly - tested to breaking point by the signing of the generally useless and overpaid Eric Gates.
Kelham O' Hanlon - 'Ireland's number one.' Goalie with an international cap. Possessed of incredible reserves of motivation in the face of pathetic performances in front of his goal.
Paul Proudlock - He scored a few goals, we shouted his name a few times. A character who cared about the fans.
David Reeves - £121,000 record signing. Hard working centre forward, fan favourite, goal getter, always willing to put in 90 minutes graft.
Kevin Rose - Successor to transferred Dave McKellar in Clive Middlemass' greatest team. Had about half McKellar's class on a good day. Didn't have that many good days.
Nigel Saddington - Lanky, assured defender with scything tackle action when required, and sometimes when not required.
Richard Sendall - Almost a useful front player by the standards of the late eighties, early nineties. Then again, the competition included Tony Fyfe and Brent Hetherington.
Jeff Thorpe - Utility player brought through from youth ranks. A real prospect early on in his career. Injury prone later, but never faulted on effort.
Mick Wadsworth - A genuine coach. The best manager we'd had in ages. Appointed in the summer of 1993. Delivering by the end of his first full season.
Derek Walsh - Scots midfielder who could score. Good enough for the plodding sides of late eighties, early nineties. Later, a valued player at Gretna.
Keith Walwyn - Mentioned in chapter two. All heart and always willing. Muscular striker, on the downward slope by the time he arrived at Brunton Park.
Andy Watson - Pretty much the only thing worth cheering outfield 91/92. Sold for a pittance the following season cos we were skint.

9 Mike Graham

I didn't start looking like Don O' Riordan. I didn't start dressing like him. It was more an attitude thing - a necessity. Carlisle and I had drifted away from each other in some ways. As they'd plumbed the depths of a 91st place finish I had headed in the other direction. In the day job there were no YTS in sight and I'd written a new Media Studies programme which was gathering impressive student numbers. I'd also started teaching people to write. Not in the a-b-c sense but in terms of Creative Writing, making a few quid and dealing with the things you always wanted to write down. My writing course had gathered a mass of bodies. I had also started collecting cheques and credits on a regular basis as a writer. I'd started a 'target practice' period in which I'd line up material for any publication that looked likely and send it out. If they published it, I'd send more. If they didn't, I'd curse them for about five minutes and figure out how to recycle the rejected ideas.

The results had been interesting. In the same week that I 'cracked' the worthy *Times Educational Supplement* I also got my first jokes into *Viz* comic. *Viz* paid better and didn't butcher my copy, so I sent them some more stuff. The roots of this new branch of income went back to the end of the 1985/86 season. It was around this time I started letting rip with writing that began with little more than an idea of how to be funny. It drew on my experiences of being a Cumbrian, a football fan and someone with a sick sense of humour.

On the last day of that relegation season Carlisle United staged a pitch invasion and general ruck at Oldham. After the 2-1 defeat that ensured our drop into the Third Division the police waded into the Carlisle end at Boundary Park and Paul Dodd, amongst others, got coshed. I wasn't there, I just read the account in his book. Carlisle were earning no friends with this approach to solving problems. The odd thing was, I was starting to write demented and sick prose that was finding friends who sat behind editors' desks. The closer I got to the literary equivalent of a football riot, the better the chance I had of getting my work accepted. I could fill paragraphs with little more than obscenities and graphic descriptions of violence. In return I'd get a reasonable cheque. Hell, this was fun.

It was *Viz* and their ilk who turned me into Don O' Riordan. The great thing about Don was the way this classy leader of men hid the heart of an executioner. He clearly enjoyed the lowest of tackles and the most pointless of fouls for their simple artistry. Part of the pleasure of watching him was the surprise of the opposing fans who didn't see it coming. Don could wait over an hour for his first assault, playing with confidence and class, lulling opposing fans into a false sense of security before... WHAM!

OPPOSITION FANS - 'Off, off, off, off, off, off.'

BLUE ARMY - 'He fuckin' dived.'

I didn't write that much for *Viz* but the success of this comic opened the floodgates for others. By 1988 *Viz* wasn't so open to a freelance writer. The management of the comic had gone into a deal with John Brown publishing which left a lot of the administration in London and freed up the creators of the comic, who worked out of Newcastle, to do what they did to perfection. Let's give editor Chris Donald his due here, the bloke is near enough a genius. I never made that much money out of his publication but without the stunning sales of *Viz* there would have been no *Brain Damage, Gas, Poot, Smut, Zit, Ziggy, Pulp, Acne, Gutter, Gutted, Elephant Parts* or *Head.* And I did okay out of that lot. Two years after selling my first item to *Viz* I was starting to cream it with the competition. This, in turn, presented one small problem.

At work, there were people who had earners on the side. These went from dealing car parts to taking pictures for soft porn mags. On one celebrated Monday morning I ended up covering somebody's class because he'd just had an irate punter on the phone. The lecturer in question - who shall remain nameless - was jobbing as a carpenter and had done a roof repair over the weekend which had started leaking in the early hours of Monday morning. He nailed down the offending fabric and I flannelled in front of his students. There was an uneasy acceptance of this moonlighting amongst those charged with managing us. In this context, my 'jokes' presented something of a moral problem. On one occasion a secretarial lecturer saw some of my work. She had no idea it was mine and she was so shocked she said she'd take the 'joke' to her church so they could pray for the people who read such garbage. Trust me, it wasn't that bad, you've heard worse 'jokes' if you go to football matches.

So, in the two years it took Carlisle to fall from staging a riot as they left the Second Division in 1986, to staging a non-turnout as they fought out a pointless away win at Cambridge which ensured 91st place, I went from sending in hopeful copy to *Viz* comic to earning enough of a regular income to call myself a comedy writer. I also went 'underground' after a fashion. I was still the same person at work but some of the things I was writing weren't getting discussed with my work mates. I was Don O' Riordan simply because the organised creature on the outside was giving way to the headcase inside when I wrote.

When the comic competitors to *Viz* arrived they went all over the place in terms of style. Puerile, smutty and sick, sick, sick. So, writing for *Zit* wasn't the same as writing for *Ziggy,* but they all demanded regular piles of copy. This meant turning it round at a phenomenal rate. For four years I would work for a couple of evenings a week, slap on some decent music, sit down with a pile of empty sheets of paper and knock it out. In the eighties this meant hammering it out with a typewriter. By the end of this period I had a state of the art laptop. Once I wrote something for *Viz* suggesting that Jimi Hendrix was alive and well and working in 'Chickpan' in Carlisle. But one item might also be a collection of thirty readers' letters or Top Tips. The Hendrix joke came from a pub conversation I'd had years before when a gang of us would compensate for the fact that nothing ever happened in Bothel by inventing things we'd seen. 'Lynyrd Skynyrd didn't die in a plane crash. I saw that Ronnie Van Zandt fixing tractors near Egremont the other day.'

I knocked out a few thousand items in this time. Keeping tabs on all the work was hard. The items varied. Sometimes I wouldn't see them printed until months later by which time I'd wonder if they were mine. I needed to be accurate since I was paid by what I got published. The readers' letters were a real problem. A couple of lines, knocked off in seconds. I took to sticking names I knew - like Carlisle United players - in my work. I'd started something. Within a few months I noted Leeds United and Newcastle United names amongst the *Viz* letter writers.

I'd sit down and knock out jokes from 5-30 to 9-30. The paper was blank and I'd start with an idea that occurred to me there and then. Working at this pace, being in effect a sit-down comedian, I was bound to go back over ideas and themes that were already stuck in my head. Carlisle United were everywhere. In the first edition of *Brain Damage* 'cash crisis club Carlisle United' re-signed one of their old players. The joke was that the player in question was 72 and he was obviously going to get massacred first time out. I'd based this story on the 'freescoring' Jimmy McConnell, a United legend from Division Three [North]. Elsewhere I sold a joke questionnaire to another comic. In this one you had to decide whether your Dad was a Third Division footballer. The questions asked things like what your dad was like on Saturday night and how he reacted when he saw Jan Molby on the telly. If he blurted out 'That useless fat bastard, I could spray out a few passes for the money he earns,' your dad probably was a Third Division footballer. Okay they weren't the greatest jokes but I soon discovered I could cut this stuff almost exactly to the needs of the different comics. Carlisle United were perfect subject material in each case and - sad to say it - they supported my attempts to work them into jokes with a pathetic start to the 88/89 campaign. Mid-table mediocrity hardly does it justice. Imagine if your team managed their first league win on 15 October. Imagine in mid-September reading: P-5, W-0, D-5, L-0. In a word, 'consistent.'

This was a parting of the ways for Carlisle and me. Compared to them, I was doing pretty well. Their place in my life was now something to do with maintaining the familiar feelings of being a Cumbrian and maintaining my loyalty. I learned something about how much I cared that season because we were almost as bad as the year before. There were encouraging signs. Nigel Saddington's arrival in the defence had added some pace and an ability to read the game. Richard Sendall had a similar level of vision up front and we could always console ourselves with the thought that he wasn't Tony Fyfe or Brent Hetherington.

Paul Proudlock had arrived by the end of the season. He scored goals with the odd rapid pounce on loose balls. Proudy could even slip an opposing defender or two. But, when all of these revelations in blue shirts were added together there was only one conclusion. A few years earlier we wouldn't even have considered most of these losers. To be fair to some of that team they'd seen better days at other clubs. I've seen it argued elsewhere - like Mick Mitchell's book on Carlisle United - that Proudlock had real skill and would have shown it in a better team. Well... maybe.

I knew this team were limited but I still cared more than I could say. I might have been writing jokes that regularly involved Carlisle but the truth was, they were in my thoughts so often that the ideas just kept coming. Stuck in Chelmsford I'd get to away games and see the odd bit of excitement. The 88/89 outfit only scored four goals on two occasions. Once they dumped Telford United out of the cup and once they thrashed Peterboro. Hell, it was worth the run up from Chelmsford in January for that demolition of 'Posh'. John Halpin - recovered from a broken leg - gave the Peterboro mid-field a lesson in creating space. The chunky frame of Mike Graham got itself on the end of a telling strike on goal. It was plodding, percentage football all the way. The opening of season nightmare of nine games without a win eventually gave way to a steadying of nerves and a general slog for points. The improved results owed a good deal to the return of Dave McKellar in goal. We briefly had a useful defender, Steve Harkness. He was there and gone so quickly I managed to miss him. Saw him on telly in a Liverpool shirt though - the verdict: he was too good for us. Hell, Bill and Ben the Flowerpot Men would have been too good for the teams I saw in some games that season. Early on in the campaign we chased Cambridge United around for ninety minutes. How the hell we scored two that day, I'll never know. Derek Walsh, a surging midfielder with an eye for goal, did have a decent game. Walsh was a tryer in a turgid team. He might have been an attacking midfielder but he was treading the turf in an attacking midfield tradition that included the likes of Chris Balderstone and he wasn't in that league. I saw Walsh play an inspirational game, masterminding attacks from midfield. This game was in 1995 and he was playing for Gretna. In a Carlisle shirt in 1989 he had to sweat to stay with the play.

Carlisle were skint and Clive Middlemass had trodden this league road before with Workington. He was working hard to motivate and he did pull organised performances from a team that was thick with plodders. I'd managed to talk a few others into coming along to games - Jane's mate Richard Courtney for one. He hadn't been to a game for ages and worried about crowd trouble. Crowd trouble! That far south you were lucky to see a crowd in the Carlisle end. The Abbey Stadium, Cambridge and Layer Road, Colchester provided their predictable rattling emptiness. Colchester scrambled a point against us and fielded the fattest goalie in Christendom. I lost the match programme years ago. I think he was called 'Sumo.'

We had a team who were trying but clearly outclassed by anyone with more than fifty pence in the transfer budget. I cared enough to go anywhere within striking distance of Chelmsford in the hope of a miracle. 4-1 at Peterboro was a miracle in those circumstances. I talked Richard Courtney along to the Colchester game and we had to jog the length of Layer Road to make the kick off. In the car I talked great Carlisle teams and classic cup-ties. At the ground we got a low-grade encounter with twice as much fury as skill.

The more Jane, Owen and I became a family the more I managed to work some football into our lives. We took Owen to his first football games at Chelmsford City. Chelmsford briefly had an out of contract Alan Brazil at the start of one season. Their 'stadium' was ten minutes walk from our front door on a bad day. I could sprint back from a game in time for the classified check on BBC1. By 1988 we were leaving Chelmsford City and a few friends well behind. Hacked off and bored with further education Jane had jumped ship in 1988 and landed a training management job with Kent County Council in Maidstone. This meant moving and we bought a house in Bearsted, on the edge of town and near the country. Jane's positive and capable side took us to Maidstone, held us together and gave us both a sense that this move was right. Cumbrian to the core, I was the one who had to be persuaded to have faith in change. We'd gone from falling in love to pulling together through a few challenges. The three of us were a family beyond any question by this point. We shared more than we had with anyone before and the problems, once sorted, helped us to keep on building. In the great Bob Stokoe tradition it wasn't always pretty, but we got results.

The same - more or less - was true with my expanding writing career. I'd started to understand what I was doing. I realised the best jokes are those that mix honesty with their authority. Don O' Riordan was funny because the flattening challenges had an honesty and surprise about them. We saw a character showing himself in his true colours and loved the shock of the opposing fans. I never felt dishonest abusing a ref for taking Don to task. Paul Fitzpatrick, Nigel Saddington and Darren Edmonson, on the other hand, could make me wince. A bit excitable was our Nigel.

My Dad once told me about a conversation he'd had with a mate who was partial to a bit of bird shooting. This mate of his once started on to my Dad about that adrenalin rush, the dry mouth and the tingle of anticipation he got when the birds were about to fly in his direction. 'You should try it when they're firing back,' said my Dad. I could picture that conversation. My Dad giving it a complete deadpan delivery and just letting the line hang there. That Don O' Riordan moment when you realise the character you're dealing with, isn't quite who you thought. In the circumstances the line was a comic gem because it had authority and honesty.

My Dad had tried it when they were firing back. 'They' were Japanese, the war was long over. The Japanese in question were out in the jungle and they weren't up for being taken alive. Later on, my Dad took a boat load of them - all alive - for repatriation. He had to go down to the hold amongst them but he wasn't allowed to take a revolver in case they got it off him and started blowing their own brains out. Yeah, come to think of it, there are worse jobs than teaching the YTS.

Put yourself into that situation. Those unseen psychos in the trees might announce themselves at any point with the chilling crack of rifle fire and the sight of your mate's head exploding. You can move in on them, but you're not supposed to kill them. As a lieutenant - which my Dad was at this point - you're obliged to carry out your orders, dangerous as they are. As a squaddie, under direction from the lieutenant, you probably don't give a shit. You just want one clear shot at the git in the tree. The more I think about that, the more I understand where my Dad developed his ability to see problems from a few angles. In the circumstances humour matters. It lets out the frustration and the feelings of helplessness. Without it you're insane. It's probably the most intelligent and useful weapon at your disposal.

You could be on a football terrace watching Eric Gates arrive three weeks too late for a decent pass. You could be emerging from the stinking hold of a ship whilst the Japanese prisoners stayed below deck and away from the chance to throw themselves over the side. You could be facing the bunch of YTS students for the third time in a week. In all three cases you could be facing a situation that made you wonder whether you had the ability to make the right choices in life. Without humour, you wouldn't have much else going to give you a sense of your own self worth.

I was writing jokes at the end of the 'Alternative comedy' period. A predictable quip from people who didn't get the alternative humour jokes was that the alternative to comedy is not being funny. Bollocks! The alternative to comedy is Fascism. If you don't believe me, go up to the guy in the tree, the one who just shot the sqauddie through the head, and try and tell him a joke.

I loved watching Don O'Riordan because - like my Dad - he had that quality of pulling a stunt when the audience didn't see it coming. The same thing I was trying to do with my writing. An example from my Dad's life: John Major's government passed a law to stop illegal gatherings of any kind. Soon after, a few coppers were hanging round the entrance to the forest track that ran down the side of Dad's house. The coppers thought they'd gone there to break up the hunt protesters. They hadn't reckoned on getting more trouble from a bloke in his sixties. My Dad got talking to one of them about the unlawful assembly law. 'It's not right is it?' said Dad.

'Well, I wouldn't like to comment,' said the cop. At this point, my Dad's mate Bill came wandering down the road with his dog.

'There's two of us now,' said my Dad, 'Are you gonna break this up?' Etc etc. Ten minutes later, having run through several of his friends who might just drop by if they received a phone call, asking for guidance on exactly how far he should stand away from everyone else and whether raising his hand to scratch his head was a threatening gesture, my Dad gave it a rest and the copper got back to throwing threatening glances at anyone with dreads and a pair of combat pants. Some coppers eh? They hate it when you try and reason with them. Like I said, the alternative to comedy is fascism.

Roughly speaking, it's the same thing on a football terrace. Or it was during the early days of the Middlemass regime at Carlisle. Swearing, abuse, and some timeless one-liner humour. All of us in search of that moment, that release to capture the emotions we were feeling. Years before, I'd ranted at the mistakes of our greatest ever team as the First Division proved it was a class above some of their best ideas. I'd done it in a pathetic way, copying the phrases I'd heard at school and firing them word for word. By the nineties, I was a bit sharper. I could see humour from all sides.

One of the best lines I ever heard came up at a Workington match. It was 1994, Workington were 2-0 down at half time and the weather was shite. The bloke heading for the half time pies in front of me was mumbling to himself. His mate looked him in the eye. 'Smile man,' he said, 'Yer a lang time dead!'

Too bloody right.

You had to be there. Hear the deep drawl in the voice. Dark tones, like the grim reaper. I love West Cumbrian humour and when I got the chance to knock out 'jokes' by the truckload it was the deep, dark West Cumbrian stuff that hit the paper. The stuff that poured out was the stuff that ran round my mind and a lot of it was linked to football. I might have based some of the jokes on Carlisle. But, at the time, like most of the others on the terraces, I was coping with some problems on the pitch.

Middlemass was up against it. No money, not much competition for places in the team and a smattering of ambitious teams with decent budgets in the same division. We needed laughs badly between 1988 and 1993. It was the only antidote to the shuffling and sorry showers of shite we saw wearing the famous blue shirt. I don't want to go there in detail. When Carlisle needed me most, I was there. I parted with cash knowing full well that Mike Graham, Eric Gates, Tony Fyfe and John Holliday were waiting on the other side of the turnstiles. If you saw these teams too, you'll know what it took to stay loyal. I'm going to bottle out here. I don't want to go through every mind-numbing encounter of those sorry seasons. I'll hit on a few games that say most of what matters.

Despite the 4-1 thrashing of Peterboro in January 1989 a more definitive match that season was probably the late September encounter with Cambridge - full of goals and incident. Mistakes played a big part in both. We battled, but we were no better than Cambridge and the full-on, blood, guts and mistakes football ended with them 3-2 ahead. They wanted it more, so they won. There were things to cheer that season, mainly the fact that Middlemass had put enough shape in the team to avoid the pathetic levels to which we'd been sinking twelve months before. But, in the annals of Carlisle United, it was a mediocre season punctuated by one highlight. A massive crowd for a third round cup tie with Liverpool at Brunton Park. Okay, Carlisle got stuffed 3-0 but in a season of non-events, this was a highlight. Put it this way: 1988/89 - P-46, W-15, D-15, L-16, goals for 53, goals against 52, points 60, position twelfth out of 24. Mid-table mediocrity.

By the point at which we knew the final judgement on our mid-table fate, events had put this into another perspective. There had been some bad feeling in the crowd on Boxing Day, mainly to do with the lack of covered space, slowness of the half time queues and the presence of some obvious 'fairweather' supporters, there to collect ticket vouchers for the forthcoming Liverpool cup tie. Some people thought this amounted to a problem. The pulling power of that Liverpool team would put our petty sqabbles into context a few months later when, with Wembley in sight, the team prepared to take on Nottingham Forest at Hillsborough in the FA Cup semi final. British football's greatest disaster sickened every true football fan, including those of us used to empty spaces on the terraces of the Fourth Division. As Nick Hornby would later observe, there never had been a plan to prevent such a disaster. It could have been any of the massive First Division giants that day. Liverpool's fans were unlucky to follow such a good team. Their regular presence in major games at 'neutral' grounds made them more likely to be the sacrifice that football was going to make before coming to its senses. It could have been Arsenal, Manchester United or Spurs. Sooner or later, some massive crowd was going to fall foul of the fatal combination of fences and policing that equated thousands of fans with herds of cattle to be channelled and contained. By 1989 I'd been in crowds bigger than that assembled at Hillsboro, but I'd been watching rock stars at the time. I'd shuffled through tunnels thick with bodies pushing each other. I'd stood on stairways deep with row on row of people all ready to fall if someone made a slip. At the end of a season that hardly warrants a mention in the official history of Carlisle United I'm willing to bet I did the same as many other Carlisle fans, by thinking long and hard about those people at Hillsboro. Like I said earlier, Bill Shankley was a great man. Ironic that it should be the club he led to greatness who would remind us that a game of football is a hell of a lot less important than a matter of life and death.

The 89/90 season showed that Middlemass had resolve and discipline. Okay, he also had some class. Dave McKellar still had what it took for sure, remember, he hadn't yet played that Rangers reserve match in front of 10,000 fans. On the scrapheap half a career before, he still had some of his best days ahead of him. Some of his very best saves were there to enjoy as Carlisle, improbably, went to the top of the table.

I saw them win that year. I even saw them dominate. Oddly, the two defining matches that stick in my mind are defeats. At Southend we were back in the news. I read two papers that day talking about the top of the table clash. First against second, at Roots Hall. Southend ran out 2-0 winners. We ran out 2-0 winners in the competition to have men sent off. Frankly, I didn't have a problem with either dismissal. Middlemass had a team that could channel aggression and run on organisation. In the great Stokoe tradition this was a team built around the players he had. Probably not the players he wanted. He got them working to their strengths. When they were outclassed, as they were by Southend, the frustration could boil over in seconds.

Still, for most of that year there were things to celebrate. Proudlock could run, McKellar's goalkeeping was dependable. Saddington and Fitzpatrick were a cause for confidence at the back. The muscular Keith Walwyn was committed to the point of pain. A guy with real heart. Walwyn's eventual fate is another of those dark ironies of football. He ended up playing non-league football for Kettering Town where his career was ended after the striker who was all heart suffered a heart attack on the pitch. In April 2003 he died after heart surgery, he was 47. One abiding memory I have of Walwyn is him chasing at full tilt when they were already played out of the game at Southend. He pulled his hamstring. He hopped high into the air, it was obvious he'd got a serious injury. His face was screwed up in pain but he was still looking at the ball as it rolled away. He might have been on the way down when we signed him, but Walwyn gave everything he could.

We chanted 'We've got Pele,' when he touched the ball. The point being, Walwyn was black. The fleeting Carlisle career of Gary Fulbrook hadn't done much to familiarise us with black players in a home shirt. That 'Pele' chant said a lot about our level of racial awareness as Cumbrians. Like I said earlier, we never considered chanting 'We've got George Best' when Frank Barton got the ball.

Let's get a few things straight here. I'm proud to be a Cumbrian. It is the only place on this Earth about which I care enough to feel genuine emotion when I arrive and when I leave. If I have any nationality, any sense of pride and identity I'm not English and not British. I'm a Cumbrian. When I die, wherever I might be living, I'm going back there. Over the years I applied for every believable job I could find in the county. I've attempted to argue my way into positions I wouldn't even consider in the south. I love the place in which I was born, and its people. In the way of real love, I love the place and people despite its faults. The only real frustration is the lack of decent jobs. But it has to be said. Cumbria can be insular and inward looking. I've never known worse racism than the stuff I've encountered from a few Cumbrians.

We've got to get this in perspective, your average Cumbrian is as decent and reasonable as your average person from anywhere else. Every football ground has seen its share of racist chanting. Some of the worst racism of all, both football and non-football, is housed near to where I live and work, in Kent. The thing about Cumbria is that ignorance can survive because nothing challenges it and I've seen it happen. When I lived up there, some people I knew had the arguments well rehearsed. The stuff about anyone black being lazy, nicking our jobs and the rest. In the last summer I worked at the factory in Wigton there was one black student doing a summer stint. Abdul was, I suppose, originally North African. In reality, he came from Leeds. I got on well enough with him but we spent more time talking about music and football than our home towns. Some people I knew weren't all that keen on a black guy working around the place and I heard the usual banter about 'them' being lazy gits who were just into chasing women. Abdul was a character. He did chase women, he even made a pass at a girl who'd gone out with me one night. On one celebrated occasion a whole crowd of us, including me and Abdul, had shifted a stack of drink knowing full well we had a seven o' clock start in the fitting shop the following day. I saw him clock on and I didn't see him again until we were clocking off. I asked him about that as we wandered up into town. He told me he'd been so wrecked he'd spent most of his 'working' day asleep on top of a furnace. He felt loads better for it and his hangover had cleared itself by the middle of the afternoon.

Abdul was a real character and I saw him work hard for most of the factory stint. He was also well aware of the stick he was taking from a handful of people. On one occasion the two of us were throwing chunks of old masonry into a heap to be taken away. 'Bloody good practice for stoning the police,' grinned Abdul. Well, it was that 'riot' summer and The Specials *Ghost Town* was on top of the charts. After he'd gone I heard some people saying 'they' were all like Abdul, the day asleep on top of the furnace had become a legend. Add a load of prejudice, one bloke who was - in reality - just like the rest of us, and you've got proof of a bullshit argument. That is Cumbria at its worst, because we don't get tested against the ideas and attitudes of the rest of the world. It's a different kind of racism to the stuff I've heard in the multi-racial south. Where I live now, the ignorance is a lifestyle choice made by narrow minds who'd sooner keep it simple. In reality, a lot of them already know they've lost the argument. Oddly enough, in a place like Cumbria, we sometimes end up acting like a threatened ethnic minority, afraid of losing everything if we break out too far into the wide world.

So, we had a hard working striker called Keith Walwyn, he was black, he was a crowd pleaser and he gave everything. In the end, it wasn't quite enough. The last game of the season pitted Carlisle against Maidstone United. We were in a play off place but the points were tight and Maidstone, one point behind us, needed to win to get a play off place. There were a few teams challenging for the places that day and I tried to explain the ins and out of the maths involved to

Owen as we drove to Dartford for the game. In another ironic twist in the history of my love affair with Carlisle United I'd moved to Maidstone in the year their team started a successful charge for league status. Maidstone United celebrated their achievement by selling their London Road ground and moving their home matches 30 miles up the road to Dartford. So, on a blazing May afternoon, Owen and I took our seats for the end of season showdown in Dartford. Along with the Southend match, that clash with Maidstone summed up everything about Clive Middlemass' greatest season.

Kevin Rose was in goal for the last sprint toward the play off show down. Our league form and position had dipped from the top spot. I'd seen a true freak of a result when Colchester - who went on to finish bottom of bloody everything and get booted out of the league - hammered us 4-0 at Layer Road. McKellar had been at Colchester. In fact, he was there for the sequence of six straight defeats that saw us drop from leaders of Division Four to one place outside the play off zone. I've met a few football anoraks over the years but nobody who could tell me the last time a league leading team suffered six straight defeats. For all this, McKellar was still guarding the goal as well as he could. The balls hitting the back of the net were coming from opposing players with yards of space to run and strike. These players were getting possession because we'd surrendered the midfield and chosen to play Craig Goldsmith who could disappear without trace for 90 minutes on a Saturday afternoon. I'm not saying it was all his fault, he just seemed to symbolise the growing problem.

As other teams became more organised the gaps in our planning and skill began to show. The fact we were prepared to sell McKellar to Kilmarnock said everything about our levels of ambition and ready cash. On 5 May, Maidstone had a younger, faster and more confident team and they charged at us with attitude from the start. We were a goal down before we knew what had hit us but Walwyn's strength, fight and constant running got us even, at which point we were over the wall in numbers. 'We' in this case means the Blue Army one of whom connected with Owen's head on his way across. Down the front and in seats, with Owen only eight years old, it struck me I'd got a problem. We were getting pasted on the pitch, despite the equaliser, and Carlisle did have an impressive track record of going over the wall when crucial games were going the wrong way. A Kent cop offered to get us out, I didn't want it but the second time he offered I ended up making a real head vs heart decision and allowing the cop to find us a safer area... in with Maidstone fans.

On the day we were given one option of which part of the ground we filled. Terracing would have offered us a safe place out of line of the pitch invasions and surrounded by the comforting noise of the Blue Army. As it was, I got to stand in a less than full area with some of the most peaceful fans I've ever met. Unbelievably, this laid back pack were watching their team make the play offs in their first league season. I think one of these 'home' fans managed to raise his hands and clap a couple of times. Well, by the time Maidstone had scored their fifth goal and broken our solid defensive line for the twentieth time these southern fans might have felt a vague stirring of passion. Owen, had a great time chatting away to the home support and enjoying the quality strikes sailing past Kevin Rose. It has to be said, this was not a great team performance but Kevin Rose was never the greatest goalie. The defence in particular were short on confidence. The running joke about Rose was an oldie but goodie. What did Kevin Rose and Michael Jackson have in common? ...They both wore gloves but nobody knew why.

We scored a second goal, not that it mattered. All we had to do was wait for the results from the other games. Chesterfield had stolen the last play-off place. That summed it up, really. Had we sneaked into the play offs we could have made some useful money, we'd never have made it to Wembley, let alone the Third Division. Had any miracle put us into a promotion place that season we would have been slaughtered in the league above. You could blame Middlemass but he had achieved more with this bunch of journeymen than anyone could reasonably expect. The thoughts in my mind coming home from that game were a dark mixture. This team and this level of finance were marooned in the Fourth Division. Up against a team with some pretensions to class - like Maidstone or Southend - we looked bloody ordinary.

Craig Goldsmith had played as a sub in the Maidstone game. Or, to be exact, we'd seen Steve Norris go off and Goldsmith come on. From that point we were down to ten men. Later that night I turned on the TV and watched Sting playing a benefit gig for the relatives of the disappeared. He dedicated one song to the friends and family of Craig Goldsmith. We didn't have anything to look forward to but we still had a hero. Thirty-four year old Keith Walwyn ran so hard in that final game that I have a picture of him fixed in my mind chasing a hopeful forward lob with almost no hope of connecting.

That was our greatest season under Clive Middlemass. The following season was a return to old ways. Newport County were long gone, but the press gangs were obviously raiding the infant schools in Wrexham, Aldershot and Halifax. Meanwhile in York, unemployed waitresses were begging any tea-shop with spare change for Saturday afternoon jobs. The alternative for unemployed girls was to be stuffed into the back of a van, roughly scrubbed over with boot black to create a fake five o'clock shadow and turned out in red shirts as York City. Yes, the bottom of the league really was that bad in 90/91. Thank fuck for the desperation in those teams because we weren't a lot better. To make matters worse there was no London team in the bottom flight and - apart from Maidstone and Gillingham - my nearest matches took in two hour plus trips to Peterboro, Northampton and Lincoln. As with Newport's monumental suicide run in 1988 our league survival depended completely on everyone else's tragedies. It was the sorry excuse for tactical master plans on offer at places like The Racecourse

Ground, Doncaster and The Shay, Halifax that we had to thank for our twentieth position. As we had in 1988, we faced a last game on a balmy May afternoon with nothing to play for and a pathetic crowd gathered to watch. Sincil Bank, Lincoln had been playing host to non-league football when we'd been holding a steady 91st place ahead of Newport in 1988. On the evidence of that season, when we'd come alive to hammer Cambridge on the last day, I thought I could expect another fighting performance in the face of a pointless game. I was wrong.

6-2 - I mean, six fucking two, they beat us. I'd seen Carlisle let in five goals on the final Saturday of the previous season. At Lincoln they let in five goals in the second half!!!!! This was the bitter end, in more ways than one, John Halpin came off the bench, gave it some commitment and walked out of our lives to play for Rochdale. Well, you can't fault him for wanting to go to a club with more ambition eh? Last game massacres were starting to look like a great tradition. The players got off lightly. From where I was standing it didn't look like they managed to wake up in the ninety minutes. For fuck's sake lads, it's almost three hours each way from Maidstone to Sincil Bank. You could've made an effort. I bloody did.

It's time to talk about the 91/92 assault on the Fourth Division title. Going there hurts about as much as revisiting the Fulham cup defeat in that First Division season. You want to know how bad it was? Then let's go to the game that is, without doubt, my worst ninety minutes as a Carlisle United supporter. And let's talk about Mike Fucking Graham. Graham had been there for a few years and he'd given a good account of himself. In the 89/90 side he'd worked manfully to hold back the tide of opposing strikers. But, on 12 February 1992 at Watling Street, Dartford, he stepped permanently into my nightmares to such an extent that I've made him pay for it off and on. It's taken over a decade for me to mellow. Some of the revenge I've taken seems pointless and stupid now. Somewhere in the middle of *Raiders of the Low Forehead* - a sicko novel - out of print these days, you'll find a character: 'Back-pedalling as furiously as full-back Mike Graham faced by tricky opposing strikers in the year Carlisle United finished bottom of bloody everything.'

It was only people taking me to task after the first edition of this book that finally brought me round. But Graham fucking tested me, alright. I know I love Carlisle United because what I'm about to tell you still hurts. I am old enough and smart enough to be above this. But I still remember some games, and one in particular, with horror. In 1992 we finished bottom of the league. Only the folding of Aldershot saved us from a certain exit. This was, unquestionably the worst Carlisle team I've ever seen. The 5-1 hammering by Maidstone United on a freezing February night in Dartford was unquestionably the worst performance I saw that year and the 944 spectators who bothered to turn up amount to the worst crowd I've ever seen at a serious Carlisle match. On that night Mike

Graham was unquestionably the saddest pile of festering garbage shuffling around in a blue shirt. I can still see his furious back-pedalling as Maidstone came forward and turned him over and over again. Maidstone were not that great. Mike Graham was a fucking nightmare. He hunched his portly shoulders forward, pounded like fury with his feet, spread his frame as wide as it would go and still failed to make contact. Time and again his patch of defence was surrendered as the crosses rained in on Kelham's goal. Graham hadn't the pace or the skill to stop it. His knees were shot, there was nobody in the squad to threaten his position. That game was like watching an autopsy on someone who was still alive.

Worse, in the next seat was a ground-hopper. Watling Street, the Dartford home of Maidstone United, was almost his last ground. He noted the pathetic 944 crowd and took pleasure in informing me he'd never seen a crowd under a thousand. At least I got away from him at half-time. But it was a crap night.

In the season prior to this, our leading scorer - Eric Gates - had displayed the mobility of a one-legged zombie with his foot in a wheel clamp. The 5-1 hammering in February 1992 came after a very brief period of early season hope. Gates had gone and Doncaster were humiliated in an opening day of the season away victory. By February our only hope was in Aldershot's bank balance. 'Depressed' doesn't do justice to my feelings that night. I knew then, more than I'd ever known, that I was welded to this team and their fortunes for life. If ever I could have walked away from Carlisle United it was in the days that followed that complete capitulation. We had little to cheer us up: the skill of our striker, Andy Watson, the class of Kelham O' Hanlon. Trust me, the worst days of Roddy Collins were more entertaining than that night.

By this point I'd got a job in Dartford. I'd risen into the management sector and taken on a team of staff. On my first day I was confronted by a desk a foot deep in unsorted paper and a filing cabinet neatly arranged in alphabetical order. The filing cabinet was empty of files. I wasn't so much picking up a new job as registering my predecessor's cry for help. There are a lot of things you could say about this situation. I'll restrict myself to two. Firstly, it was obvious I'd got an uphill struggle on my hands. Secondly, I'm still working in the same place as I write this.

It was made harder because the previous six months had been the happiest of my working life. I'd been working as Publicity Officer at Thurrock College, my writing was getting published by the ton and opportunities kept coming my way. Above all, I was having the best laugh of my working life. The adult comics now included the mega-sick *Ziggy*. *Ziggy* was hell-bent on getting noticed by going over the top. I did a couple of jokes for them that got minor complaints and attention and then pulled one that made half a page of a national newspaper. Give the tabloid in question their due, they did something moral. They were so offended they refused to name the magazine. The publicity would have been worth somewhere between ten and twenty thousand sales to us.

I'd met the odd reader of my stuff by this point but in 1990 I did the Comic Art Convention in London, speaking about writing sick jokes for a living. I met some fans there. Once I sussed that they weren't about to knife me for the stuff I was writing we got on well. I'd even started getting some loony fan mail from writing about the paranormal.

I could work all day at college, write this stuff in the evenings and come away feeling wide awake. It didn't matter how mad the ideas were, someone would buy them. Okay, I had the odd loser. My comic superhero - Captain Penis - who had a three foot erection, a permanent state of sexual arousal and a nifty line in using the appendage to fight crime stiffed out for real everywhere. On the other hand, stuff I thought would never go was snapped up and followed by cheques dropping through the door. I moved jobs because a promotion offered itself, and offered me more money. I'd worked myself up the ladder. Then again, that didn't necessarily make it feel better. Eight months into the new job, that night in February 1992 depressed me all the more because I knew that, like my team, I was reduced to struggling against daunting odds with no guarantee of getting a result. Carlisle and me, needed hard work and some new faces in the team.

We could both remember days when there had been a sparkle to the whole thing. What sparkle there was as a Carlisle supporter often came from the company at the games. In that desperate 'bottom of the league season' I managed to enjoy two games. On Boxing Day 1991 I finally persuaded my Dad to come to a game. They don't come much more hopeless than a bottom of the table encounter and Carlisle v Doncaster promised nothing for the discerning fan. For me and my Dad it was another part of the growing pattern of his life alone. Five years into being alone there was still a sadness in some of the things he did. He couldn't share anything with the person who'd mattered most. In the face of this, he did things he would never have been able to share with my Mum, because he'd never have talked her into them. A long trip to the Cape Verde Islands put him just about beyond civilisation. On Boxing Day Carlisle won 1-0. The football was pathetic. Simon Jeffels got the only goal. Jeffels, like Paul Proudlock would end up in non-league football in his mid-twenties. Let's face it, this team was short on class.

What I got that day was a chance to talk to my Dad. We got decent seats in the main stand, I pointed out every other location at Brunton Park in which I'd stood and filled him in on a part of my life that he'd missed. He, in turn, marvelled at the quality of the view. A rugby man through and through, my Dad could appreciate a quality move and, looking down on the action, he got a few moments to applaud. Well, Kelham and Andy Watson added what class we had. What mattered most was being together and sharing some father and son time. The strange thing was that, in an odd way, I was the dad. Brunton Park was new to him and he registered the importance of the result only because he understood the maths. To me it mattered emotionally that the score gave us some space over Doncaster and it might have kept us off the bottom at the end of the season. In the end it didn't matter at all. In May we chose to stage our traditional, last Saturday, full-blooded surrender. On 2 May we were second bottom in the morning and absolute bottom by twenty to five after play-off chasing Scunthorpe hammered us 4-0. Doncaster, bottom that morning, climbed into Carlisle United's traditional 'one off the bottom,' league slot.

Carlisle were down to their loyal support. They hadn't much else to depend upon. I knew how they felt. Then again, my loyal support - Jane - had become my wife in the summer of 1991 and by the time I talked her into going along to the Gillingham away match in March we were expecting a baby. I'd like to think that Thom got his love of football from that game. In reality, this is garbage. He got it from growing up in the south and watching Arsenal on television, talking Arsenal with his mates and loving the proud red colours of the Arsenal shirt. However, the first game Thom chose to attend was a Carlisle away match at Southend in 1997. He first went to a game inside his mother in 1992 as Carlisle played Gillingham. And we won. For years I would argue with other fans about this game and it would be over a season later, on a train back from Northampton that I would finally find a fellow witness - a certain Phil Lorimer - who saw what I saw. Honest, John Holliday had a good game. The misfiring man-mountain of moderate abilities managed to mess up the best that North Kent could throw in his direction. Sometimes his enthusiasm and unpredictability achieved things by accident. For starters, the Gills could hardly cut off his headed passes when Holliday's lack of accuracy left you guessing until the last minute where they would land. That was a magic afternoon in a pathetic season. It was our second, and final, away win of the season. The excitement of watching a clumsy assortment of journeymen, strengthened by Andy Watson, Kelham O' Hanlon and the briefly on form John Holliday had Jane out of her seat and may just have pumped a drop of adrenalin through Thom's growing veins. His slowly forming ears may have heard the roar of the crowd, such as the 'crowd' was in our end. It was, quite simply, a magical, lucky, exciting afternoon. We struggled to match Gillingham on skill. We matched them on running and out did them on luck. The proof that something almost unfathomably strange was happening that day was on the scoresheet. We won 2-1. Our goals were scored by... Holmes and Watson.

Great game, shame about the rest of that season.

In May 1992 we finished bottom of the league because we were bottom of Division Four. The following year we still managed to make it to Division Three. That year the Premiership was created and the three divisions beneath the top flight put a positive face on the fact that they appeared to have been cynically cut adrift. From now on there would be nothing below the Third Division.

By this point we had Aiden McCaffery as manager - another one taken from within the playing ranks. McCaffrey's first team appearances were limited to the season in which Newport did us all a favour so he was under no illusions. In April 1991 he inherited a team already doomed to finishing in the bottom block of the league. He managed them through the worst season in the history of the club and was eventually booted out in September '92 to make way for David McCreery. As Paul Harrison put it in *The Lads In Blue*: 'His predicament was a difficult one, few managers would have stuck it out for so long.' McCaffrey had no money to spend and little in the way of real talent at his disposal.

Few sets of fans would have stuck it out so well either. By the end of the 1991/92 season there were intense discussions about the unthinkable. Part time football was one possibility - it was well known that the club would accept any reasonable offer from anyone who wanted to buy it outright and there was talk about the Scottish league. This last area has been the subject of constant rumour and speculation. Hell, opposing fans regularly chant, 'You're just a small town in Scotland.' The rumours are strongest when our form is weakest. With regard to the Scottish league there are some standard arguments:

- The longest round trips in the football league in any given season invariably pit Carlisle against the likes of Torquay, Exeter and Gillingham. Nowhere in Scotland is as far from Carlisle as these places.

- Carlisle is so far from any English club - almost 60 miles from Newcastle - that we have no local competition. Queen of the South, in Dumfriesshire, are about as close as Workington.

Alongside these there are a few sound financial arguments. As I write this, Carlisle have a 16,000 capacity ground. This puts them on a par with credible Scots teams like Dundee, Kilmarnock and St Johnstone all of whom have recently staged assaults on major silverware, and/or qualification for Europe.

The more you think about it, the better it gets. I've held such arguments with uncomprehending work mates. Carlisle's support veers wildly in good and bad years. That bottom of the season run in 1992 saw pathetic crowds. Having said this, an assault on the Scottish Premiership would bring the crowds back and this is where my workmates get worried about my sanity.

Apply a little crude maths and what I'm about to say looks saner than you think. There are teams in the Scottish Premiership sustaining successful seasons on an average gate of 8-10 thousand. Allow for the massive away support of Rangers and Celtic and you've got plenty of punters on some gates even if your entire home support takes the day off. Look at the middle of the Scottish First Division and you'll see gates and teams who couldn't survive against the likes of Lincoln City or Northampton. The gulf between first and twentieth place in Scotland is immense. The team in which Mike Graham 'enjoyed' his final season at Carlisle would have been good enough for an untroubled season in Scottish League Division One. Stranraer can reach that league!

Allow for the marketing potential of a half decent English - i.e. better than

Berwick Rangers - team in Scotland and you've got headlines every week and a pile of travelling support willing their boys to beat the English! The policing bill might go up but so would the crowds. I love Carlisle United but even I would admit they couldn't realistically oppose the likes of Celtic and Rangers, but there are few other teams north of the border who would pose an impossible task. Aberdeen, Hibs and Dundee United would certainly put more on the gate at Brunton Park than Torquay or Leyton Orient and, given the fact that these teams would all come twice a year excluding the cup games, you have the makings of a useful income and an attractive package. My workmates think I'm insane suggesting a club that has fallen to The Conference could survive so high up in Scotland.

I don't want anyone at Carlisle to seriously consider this at the moment because I live in Maidstone. Give me a job in Carlisle and I might feel different - love has a selfish element. We tend only to love those people and things that can give us something meaningful in return. Deep down, I care so much that I want Carlisle to do well. My head says they would do well in Scotland. I would struggle to survive without a close up fix of my team.

In the summer of 1992 the hope, like the league position, was at rock bottom and any constructive suggestion was up for consideration. The rest - as they say - is history. Michael Knighton ended one lot of speculation by taking over the club. In the end, he started an equal amount of speculation but, in those early days, we heard out his ten year plan for Premiership action; we marvelled at the fluid movement in the early season team and felt more relief than we could usefully express that we had been spared the worse options on offer. The much-maligned Aiden McCaffrey was on his way. David McCreery was in and a few new faces had joined him. On 18 August 1992 I took the whole family along, Jane well pregnant by this point, as Burnley surrendered to a performance packed with movement. The skill was intermittent but this looked like a new team. Hell, we were so good in that 4-1 Coca Cola cup win that Ricardo Gabbiadini looked good. He even scored, twice! The highspot of the night for me was the early back pass from Burnley in which they managed to forget the new back pass rule. Ricardo's first goal for Carlisle came from the resulting indirect free kick. Thom, still inside his mother but considerably larger than he was at Gillingham the previous season, stirred as Ricardo drove home.

A few months after I'd seen the worst team ever to trade under the name of Carlisle United I was now watching an outfit that had some pretensions to class and a smattering of talent. Okay Kelham and Andy Watson were still on board but we also had two good young prospects from the youth team, Jeff Thorpe and Darren Edmonson. A young midfielder signed from Swansea called Simon Davey also looked impressive.

Normal service was resumed at Colchester, Barnet, Lincoln and Gillingham where narrow defeats on the back of fighting performances were the order of the day. I only saw Carlisle win during home trips that season but I still came away encouraged. Like my job, I knew it was going to take a long haul - some new ideas were working, some weren't. On the negative side we tried out the forward 'talents' of the woeful Jason Prins, who at least had the excuse that he was hardly out of nappies. We also offered John Holliday another bite of the cherry in the hope that he could rekindle whatever it was he had kindled that afternoon in Gillingham. He didn't deliver. We delivered him to Mansfield Town but he was back in Cumbria, at Workington, pretty soon after.

In late October Jane and I became parents to Thom. He arrived late, chunky and startled. Nothing before or since compares with seeing his entry into the world, holding our little bundle of life or looking into his eyes as he tried to make sense of those first moments. Like all babies, he would disturb our sleep, rearrange our lives and frustrate our efforts to comfort him. But I'd never known love like I felt then and Thom's first months were more contented and happy than I'd dared believe possible. By any standards he was a good baby and his sleep was usually so contented that his soft breathing was more musical, and more magical, than anything I'd ever heard.

Football was out there if I still wanted it. But, faced with a Gillingham strike in the second half of a tight game, I found myself still feeling good. We were both in the bottom bundle of clubs, although the monumentally crap Halifax Town were providing the - 'we'll never be that bad' - cushion of hope. In the circumstances I could come away from the Gills defeat almost glad for Gillingham. Given their proximity to my home I wouldn't wish any ill on them. The only really bad news that season was the transfer of Andy Watson to Barnsley. But our baby son was magic, and a Saturday afternoon that took in a trip to Pizza Express and a chance to feed him a bottle was preferable to a windswept terrace a grey sky, and a point at best. I still stuck with the football, but there was a feeling that it was on hold until Thom could make more sense of the world for himself.

Michael Knighton duly obliged by saving the surge until that time. Thom was toddling, the winter of 1993/94 was rolling around to a half-cocked spring and Jane and I booked a holiday. Predictably, I scanned the league tables, doubtful about the wisdom of booking on the play-off dates. In the end it seemed unlikely, Carlisle were fourteenth. A few months later, we made the play offs and I lost sleep in agonies of split loyalties. I wanted promotion badly, but on the day of the final, I would be thousands of miles away.

We made the play-offs and over two legs we caved in to Wycombe Wanderers. I faced the result with a mixture of disappointment, relief and guilt at feeling relieved. In the end, it was a fair result. In 180 minutes of play off football we found the net once, with a penalty. Wycombe won promotion in their first season.

We gave them a helping hand by scoring their first league goal on a hot

August afternoon in Carlisle and then losing to them away in December. Shame, Wycombe's ground is within easy travelling distance for the south east Blue Army. We travelled badly in the south east that season but the quality of our football was improving. The addition of David Reeves was a clear signal of intent. We'd signed the lanky workhorse of a forward from Notts County for £121,000. The fee was a club record and an indication of the Knighton style in which stunts and gestures would feature prominently. Knighton had gone £1,000 higher than the fee we paid for Gordon Staniforth. He had - apparently - set out deliberately to give us our most expensive player, at the cheapest possible price.

Our surge up the table in the last quarter of the season owed a lot to Reeves' eleven goals. The confidence was there, the new boss Mick Wadsworth was gradually blending a shape and sense of style into this side. Hell, we were a footballing side again. I'd forgotten what that was like.

Oddly, the most positive, emotional football experience I had that season came on 4 April. We were up at home over Easter. Thom was old enough to recognise his grandad and he, Jane and his grandad were enjoying some quality time in Workington! I'd gone to see the Reds against Great Harwood Town with Wayne, a lad who lived up the road from my Dad and ate and slept football. Carlisle United kicked off in Crewe that day, facing a home side fancied for automatic promotion.

In the Workington team I saw were Jason Prins and John Holliday. In the blustering Solway wind, Workington struggled, squelched and surrendered space. Ace defender Paddy Atkinson - late of Hartlepool and eventually of York City - was all that stood between the Red Army and a complete massacre. Holliday was a strange sight. His heading 'skills' were well employed on set pieces. Any dead ball led to a long wait as the massive, misfiring defensive enigma trotted slowly into the Great Harwood penalty box. The dead ball was lofted slowly into orbit where Holliday would use his massive frame to ensure first connection. Big John's gangling inaccuracy meant the ball could land anywhere and the opposing defenders hadn't a fucking clue how to deal with him. John's mission was to knock the ball back where the beer bellied frames of the forward playing 'lads' were splashing in for a crack on goal. At their worst I've seen Carlisle play kick and rush football. This was an average season by Workington's '90s standards and they were playing rush and try to kick football. Incidentally, they lost.

Two years before we were so desperate that Holliday and Prins had offered hope. Now we were so good that I couldn't wait to cross the road, get into the Safeway's cafe, wait for the rest of the family and listen to the game I'd been thinking about all afternoon. The one in Crewe. We'd won a hard fought encounter 3-2, scrambling a late winner off a free kick. Wayne had a radio and we listened in close to the crackling report. Hell, it took me back, listening to a report of a Carlisle team on the verge of something. Okay, it was only fucking Crewe, but two years before we were barely fit to lace their boots.

How the hell could I have doubted them when they were fourteenth and booked a holiday in Menorca that coincided with the play offs? Two days before this final I was telling the guy in the next apartment about my near miss of the play offs. He shrugged, stared into space and struggled to put a sentence together as he confessed he was a Preston fan. He'd done the same thing and nowhere on that end of the island seemed able to put on a Sky broadcast of the Division Three final. In the end he downed beer like there was a hole in his stomach as he suffered through ten minutes of highlights of a Wembley final in which Wycombe put his heroes to the test and beat them. I felt for that guy.

I also reflected long and hard on that season. Knighton offered us drama, promises, stunts and an end of season cliffhanger. A formula that would repeat itself for years to come.

10 Kenny Lowe

Mentioned for the first time in this chapter:

These are my opinions not facts. Others - especially those mentioned below - are likely to disagree.

Tony Caig - First choice United goalie for 94/95, product of youth policy. Great shot stopper, suspect on kicking during the early part of his career.
Dave Currie - Well travelled thirty-something striker. On his way down the league. Miraculous first touch and deft striker of the ball. Faulted by some for lack of effort and by others for the kind of arguing that attracts yellow cards.
Rory Delap - Gawky prospect with speed and vision. A promising rumour at the start of the 94/95 season. Eventually a Premiership regular.
Tony Gallimore - Classy left back, signed from Stoke. Found his feet at Carlisle and made a massive impact with 40 appearances in 94/95 season.
Joe Joyce - Experienced and intelligent defender. Signed in player/coaching role. Still cutting it on the pitch in 94/95 season.
Kenny Lowe - Much travelled, seldom established midfield/forward/waste of space, briefly on loan 94/95. Subsequently a titan in the dugout at Barrow.
Richard Prokas - Utility player, mainly mid-field. Second to none in commitment and a worthy fan favourite. Progressed from youth team for start of 94/95 season.
Shane Reddish - Bargain basement relic of a bygone age, out of time by 1994 and outclassed by the rest of the squad.
Rod Thomas - Mentioned briefly before but this chapter is his era. Skilful, diminutive, dread-locked forward, England schoolboy, youth and under 21 international. Briefly revived stalled career at Carlisle.
Peter Valentine - Solid central defender, always willing to give it a go, short on style.
Dean 'Deano' Walling - Lanky and unflappable defender, former striker with non-league past. Found his niche at Carlisle with silky performances in defence supplemented with precise goal getting strikes, especially from set pieces.

When the dust settled on the promotion campaign of 1994 I knew a satisfaction that stirred a strange mix of nostalgia and anticipation. At their best Carlisle United had earned a reputation as an unwelcome nightmare on the cup campaign of any fancied team and a tough run around in search of points, with some unwelcome Cumbrian weather thrown in, for any evenly matched team. But their 'best' meant the seventies. That sprint up the league in 1994 reached parts of my mind that had been in cold storage for years.

Listening to the final moments at Crewe on Radio Cumbria was a minor incident but it brought back the past. I could picture the last few frantic minutes of that game. Carlisle setting up a free kick. Davey poised over the ball and a sense of purpose in the tension. An accurate strike, Rod Thomas darting in to cause confusion, Crewe's organisation surrendering to the pace and pressure before Rod with his close control and speed dived in behind to deliver and take the points north.

I wasn't there., I'd spent the afternoon watching Jason Prins and John Holliday safe in the knowledge that they weren't on the books at Brunton Park. After a few false dawns and more turgid encounters than any loyal fan should ever have to endure, there was now an air of expectation about this outfit. My childhood memories of picturing games I didn't attend and expecting a win regardless were being fired again. We had hope.

Then again, there were Knighton's over-blown and self-aggrandising touches everywhere. Mick Wadsworth was 'Director of Coaching,' that's a manager to you and me. Carlisle had a youth academy. It had seen the likes of Jeff Thorpe and Tony Caig into the first team and several other fresh faces - Delap, Prokas etc. - on the team photo and so there was - arguably - a top to bottom coaching scheme that demanded an overall director. In the end, having a 'Director of Coaching' in the Third Division is like calling a dustman a refuge disposal engineer. It tells the world you've got ambition, but they'll only notice when you deliver something above the usual standard of service.

The fixture list appeared, I started making plans. Nothing was going to keep me from Barnet and Fulham, Northampton was worth the trek and I'd get in as many at home as possible. We opened against Wigan who had finished in the bottom four in May. As a Cumbrian, I don't expect decent weather this side of a charter flight and a gaping hole in my wallet. There is always that odd feeling that you've dreamed that first balmy game of the season. In hot sunshine we beat Wigan 2-1. Reeves and Dean 'Deano' Walling made the difference on the day. The air of unreality grew with the passing weeks as win piled upon win and a yawning gap began to open up between us and the pack. Week after week we rattled in 2 and 3 in response to the opposition's ones and zeros. I went through shock, disorientation and what passes in the mind of a Cumbrian for deep thinking. By 5 October the Blue Army - with several away shirts in evidence - were piling into Loftus Road for a mid-week collision in the League Cup. I'd come to a realisation of sorts and I'd argue I was a slightly different supporter to the guy that had seen that opening encounter.

Losing 3-0 on aggregate to QPR was the first real defeat of the season. We'd avenged a first leg loss over Rotherham earlier in the competition. The work rate from the players and the sense that - even at 3-0 down on aggregate - it mattered to chase every ball, were a healthy sign. Still, the whole thing felt unreal to me. Partly, I'm sure, this was down to the situation. The usual will I/won't I debate about going. The worry about missing a train by five minutes, getting home an hour later and being knackered the following morning. But there was more to it than that.

Football crowds change imperceptibly from match to match. Carlisle away in the south east pull an odd assortment of interested ex-pats, addicted types, Cumbrians with an unhealthy interest in bum aching coach journeys, over-priced motorway food and reading the tabloids down to the small print. Add the odd curiosity seeker - and I've met some really odd ones in Carlisle crowds - and allow for the small changes with each London borough, weekend/midweek games, the month, the weather, the seaside towns which host low grade football etc, and you've got the ever changing south east away crowd. The mixing of the mystical formula on 5 October 1994 put a few professional types into the Loftus Road crowd and a number of interested bystanders carrying the hope they would see an upset. You can get too analytical about this stuff but the feeling of unreality hit me several times that season. Never more so than that night because - after an age in which it was unthinkable - Carlisle United were, by general agreement, good enough to punish anyone. A few neutrals, believing an upset possible, were in our end.

Speaking of the odd people you meet in crowds... within a couple of years I would find myself on a rain swept seaside football terrace standing next to a bunch of Americans who had targeted Carlisle vs Bournemouth because they wanted something 'authentic.' Hell, they'd done the Chedder Gorge and an English country pub, what else was there?

In the face of the consistent changes it makes sense, every once in a while, to consider your own reasons for being there. In the space of that Coca Cola/League Cup tie - 20 September to 5 October - I'd found myself thinking hard about the whole thing and why I was there. The surest sign that something was wrong was the inexplicable relief with which I greeted the news of a 0-1 defeat at Carlisle on 20 September. I want Carlisle to turn over fashionable teams, London teams are a particular want in this department. Maybe I just didn't fancy the bleary train rides home on freezing Tuesday nights, the higher gate prices against the lower chance of a certain win, the stubborn refusal of my eyes to open the following morning, and the clock watching in the afternoon waiting to fight the rush hour on my way to some seldom visited ground with no fondly remembered burger cabin. If QPR had put four past us at the first attempt then a trip to the return leg at Loftus Road would have been easier to reject out of hand. Well those were the logical reasons for welcoming a defeat, but they'd never made me feel good when we took a stuffing before.

Frankly, by September 1994 I was having an identity crisis as a supporter. I might have been coming up to 35 but this was not a mid-life crisis. I'm hoping to avoid any crisis at any time in my life. My strategy is foolproof. I've spent my entire adult life so bloody confused about what it all means and wondering where the hell I fit in that no birthday can make the confusion any worse. I worried seriously about why I was so relieved at that defeat. I had started to worry at it hard as I shuffled through Euston station at the end of September on my way to Northampton.

What I think it comes down to is this. We match ourselves with the people in life that reflect the way we see things. That's certainly true with our choices in music, television or whatever. On the face of it there is a difference to the way we support football teams and the way we pick our favourite rock stars. The unwritten rules of football give you a choice of glamour or local. You all support the local club and pick a glamour club that you follow on TV. Well, that was the theory for my generation and we've already established that 'local' to me meant a choice of Carlisle and Workington. At the start of the 94/95 season it struck me for the first time that it isn't that simple for your whole life. Asked up to the end of the previous season I could give a straight answer as to what a fixture list was doing on my computer diary at work, why I bothered heading to Barnet on a wet Saturday and the rest. Depending on the person asking the question my Cumbrian roots, our place as a little known outpost of England and/or great Carlisle tradition of the hard working footballing side would feature. The first round of the Coca Cola/League Cup tie with QPR had taken place in Carlisle on 20 September and, reading the report in the paper the following morning, I'd felt an odd mixture of emotion at the 1-0 defeat we'd taken. The fall out of the strange elation at the defeat by QPR, turning over in my mind for half a week, told me that these pat answers were bollocks.

I'd stuck with Carlisle for many reasons. But one that I'd missed was the way their progress and attitude had strangely mirrored my own over the best part of two and a half decades. This was something of a revelation and it struck me, in the manner of all great revelations, in the most unlikely place. I've had a few interesting experiences in train toilets over the years but getting hit with a life defining revelation on a Saturday morning ranks as one of the most memorable. What it comes down to is that, in an odd way, following a football team does match the personal qualities we see in rock stars, actors and others. Teams can have such a quality. Football lends itself to this more than you might think. From one angle the whole beauty of football is the different meanings it can have for everyone. Mike Graham's furious back-pedalling stays with me as an image of panic and hopelessness from the darkest period of my existence as a United supporter. Then again, I was having a few dark moments of my own at the time. That pathetic crowd we fielded in the bottom of the league year matched my view of life at the time as well as any Smiths' album or gritty movie. The illusion - and it is an illusion - is that we have more choice over the records and movies which take our cash than we do about the football teams we support. In 1994, by contrast to the bottom of everything season, Carlisle and I were heading in different directions. I went through life at the time coming home knackered, struggling to fit more work into less time than I'd ever had and knowing that none of it was as important as grabbing what quality moments I could with Thom. Quality moments on the pitch had been at a similar premium for years but now - even in the jaws of a home defeat by QPR - we were a quality outfit.

Carlisle United weren't matching my expectations of life, they were bloody well exceeding them. I couldn't read a grim northern slant into their games because there was a confidence and quality about everything they were doing. The only thing that matched the way my life was going was that we'd got beaten. Don't get me wrong, I didn't want the rotund back-peddling nightmare Graham and his cronies to return. I just needed to adjust to the new situation, to make some sense of a confusing feeling that had dogged me for a few days. I was a Cumbrian, they were my team and the reasons I'd loved them all along were still there. The discomfort so far in the impressive season was like supporting your other half through a tough set of exams and then not being able to say you were jealous when they landed a better-paid job than you. You might feel a bit odd but you'd still sleep with them. In the end, because it mattered enough, you'd work it out, and you'd both be better for it. I owed this team more support. I'd let life dictate to me a fair bit and all I had to show for it was a few more quid in the bank and a mountain of work on my desk. I sat down, got stuck into my copy of *The Sun* and looked forward with confidence to enjoying an away win.

We were going to win, of course. We were three points clear of the pack. There they were almost propping up the football league. Northampton's home at the cricket ground was far enough from the station to leave an away fan equally confused every year. I never did memorise the route. That day I asked for directions a few times. One guy told me the game was in Carlisle, a bloke in an Arsenal top didn't know where the ground was.

Shuffling to my seat meant wandering in front of the away team bench and I got in a cheery chat with Jeff Thorpe. Just before kick off, the empty seat next to me was filled by the ref's wife, a looker. He might not have parents but this ref was doing alright. I started to get edgy. What happens when you want to get up and scream for an offside and the wife of the guy who denied it is practically sitting in your lap?

Northampton played like a team second bottom of the whole lot should play - they were fucking angry. Not too skilful maybe, but they ran at the game like they wanted some result. The nerves were bloody transparent when chances and half chances were snatched by panicking forwards. They could string their passes together, but in front of goal they weren't accurate enough. Carlisle were penned back, but when they did break free they had time and skill to measure the attacks.

The first sign that something was seriously wrong came with Rodder's first touch. A skilful shimmy turned into some inspired break-dancing as he lost control on the low grade Cobblers' pitch. 'He thought the pitch was a bit uneven,' said Mrs Ref. Uneven, it was obviously uneven. Roderick's flailing dreadlocks were just about visible from behind the nearest hillock! Let's add 'heavy' to the criticisms of the pitch and mention the wind that was blowing into Tony Caig's goalmouth.

With massive defensive clearances doing a swift one eighty turn, United were up against it until half time. Still with most of the first half gone I wasn't worried. We were soaking up pressure but that's why we bought Deano. Tony 'Gally' Gallimore and Joe Joyce were superb at the back. When Northampton scored I thought back to the revelation on the train and didn't even consider feeling good about it. We had skill, we had shape, we had pace and more points than this lot would see before March. Half time was approaching and with that wind being worth an extra man in midfield I was figuring two or three for us. To be fair, the signs were already there that we needed the extra man. Kenny Lowe was definitely mentioned in the team check at the start but he must have been off getting in the pies because I didn't notice him playing football during the first 45 minutes. Elsewhere the pace was lacking, probably on account of the miles run in pursuit of QPR a few days earlier.

We broke out a bit more in the second half but from the restart I realised I'd been wrong about that wind. All we could do was hold them, we were still getting caught on the break. The conditions demanded short passes, simple moves and several miles of running from every man. Give Northampton their due - they were doing all of that. The older heads in the away pyjama strip could be seen doing their best to calm things down and David Currie's gob was getting as much work as his legs in this department.

This was a job for a director of coaching and Wadsworth duly responded. I finally spotted Kenny Lowe - he was the one heading for the touch-line. His number was up, thank fuck. So was Valentine's. Poor old Pedro looked knackered but then he had spent 90 minutes marshalling a defence against the might of Les Ferdinand a few days before. As for Kenny Lowe I'm glad he was a loan job if we'd forked out as much as ten grand for the sod on that form I'd have been back down to the bench for a chat. Players have come and gone over the years but Kenny Lowe - a short lived loan signing from Birmingham - continues to trouble me. I saw his only start in a Carlisle shirt. He made one more appearance as sub and was promptly despatched back to St Andrews. In my mind he is forever marooned in a fast moving mid-field, lacking match fitness, chasing a pass that has already fled and battling a hard wind into the bargain. At the end of the season I voted for Kenny Lowe in a United fanzine poll as the biggest waste of space I'd seen that season in a Carlisle shirt. In fact, I saw him play for around an hour. The only other time I remember seeing him impress I caught sight of his thin frame and thinning thatch as he made a workmanlike attempt on goal in a Birmingham City shirt the following season.

Amazingly Kenny scored impressively in the biggest waste of space category in the fanzine that year; he walked the award with more than double the votes of his closest competitor, Shane Reddish. There were good reasons for voting for Reddish. He was a genuine throwback, signed at the end of a poor season. He'd clocked up over 30 appearances to the start of the 94/95 season. He'd even scored, but he belonged in the aimless outfit he'd joined in 1993. We got better, he looked worse. Lowe was simply on trial and we were glad to see the back of him. So what was it about Kenny-fucking-Lowe? You've got me, but he still gets abused on our message boards despite his heroic exploits in the dugout at Barrow.

Kenny Lowe walked out of my life with half an hour of the Northampton game to go. With Prokas and Edmonson on we hit the heights. The first move of the new line up saw a quick cut through mid-field, a tidy ball out to the left, some deft control, a pass and Reevesy was one goal nearer being the leading scorer in the division. Then Northampton threw the script away and scored again. The announcer claimed it for one of their own. A Blue Army inquest on the train to London agreed Joe Joyce had been the last to touch it. I didn't have the angle in the cramped stand to know for sure. If it was Joe it was bloody cruel luck because his cool and vision had done a hell of a lot to hold back the scurrying maroon tide for most of the afternoon.

We chased the game but didn't get back in. Our first league defeat of the season. Two games against southern teams, two defeats in one week and I went home happy from the second one. Genuinely happy. Having figured out why I'd been quietly relieved the first time, seen myself for the quietly miserable sod I was becoming and deciding to get behind a winning team they went and fucking lost on me. I went home happy because I'd seen them chase, show skill and somewhere deep in the confused cesspit - the nearest thing to a 'mind' I can muster - I knew I'd seen a team fit for promotion. When they won or matched Premiership opposition I got nervous and confused. When they lost to a bunch of darting and desperate crapites I came away happy and confident of promotion. Funny old game innit?

Northampton was memorable for another reason. On the train home I ran into 'Foxy Ferret' Phil Lorimer. Phil was talking with another ex-pat, Sean, from Workington. The memorable bit about Phil is that I would see him on and off for years at United games and he would be the most visible - and the most inexplicable - of the group of supporters I got to know. Phil made an impression on me because his reasons for membership of the Blue Army were unusual, to say the least. Phil is/was from the south coast. He makes/made his living transporting greyhounds, travelling in and out of Cumbria. He has explained on at least three occasions how and why he came to adopt Carlisle and - in the manner of a great Frankie Howerd performance - it always made sense when I heard it and disappeared like morning mist when I ran it through my mind at other times. Being a southerner Phil clearly had a choice. Why he continued the loyalty through the unmitigated shite of the season from hell in 1992 beats me. But Phil and I really clicked when the conversation swung round to nightmare players. We abused Kenny Lowe that afternoon, Sean chipped in with others - like John Holliday - and I mentioned Holliday's stormer against Gillingham. Phil had been there and backed me. In such moments bonds are formed.

Phil Lorimer wouldn't come to my funeral for two good reasons. Firstly he's unlikely to be that bothered and secondly if I did beat him to that great windswept terrace in the sky he'd never bloody well find out. So why would I feel kinship with this bloke? Not because we shared a schooling or even a county when we grew up, not because we were drawn to Carlisle by a rich and rewarding tradition of playing entertaining football and not because the experience of watching a hard fought bottom flight tussle in a howling gale at a crumbling cricket ground offered us that incomparable big match atmosphere. I reckon we belong together because our needs were met by Carlisle United more than we would ever want to admit.

It's worth a thought: the travelling Blue Army are the same odd assortment that any team shackled with descriptions like 'regional' and 'unfashionable' would pull. When I've wandered out to the car park at Brunton Park in recent years I haven't as a rule been knocked out with the quality cars and dripping wealth mustered by the likes of Shrewsbury, Hull, Stevenage or Leigh RMI. All clubs can talk about ambition, but most of us have also seen our teams surrender on a Saturday afternoon. So why would any sane person give up time and cash to check them out? We might say they are 'our' team, except that they aren't always our local team. We might link our support to some past good experience but that is - roughly speaking - the equivalent of trying to muscle your way into bed with someone else's wife because the pair of you once went all the way with her parents in the next room when you were fifteen. Who cares if she's still pretty, is it honestly worth a night in hospital? We have a choice and we've had one all our adult lives. Whatever we say, we go because we want to and we want to because deep down our teams reflect our lives. Not totally, and not in some pretentious bullshit way that links Rod Thomas' weaving his magic through a pedestrian defence with our own hopes of escaping a dead end at work. In fact, for the most part, it's so bloody simple it's frightening. Most of us 'rank and file' supporters follow ploddingly average teams with ambition before returning to our ploddingly average lives in which we set targets and work forward ploddingly. Whatever we say about local teams, footballing traditions and the rest we seldom spend time in the half time queues admitting we have a choice about whether we are there. In fact, you are more likely to hear complaints from people who claim they have no choice.

The proof that we have a choice is in the absence of huge numbers of flash cars from the travelling fleet. Conspicuously successful people are more evident in the quality seating areas of Premiership high flyers than they will ever be at Brunton Park. Phil Lorimer and I support Carlisle because our allegiance has paid off in a manner of speaking. We've spent years watching teams that have matched our vision of life. Deep down, we've got to be optimists but we've also got a realistic streak strengthened through years of slogging to make a living. We're both likely to seize opportunities and make the most of their possibilities, which, in a manner of speaking, explains why we would seize on the clumsy efficiency of John Holliday and briefly believe he could be the answer to our defensive problems. It sounds grim although it isn't really all that bad. The sense of companionship is real. All the more so because the bonds go deeper than the action on the park and deeper than the jobs we do. The real pessimists - the ones for whom life can be truly grim - gave up years ago and you might catch some of them dragging around with their wives on a Saturday afternoon debating the merits of buying a new towel rail. Ask 'em about football and they may say they packed it in years ago because there was no point. They'd sooner get something done on a Saturday afternoon. I'll join them myself the second I get an adrenalin rush looking at a towel rail!

Taking this logic a little further it is no wonder that the massively successful tend to avoid the lower division teams. There always were those with talents far in excess of their classmates and the other kids in the street. For a while in the late years of junior school and the early years of the psychopathic comprehensive there is the tempting illusion that none of us are that different. The 'different' kids, often conspicuous by the fact that football matters less for them at ten years old than it does for most of us, tend to be the first to depart the fold. The ones who really get on from your class in school usually are the different ones. The ones who don't sell out or allow the local headcases to beat the ambition out of them. These people are likely to find the kind of bullying meted out by lower division defenders to a fledgling talent like Matt Jansen or Peter Beardsley a little too close to home. If life's high achievers need football it is often a fashion accessory, like designer stubble, or an opportunity to power lunch in an executive box. It has to be said, there are executive boxes in the lower divisions, but if anyone is power lunching in these the chances are that the discussions revolve around cleaning contracts for an office block or two.

The point is that much of this behaviour and allegiance, the way the ramshackle army of travelling support gather together and unite, after a fashion, for a couple of hours on a Saturday defies logic. You could adopt a team because of their great footballing tradition but put this logic to the test and its complete bollocks outside of the Premiership. You could argue that Carlisle are a footballing side with a pedigree worth defending. But, that argument was history by 1994 despite the flashes we'd seen on the pitch in recent games.

No side that has sunk as low as we have over such a long period can seriously claim to maintain a great tradition. When you are reduced to journeymen pros, a youth policy and the kind of 'talent' that leaves you change from £50,000 the best you can realistically hope to start with is ambition, attitude and a few useful skills. Okay, we had a 'Director of Coaching' by 1994 but you could have called Mick Wadsworth the 'ring master' for all the difference that made. And anyway, the man who takes on the development of hopeful talent in a lower league club is also part of the sales force. Mick Wadsworth achieved a lot for Carlisle and one honest measure of that is the presence of his former players in higher placed teams than ours over the future seasons. He found the best and brought it out. Wadsworth's subsequent career has hit some lows - a poor performing national side in Africa and assisting at Shrewsbury being two cases of note. Then again, some of us in the Blue Army still imagine a mythical return - and he's also achieved the near impossible. You could pack the entire fan base of Scarborough Athletic onto an Inter City train and leave a few empty seats so how the fuck does a team with a start like that make the Third Division play offs in 1998? Because Wadsworth, on form and motivated, is in the dugout.

So, anyway, Carlisle started the 94/95 season well. We took our first league defeat at the end of September in Northampton and within a few days we were dumped out of the Coca Cola/ League Cup by QPR. Somewhere along the line I got to thinking about why those of us who turn up on a regular basis actually bother which, naturally enough, led me to figure out why I put all the effort in myself. The conclusion was that I belong with them because I can't identify myself with the world's high achievers but I'm not ready to limit my ambitions to redecorating the bathroom on a Saturday afternoon.

As the song says: 'I'm Carlisle till I die.' And for the rest of that season we were all reminded how good that could be.

11 Paul Conway

Mentioned for the first time in this chapter:

These are my opinions not facts. Others - especially those mentioned below - are likely to disagree.

Paul Conway - Wandsworth born 'American' mid-field ball winner. Son of former Fulham idol Jimmy Conway, who moved to the USA, allowing his son to grow up stateside. Generally impressive on positioning, distribution and work rate.
Tony Elliot - Well travelled reserve keeper. Agile, brave and maintaining the great Peter Shilton tradition of extending his goal area to the half way line by means of loudly barking instructions at the defence. A favourite with me if not the managers charged with selecting him. Later a goalkeeping coach.
Peter Hampton - Long serving physio. Shortish dark-haired dead ringer for Mick Wadsworth giving the physical and mental master planners behind United the bizarre appearance of twins.
Steve Hayward - Attack minded midfielder with strength, accuracy and a level of nerve and commitment that was seldom found wanting.
Paul McGregor - He wore a blue shirt briefly, on loan in the 98/99 season. The word 'striker' appeared next to his name when his loan signing was announced. Maybe he was a 'striker' in the great British tradition of a bloke who refuses to do the job for which he is paid. Ten games, three goals. Not a fan favourite.
Derek Mountfield - Seasoned campaigner, centre half with class, a level head and a knack for well timed - but very occasional - forays up front.
Paul Murray - Home-grown talent. Unfussy mid-fielder with high work rate and an effective line in ball winning followed by well placed lay off.

In the worst moments, I've still got memories. If I want, I can remind myself about seven months that shook the world, well they shook my world anyway. If I want to touch the feelings that remind me why it matters, why I'll stand in the freezing January rain with little more than hope and a bacon roll to keep me going, I can think back to a handful of matches that reminded me it's more than a game. Times that strengthened my hold on life. One that I will treasure for as long as there are two brain cells working with a spark between them goes back to 22 October 1994. This ranks as one of the best afternoons I'm likely to have as a Blue.

My Dad and thirteen year old Owen were along for the ride. Dad hadn't been to a football match since the grim Boxing Day encounter with Doncaster in the season from Hell. Owen was looking for the things that made him different.

He'd started telling his mates he supported Carlisle. On the way in one fan threw himself down in an 'I'm not worthy' gesture as Roderick's Ford Escort trundled into the players' car park. With a mass of newly blooded supporters backing the high-flying team the optimism was infectious. The three of us were an unlikely band - one terminal case bringing along his Dad who was in it more for the bonding/quality time angle and a teenager filling in his time. Things started off well when the team was announced - Jeff Thorpe at number 12 and Kenny Lowe's name absent. Barnet's pathetic performance in the previous season had been turned round suspiciously fast. A few minutes in, the reasons were obvious. Manger, Ray Clemence hadn't much more skill or class to call on than his team could muster twelve months before. He'd got his cloggers organised, no more. His Barnet side resembled Carlisle's best under Clive Middlemas, the team I'd seen crumble at the boots of Maidstone United the day Owen got his head jumped on.

The kick off saw Reevesy out on the right and a clear plan to get round the back with a quick move. It didn't come off but from the start we were running at them, round them and into them. When David Currie got close after six minutes they were rattled. With passes being hit accurately and moves starting from anywhere a Blue found the ball the Barnet system was under threat. Barnet played it straight and aimed to stand up and stop the opposition. Drilled and disciplined, they were there for the taking as Carlisle ran off their men and Roderick and Reevesy sought new positions. The increasingly assured touches of Paul Conway took them on from mid-field and Carlisle ran in at the defence turning them and pulling them out of position. As the gaps opened up behind the full backs the chances came. Reevesy got in a shot just after the quarter hour. Derek Mountfield got his head to Currie's free kick soon after and Barnet's counters looked weak and desperate. When Simon Davey almost got on the score sheet in the twentieth minute the whole stand was up.

This was the only occasion on which I saw my Dad genuinely worked up about a football match. One of the odd things about my Dad was his fair-minded attitude in terms of most sports. His admiration for many stars was a lesson in fair play and enjoyment without cynicism. For all that, his attitude was a world away from the traditional British fair play for which this country is famed/ a laughing stock. During the seventies the Welsh rugby team humbled the world with a legendary brand of open, skilful and running rugby. My Dad would celebrate these performances by leaving his chair and yelling 'Come on, run it, run it!' even if J P R Williams was busy cutting a swathe through the English. I don't think there's a drop of Welsh blood in the family tree on Dad's side. Dad's other passions in sport revolved around athletics and Steve Ovett, Sebastian Coe and Steve Cram got the same vocal support that was lavished on Welsh rugby. My Dad was a fast running rugby player of some distinction and a good middle distance runner at school. He knew these sports well enough to appreciate the skills he was applauding. His football interest generally revolved around high profile games. He loved Sunderland's victory in the 1973 cup final for all the romantic reasons.

He briefly saw the shape, skill and vision he'd seen in rugby games on a football pitch at Carlisle in October 1994. In the first half hour Carlisle had set up a fast moving siege of the rigid Barnet defence and the move that got Reevesy onto the score sheet after the half hour would have done justice to Dad's beloved Welsh rugby union outfit of the seventies. Dave Currie's pass inside the defence was inch perfect and Roderick ran to the by-line making space, turning in an instant and BANG!!!!!! - in stormed Reevesy with £121,000 of clinical finishing. Predictably, Barnet tried to make a fight of it. They came out, we held them and the only other real chance of the half fell to Deano off a corner.

Early second half, they hit the bar, Rod's greed and a snatched shot knackered a good Carlisle move some time after the hour and Tony Elliot saved things at the other end from a decent Barnet shot. We needed something fast to make the clear superiority count and did we get it or what? Paul Conway had been inspirational considering it was the first competitive game he'd started all season. I'd been singling him out for shouts of encouragement. Call it psychic. Call it wishful thinking. The second he got the ball off that Barnet corner and started his run goalwards I knew it was in. Okay, there was the small matter of him being in our half when he started and a few defenders and their goalkeeper being on hand to try and stop him. 'Goal' doesn't do justice to his defence defying run, perfect positioning and split second delivery of the killer shot. 'Fucking awesome' comes somewhere close. I could spoil the whole thing by heading downstairs to watch it on the video now. If I did that I'd discover it was a well timed run and a well struck shot but in my mind that goal has grown in its paranormal power because I could sense the thing as he started his run and when it hit the back of the net I was yelling so loud it felt like an out of body experience.

Davey deservedly got on the score sheet with a crisp first-time drive. And Roderick's closing goal was a deserved reward for the usual skill, even if his back heel into a Barnet gut was out of order earlier on. When the final whistle blew I'd lost all track of time and Barnet had lost the appearance of an organised football team. Classic!

A word about Paul Murray here - he was bloody brilliant and along with Conway put together the kind of flowing, skilful football that allowed the whole team to play to their greatest strengths. There were two rumours circulating about the absence of Tony 'Gally' Gallimore from the left back position - one linked it to the need to hide him from the prying eyes of Premier division scouts. Another linked it to ten pints too soon before the game. The hot rumour over the non-appearance of Kenny Lowe on the pitch suggested he was crap.

Let's get this defence shredding performance in perspective, it was brilliant. With Paul Murray and Darren Edmonson overlapping and getting in a shot each and the midfield exploring space in search of opportunities the whole team were buzzing. Reevesy, Roderick and Dave Currie made space, squeezed the ball through angles and pulled off the defence in a way that suggested a tactical master plan even if there wasn't one. Hell, being a Carlisle supporter for years I'd forgotten football could be like this. Even the team that won promotion to Division One didn't always do it so well. Given his dominance in midfield Paul Conway looked as assured as Ray Train and Les O' Neil, men who had assumed legendary status. Reeves' incisive strikes were as good as anything Brunton Park had seen in over a decade, all that and he looked more like an athlete than Joe Laidlaw ever could.

Writing it up later for *So Jack Ashurst Where's My Shirt* I thought long and hard about the words 'Total football' because they sounded so bloody pretentious. But we had the fluid overlaps, the covering for players out of position, the invention, the chances coming in from all angles. Okay, it's over the top to compare Wadsworth's generation of the Blue Army to Cruyff era Holland but Tommy Docherty vintage Man Utd are a good comparison. Alright, 'The Doc' had a class outfit with a host of current internationals but he brought players up through the ranks and bought well, just like Mick Wadsworth. Whatever, we had a successful team. Players who understood each other and showed a love of playing that created openings out of nothing.

That afternoon was a watershed, a truly transforming experience. From the second - Barnet destroying - goal I'd witnessed the kind of performance I had never seen. We hadn't beaten Barnet, we'd dissected them. Grim bottom flight reality headed off into the distance sometime after four that Saturday afternoon and remained a stranger for weeks. I hadn't been programmed for this! In the final half hour we'd played an exhibition and a team three places below us had watched. That alone is enough to give that afternoon a place of affection in my memory. Thinking back years later it matters more for another reason. My Dad had understood, the way caring parents do, that football was in my life to stay but until that afternoon he'd never really felt it. It wasn't ever likely to be his game but he was on his feet as we surged forward again and again because the shape, invention and the passion to get the job done were infectious. As infectious, say, as a team of red shirted rugby legends running around the best the other home nations could manage in the seventies. Driving home the most important things were the confidence I'd seen in that team and the points that were in the bag. Now, years later, the most important thing is that, just once, I shared an experience that special with my Dad.

'Toilet paper!!!, look, paper, fuckin' toilet paper!!!!!'

The accent was thick Cumbrian, which might explain the puzzled looks from a few Fulham fans in the same bogs but, to tell you the truth, I didn't get it myself at first. It was all a bit strange. A gents the size of an indoor gym and a floor that was almost clean. The screaming Blue in the cubicle had one up on me - he'd ventured in for a slash and discovered that there were clubs in the bottom flight who provided a few trappings that would pass for civilised, like toilet paper. He emerged, younger than I'd imagined and totally stunned by his encounter with the strange rolls on the bog wall. It struck me then that this guy had probably never seen the inside of a decent football ground. Why should he? If he'd been supporting the team for five years he'd known nothing but the bargain basement. This time around I settled into a seat surrounded by Barbour jackets, posh accents and discussions about Carlisle's chances that afternoon. The Barbour crowd in question continued the great tradition of odd people in the next seats to me at a football match. They knew their football, claimed some Cumbrian connections and knew precisely sod all about the Carlisle team other than their ability to lead Division Three. Football tourists, but then successful clubs - like Carlisle - attract these people. They saw some sights that afternoon. Elsewhere a kid from Carlisle marvelled at the surroundings and shouted, 'Look' as he pointed skywards. Figuring I'd have the chance to see a UFO at long last I looked up and saw a Jumbo jet. That lad didn't get to many away games.

Fulham had some guts and wanted the points badly enough which was just fine by me because when they ran at us the gaps at the back started appearing. In the Fulham back four Terry Angus had an attitude problem from the start, suggesting that he knew his fellow defenders were up against it. The man-mountain of blubber and bad attitude that answered to the name of Terry Hurlock shuffled around looking increasingly pissed off as Wadsworth's Academy of Total Football Excellence got the measure of the crude offside trap. The class difference told and once Reevesy had hammered us into an early lead I was back to the out of body job, with each move and skilful lay off further proof of our superiority. Fulham put in a couple of cheeky attacks, giving Caig a chance to show his class and confidence. And then... Derek Mountfield got himself on the score sheet. Let's be straight here, Derek was a defender with a defender's instincts. Brought into the side in the twilight of his career Mountfield had seen action at the very top, a championship and European glory with Everton. If he had the space and confidence to come forward, we had to be playing well.

The planes swept up into the sky at the rate of one a minute and the Carlisle kid out in the big town spotted Concorde. Soon he'd sussed that there seemed to be a fair few sightings of Jumbos and reasoned that it must be the same one going round in circles! In the second half Roderick broke, dreadlocks trying like hell to keep up with his flying feet. Hurlock's suspect fitness was failing and with the balls from midfield measuring the offside trap to perfection we were running side by side with the defence in mad sprints on goal. Reevesy missed one it would have been easier to bag. Fast crosses were squandered and when Simon Davey got one with time to spare he stopped, checked and convinced us all that he'd blown a good opportunity but when his pass connected with a speeding Paul Conway it was... FUCKING MAGIC - GGOOOOOALLLLLLL-

LLL !!!!!!!

You could look in the football statto books and discover our Wandsworth born 'American' midfielder - Paul Conway - stayed with us for another two seasons, moved to the dizzy heights of Northampton Town, struggled to establish himself and reunited with Mick Wadsworth at Scarborough, playing his part in their sprint for play off glory in 1998. But, every journeyman has his moments and during one week in October 1994 Paul Conway was magnificent. Two goals, two great games for a table topping side. No statistics will begin to tell that story, you had to be there. I'll tell you how good he was - I missed Fulham's late consolation goal because I was still re-running the Conway strike with the Blues in the seats around me.

Could it get better? Well yes, and no.

In my thirties I got a Christmas present I'd have loved as a kid. My Dad bid in a charity auction and landed a signed ball and the chance to meet the Carlisle team. When I was younger the thought of meeting the Brunton supermen would have terrified me. As 1994 drew to a close it was a curious experience. We'll take a diversion first, honest, we'll be back to football soon enough.

When they tell you the truth about Santa Claus it's only the start. My Dad once cheerfully explained to me that one role pets serve is to teach us to cope with death. They live shorter lives than we do and our attachments, though deep, don't as a rule reach the depth we get with the people we learn to love. The cheerful discourse from my Dad was heading in the direction of grim Cumbrian humour. The basic point being that we're all gonna die anyway and that little stiff upturned hamster is your starter for ten. Oh sure, it's tragic but it's also cuddly, cute, un-mutilated and seemingly peaceful. Your grandparents might pull off looking peaceful in the chapel of rest but cuddly, give me a break! It just gets worse, by way of a few relatives, at least one of whom will - statistically speaking - go before disease and decay get a chance, possibly as the result of getting on the wrong end of some unforgiving machinery that'll reduce the contents of the casket to something resembling a kebab with too much tabasco. The Grim Reaper just keeps lurking in the shadows. Those creeping dark thoughts that started with wondering about how that beloved pet might really 'be' with the angels gradually turn round to you and the fact that your fading frame won't withstand the cells from within trying to kill it, the wearing out of the vital bits of machinery and the gradual drip drip effect of the abuse you hand out to your metabolism every time you open the biscuit tin. The longer you live the more you realise those grim reminders from the Grim one are there for you and you alone. That's age and experience for you and in the face of the unavoidable the least you can do is get in the odd sick chuckle. It's worth planning ahead, because there is an ahead for all of us. I'm waiting for the day when the cancerous lumps are pushing up against my skin to give it that unmistakable bag of spanners effect, my lungs are stubbornly refusing to push against the inside of my body and that worrying pain in my chest has reduced my arms to flapping and pathetic extensions of my useless body. Maybe then I'll admit I need a visit to the doctor.

DOC - Ermmm... Mr Nixon, what appears to be the problem.

NEIL - Well, you see, Doc, it started with my hamster.

Life's like that. There is a stubborn predictability to the way things carry on with absolute indifference to our own growth and death. Football for starters. There is a point to the fining of footballers for bringing the whole thing into disrepute but oddly, it seems to me, those imposing the fines don't really get that point. They throw fines and bans at a bunch of men in the prime of their athletic lives and the highest profile penalties are reserved for the role models, those whose earning power and ability to pull crowds has already reminded them they are special. Let one of these players commit some atrocity of bad conduct and the authorities punish them with massive fines and/or bans that simply remind the world how gifted these people are. The petty machinations aimed by the football authorities at a few outspoken 'characters' don't belittle these mavericks and trouble-makers.

The game - most certainly - is bigger than any one person and the point of fining and suspending people for threatening the reputation of their sport is to remind us all that football is the constant and the people in the game are the short term means by which the game continues. If you really want to bring them down and make this point you would be better forcing an Eric Cantona or Stan Bowles to read dusty books of statistics and census data to trace the lives of past internationals. Let them marvel at the crowds in front of which the internationals of the twenties and thirties played. Let them consider what it meant in those days and then give them the task of convincing a bunch of present day Arsenal loving school-kids that they should give a shit about the career of George Male. If they fail in this task, give them 100 hours community service emptying bed pans for a bunch of terminal confusion cases with their minds stuck hopelessly in the past. You know, people who can talk about nothing other than George Male.

CASE - Wayne Rooney, never heard of him Son. 'Ere, when you've done with the bead-pan bring us me paper and then you can polish up me signed photo of George Male. Hell of a player George Male.

FOOTBALLER IN TROUBLE - Er, yeah, right.

That'll hurt more than fining them a week's wages.

As a kid I would have been humbled in the presence of Alan Ross. By the time I came to write this book he was a housing officer in Carlisle. I'd be interested to know whether his agility and work rate deflected paper from his desk as efficiently as those outstretched arms once deflected goalbound shots. I spoke to people who knew him as I was working on this book. They reminisced about his goalkeeping skills but - in reality - they were happier to talk about the man they knew. A decent bloke. One of the good guys. In the time between finishing this book and seeing it published Alan Ross died. I'd love to have met him. I would have told him that I stood on the terraces and wanted to be like him, then. Meeting him as an adult I'd have got the words out without the nerves that would have silenced me as a kid. I guess, in those circumstances, I'd have been more impressed with the qualities that his friends were happier to mention. I'd have admired the decent bloke in his fifties. The one who cared about his family and worked hard for the council. A modest man who was a priceless ambassador for the club until the day he died - the Alan Ross who gladly suffered fools, like the endless stream of long-standing fans who'd seen him in his heyday and simply had to talk about it. You know, people like me.

There is a point to the hero worship of local footballers and fleeting pop stars. These people present a picture of life that appears simple. They suggest that mastering one set of skills will bring recognition and rewards. It's not true and, around the time we discover this in life, our heroes are also vanishing, their skills unable to stand the ageing process or changes in fashion. Around the time that I met the mighty league leading United squad, I also started work writing for *The Rough Guide to Rock* writing potted histories of rock careers. I'd idolised some of the people I wrote about. Now I rang them at home in the afternoon and they were always in! I didn't spend long talking to agents or managers because the careers in question seldom warranted the devoted attention of such people. Oh sure, they might be on someone's books but if I wanted information, a quote or simply a chat I could deal with the 'star' himself. This work wouldn't generate cash so no agent or manager was going to get involved.

So, life had taught me a fair bit about heroes before I stepped into a crowded dressing room in Gillingham. It must have taught me well because I found what I expected to find. The United dressing room reminded me a lot of my time in the fitting shop at British Sidac in Wigton. At least I'd imagined things the way they would be and my own game plan went to perfection. Locate the mighty David Reeves and Rod, get some pictures, exchange a few words and split. The conversation was all a bit ordinary as well. Rod seemed pretty positive considering his absence through injury on the day. For a flashy performer on the pitch Rodders understated modest charm was a pleasant surprise and Reevesy was the business. Classic boys' own centre forward stuff and I've never read *Boys Own*. When I got out the camera for a picture of me and Rodders, Reevesy confessed that he didn't know much about photography, but he got stuck in and I'll treasure the results for as long as I'll treasure anything. The real revelation of the dressing room was Dave Currie. For a guy who's gob and attitude got so much exercise on the pitch he was a surprising non-event in the dressing room. If he moved whilst I was in there, I didn't notice.

So much for my game plan where the hell was United's? My mate Steve was with me. His occasional football trips take him to see Liverpool and

Manchester United. I'd filled him in on United's stylish and inventive play. The most stylish and inventive move of the first half saw Richard Prokas heading off the line when Tony Elliot was beaten for the only time in the game. The gap between the two teams was 32 points. By two o'clock it was 35 points. On the pitch it was bloody close and Gillingham just shaded it as the better team over 90 minutes. Somewhere in the second half a disgruntled Gill heading home addressed the Carlisle fans. He'd finally discovered the secret of championship teams - they win even when they play badly. True enough I guess. About twenty of us chipped in to tell him that Gillingham were playing badly and losing. This game was a scrappy mess looking for some shape, a disappointment after our early season adventures. But we won. Deano was having a quiet game and when we got a second half corner Steve couldn't understand why the 'Deano' chants were going up. Within seconds we were on our feet celebrating Deano's headed goal, the classiest thing United did all afternoon. Tony Elliot was superb and without him we would have gone home with less than three points. Still we were lucky. A Gill hit the deck in our penalty area and the Rainham End went mad. We shut up. It looked a clear penalty to me. The ref didn't give it, about thirty seconds later somebody behind me shouted 'The Referee is a Cumbrian.' Hell, I'm a Cumbrian and I'd probably have given that penalty.

We weren't always brilliant but it was obvious our time had come. I saw plenty of games. I think it worth recording one hard fought victory, one considered percentage game and the final chapter at Colchester. We completed the double over Barnet with a gritty performance in which we withstood their well disciplined moves on a sloping pitch, measured our assaults through their midfield and stung them with two clinical finishes from Dave Currie and Simon Davey. It mattered because we fought our way through 90 minutes and I stood on a roofless terrace chomping on rubber burgers handed out by the local YTS with coolie boxes slung over their shoulders. The tea tasted like dishwater and I had a headache from fighting the M25 traffic all the way from work and I still count it a privilege to have been there.

By Easter our lead had reduced football commentators to boredom and a greater interest in who would be champions of the other divisions. By this point we had clinched our first ever date at Wembley Stadium in the final of the Auto Windscreens Shield. I'd seen none of the games that got us there. The qualifying matches are played by region, north or south, and our opponents - representing the south - were Birmingham. Even by my standards, midweek slogs to Rochdale to take in a match were ambitious. I got a Wembley ticket. The odd tackle was shirked as the first team fought to avoid injuries. Still we kept on winning. A game that stands out for me is Gillingham, at Carlisle on 8 April. The Kent local papers had made much of the recent Gills 'Revival.' Fifteen minutes and several fouls into the game it was obvious Gillingham's revival was down to their fighting spirit. We got 90 minutes of Gills taking out any Blue with pace and vision. Hell, Revie's Leeds team were never this bad. In a word 'Cloggers.' We beat them though. The build up on Jeff Thorpe's opening goal was superb and the passing that got the ball to his feet was complete class. Thorpe played in a striking position with Reeves given space at the side to cut in and feed. Before he was clogged into an early bath, Thorpey did a brilliant job. Steve Hayward was also doing some serious stuff and his work rate was impressive. His goal was a class piece of finishing, reminding Kent's cloggers they were in the presence of greatness. Their response was predictable and directed with some force at Roderick's ankles. To be fair, Rodders had been having an off day by his own standards. That said, we still missed him when he limped off - two up at half time against a team of assassins. Shutting up shop and playing a percentage game in the second half was understandable. We were that good, reserves in the side, no real need to score again, we could toy with opposing teams and keep a clean sheet for 45 minutes.

Three days later I was one of 500 who turned up to the semi final of the Cumberland Cup. An annual knockout competition featuring teams from great football towns - Penrith, Gretna and the rest. Traditionally Carlisle give the others a chance by fielding the reserves. I saw Gretna's men turn over a side made mainly of youngsters and it was my first sighting in action of Matt Jansen who had a good game, got hustled out of challenges by solid defenders twice his size and managed to squander the best Carlisle chance of the night. Tony Elliot was bloody good and his double point blank stop in the second half was as good a reflex save as I saw all season. Given the lack of atmosphere in the under-attended game Elliot's shouts carried to the stand. The guy learned his tact and diplomacy from the great Shilton for sure and - as with Paul Conway - it pains me to record that his career carried on with a handful of appearances for us the following season before moving to Cardiff and that inevitable meeting with Wadsworth at Scarborough for the successful play off push of 1998.

By the time we played at Wembley on 23 April we were promoted. Only an inconceivable series of results could deny us the championship. Wembley was like nothing before in my history as a United supporter. Steve, who had come to Gillingham came along as did Owen whose inconsistent Carlisle support certainly extended to the big occasion.

The video of the game tells me that Birmingham City had most of the possession. Our hard-fighting performance was undermined by obvious nerves. The papers saw fit to highlight the incredible crowd and the atmosphere. With over 70,000 jammed into the stadium and Mexican waves rocking the ground this was a good advert for the great things in football. You could touch the wonder of it all in the Carlisle end. The special hats - including a stunner with a deck-chair sheep on top - are sharp in my mind. The nerves and the pumping adrenalin at the time have reduced the game to a confusing jumble in my mind. Watching snatches of the game on video, I get the curious sensation that I'm watching a different game. The main difference is that the images that stand out for me include the chances that we could have put away in normal time. From where I was sitting Rodder's chance looked like a bad miss, my video blames the pass and shows the whole move to be working at the limits. Conway got close and Deano's chance off a set piece was a better opportunity than we knew - sitting at the far end of the ground. Tony Caig managed one superb save and the team made up for their nerves with a work rate that still stuns me to this day. The covering and commitment meant that the game never let up in pace. One image sums all of that up for me, with Caig soundly beaten for the only time in the 90 minutes Deano coolly followed a looping on target ball, positioned himself to perfection and with a combination of scoop and punt cleared it. The man's cool and unflappability were never more tested. We were all proud of the team. Ninety minutes flew past in a blur. At the end of normal time my throat was shredded and sore. This game was the first senior final in the UK to hold the possibility of a 'Golden goal' finish. Peter Hampton was out there leading the efforts to revive exhausted legs.

The chance of the game being decided in a moment added an unbearable tension to the restart and the tired legs on both sides were sending passes astray. Jeff Thorpe put in a run that gave us a move and the deck-chair army, waving sheep and all, were up as one and then sighing and deflated as they sank back down. Nothing in over a quarter of a century had prepared me for those minutes. My video tells me that the quality of the action went down and yet I can still touch that tension, the sheer unreality. Whatever happened was going to make history for Carlisle. A golden goal would make football history. It fell to Paul Tait to bury the ball from a standard move. Great move, well taken goal, history made and deck-chair shirts throwing themselves on the ground in despair. I've heard people who have been shot saying you don't feel it. In the heat of battle, with the adrenalin pumping to hand shaking levels, a bullet feels more like a punch. The pain dulling impact of your body's survival mechanism and the sheer lack of anything else with which to compare the experience, make the injury appear unimportant. So it was with that goal. Given the relentless pace and tension my natural reaction was to will the fallen bodies to get back up and fight. It took hours, and the gradual appearance of familiar motorway sights, before the loss really sank in. At that time, in that place it was a stunned silence that told me things had changed. The slow realisation that I hadn't much of a voice left and that the movement on the pitch had taken on an unfamiliar and distant appearance. Distant enough to locate most of the noise at the far end amongst the most dedicated of the Brummie hordes. Paul Tait's celebrations, which involved exposing a t-shirt with a message that didn't impress the more po faced of the Midland's own Blue Army, would take some of the headlines. Following a standing ovation that came from the bottom of our very souls the Cumbrian Blue Army trooped out of the stadium and headed home without much fuss. The papers wrote up the game as a great advert for the lower leagues and a footnote in the history of the game in the UK.

We'd had our chances to win it and overall I had no complaints, apart from the final score. It would be unfair to blame anyone who missed a chance. The papers would rightfully herald the combination of a lowly final and massive crowd as a great advert for football. They claimed the golden goal as a successful innovation. On the day, maybe, but it strikes me that a golden goal finale to a bad tempered Leeds v Man Utd cup tie, perhaps one that came in the form of a hotly disputed penalty, might give the game a disaster of historic proportions. I hope I'm wrong.

History records the visit to Colchester in April as coming six days after Wembley. My mind tells me it was several centuries later. At stake this time was the chance to take a championship on the pitch. In my entire history as a supporter we'd never won a championship. The last such win had been in 1965 when we took the old Third Division by a point. I ended up escorting three youngsters into Colchester's far from impressive stadium to see a shapeless and nerve wracking struggle. We pitted our championship dreams against a Colchester side with their own play off ambitions and - arguably - more need of three points than us. It was a desperate game and I was more nervous than I'd been at Wembley. I knew I was seeing my last game of the season, I knew we were promoted and I knew we'd lost our last two league games. I wanted a win and the championship that day as much as I'd wanted anything at a United game. I saw a nervous 90 minutes punctuated by the brief joy of celebrating a Reeves' goal and the desperate willing of the ref's whistle. The added time lasted hours but we got three points and an unassailable lead. The game didn't deserve its place in our history, the pitch invasion and salute to the fans in return were a worthy finale. I knew as I clapped and cheered that team off the pitch that - come hell or Division Two - I'd love them and what they had given us that season for ever.

When the dust settled on the season Carlisle United had managed to gain 91 points losing only five times in the league all season - three of the defeats coming when promotion was secure and one of them in our last home game with a championship in the bag and nothing to play for. Ironically we lost that last game in front of the biggest Division Three crowd of that season. No team in England could match our record and David Reeves came close to leading the score sheet for the entire division. A club that had plumbed the depths three years earlier now stood on the brink of a higher league and basked in the praise of pundits the length and breadth of the country. Great things were predicted. We'd humbled the division with a team built on our strengths. The bought players had been well chosen - Rod Thomas poached from a directionless spell at Watford was every bit as astute a buy as Reevesy - our record signing and cut price Deano who finished second highest scorer. All three figured in the PFA select side of the year. Most encouraging of all was the presence of so many from the youth team. Darren Edmonson, Jeff Thorpe and Tony Caig in particular had shown their worth. The first two had been there in the season from hell and, in their short careers, they had tasted both ends of the same division and final Saturdays of complete contrast three years apart.

The Knighton era was upon us for sure, there was talk of great things and the days of the crumbling scratching shed were numbered as new plans for a state of the art stadium emerged. Die hard Carlisle fans everywhere knew a hope they could barely control that summer whilst others dredged up Cumbrian credentials, bought season tickets and shirts and planned for the all out assault on a higher division.

12 Jimmy Glass

Mentioned for the first time in this chapter:

These are my opinions not facts. Others - especially those mentioned below - are likely to disagree.

Graham Anthony - Midfielder, couldn't get established at Sheffield United, Scarborough, Swindon or Plymouth. We gave him a regular run.
Owen Archdeacon - Defensive stalwart from 1995. Classy, in an understated way.
Warren Aspinall - 'Sumo,' chunky and committed striker who included Aston Villa and Everton on his pedigree. Loaned in 1995, signed the following season, carrying the weight of our forward playing hopes, along with his own considerable bulk, a season later.
Billy Barr - Proven defensive stalwart at Halifax and Crewe, signed to provide some stability in a back line always likely to leak in Division Two.
Jon Blott - Goalie who played two games in 1985. His is one hell of a story, but it doesn't have much to do with Carlisle. We'll get to it at the end of the chapter.
David Brightwell - Experienced defender, with some practice in last-ditch bottom of the league campaigns, therefore useful in 1999.
Andy Couzens - Struggled to break into the midfield at Leeds United, dropped down to our level and got a regular run out.
Mervyn Day - Goalie with impressive pedigree. Made his final league appearances and first steps in management at Carlisle.
Scott Dobie - Youth team forward, first team regular when just out of his teens.
Steve Finney - Another net busting super hero of the Knighton era who turned out to be a well travelled clubbable sort who could score if the opposition were holding white sticks.
Jimmy Glass - On loan goalie at the end of 98/99 season who went on to star in Channel 4's *The Greatest Sporting Moments of all Time*.
Matt Jansen - We've been here before. But his Carlisle career takes place in this chapter. Phenomenal prospect, slight, fast and flashy striker brought forward from youth team. Briefly rekindled memories of a young Beardsley.
Richard Knight - A goalie. Teenager dropped in over his head as a brief stop gap replacement for the departed Tony Caig in the grim end of season run in 1999. Within weeks we would famously tell the Football League we were 'without a goalie,' a statement that made perfect sense to some who saw Richard Knight play that season.
Lee Peacock - A forward. Scots born YTS trainee became established in mid-

nineties sides. Briefly played in goal, arguably a better keeper than Richard Knight.
Gareth McAlindon - Product of youth team, playing as a teenager by mid nineties. Almost a regular by the time he was twenty.
Ross Milligan - Young defender signed from Rangers for start of 97/98 season.
Tony Philliskirk - Much travelled striker who had partnered the mighty Reeves during a spell at Bolton. Loan signing to Carlisle in 1995 with a view to rekindling the old magic.
Stephane Pounewatchy - Classy French centre back, allegedly thought he was coming to a higher flying club in 1996.
Damon Searle - Cardiff, Stockport, Carlisle. A defender who was used to ugly sights, therefore unlikely to panic when the bottom of the league loomed large.
Allan Smart - Lanky Scots striker with clear promise. Young and inexperienced when signed in part-exchange for older and proven David Reeves. Came up with the goods when it really counted at Wembley, but he was playing for someone else then.
Ian Stevens - Well travelled striking machine, signed from Shrewsbury late on in 96/97 season. In and out of Carlisle thereafter.
Richard Tracey - Teenage prospect, thrown into the thick of it when serious trouble loomed, denied his place in history by the Brunton Park woodwork.
Will Varty - Central defender who stuck to his task, and his club, when many others deserted.
Ronnie Wallwork - Another bloody loan signing. Looked useful, went somewhere else. In fact, pretty much everywhere else.
David Wilkes - Defender who played a few games up to the shameful finish in 1992, from when he joined the coaching staff.
Nick Wright - Hadn't got a game at Derby in over three seasons. Got 25 for us up to the summer of 98. Went on to Watford, and history.

The fanzines were openly speculating about another promotion in 1996. I'd started writing for the United fanzines by this point. I was sending material off to one in particular, *So Jack Ashurst, Where's My Shirt*. The zines were seeking predictions from the United faithful of our league position at the end of the season. I couldn't go with a second automatic promotion. I reckoned on a season of consolidation and a league position somewhere around mid-table in Division Two.

By the summer of 1995, like Carlisle, I had moved into a higher division. The tide of change that had swept the public services under the Conservatives turned colleges into private operations which, amongst other things, could go bust. My employers were more secure than our rivals, but new contracts were being introduced for staff. As a manager I faced applying for a new and more demanding role. These new jobs were open to applications from others but the 'others' in question would lack the experience of having done the job. In the end, many of the posts had only one applicant. I did face competition but - frankly - my own involvement in the whole reorganisation was so momentous that I can't remember who told me or where I was when I found out I'd been 'promoted.' Then again, at least I can remember being interviewed. A couple of years later the vice principal told me that he hadn't been at my interview. He was there and he was yawning right through the whole thing. I would have taken it personally, but he was yawning when I walked in so I figured it couldn't have been anything I'd said. Other colleges were sacking entire departments. For us, the massive holidays of old were the only real casualty. My new contract cut those in half and left me booking out my annual leave when and where I could. The biggest impact from my point of view was on my writing work. In the good old days where staff rooms had been home to small time spiv operators, marathon runners and people who would shuffle out and teach if they couldn't think of anything else to do, my writing work had fitted in well with the 'day' job. Writing items for sicko comics and magazines had meant I could stockpile the stuff over those weeks in the summer when I wasn't in college. Working that way was out of the question under the new pattern when I simply wasn't going to get long breaks anymore. Then again, I got a decent pay rise.

So, the new division was strange to me. I wasn't going to quit writing but I needed to rethink. I didn't have the time to chase a pile of editors with ideas but I could cut down the number of ideas and make them bigger. Pitching book ideas seemed an obvious solution. There were some things I knew about well enough to put together a mountain of words. The paranormal, rock music, football and Media Studies were the obvious areas. Well those and writing fiction. Up to this point my only book writing experience had been a mega sick 'novel' I'd started. This book dated back to 1990, a time in which I was so naive that I thought you had to write a complete book and then send it to publishers. A few people had seen parts of it, reckoning it too sick to sell. The book - sent out under the titles *Sex-Food-Violence* and *Taste the Paste* had been knocked back repeatedly. In the eighties, whilst I was writing for every sicko comic under the sun I'd headed off to a Media Studies conference. Climbing out of an underground station I ran into Brian Dutton. Brian worked across the road from Thurrock Technical College in Palmer's VIth Form College, he taught Media studies and he'd written a couple of books on the subject. Both of his books were absolute winners and I'd been nicking ideas for classes from his writing the day before I met him. We got talking about our side projects and I was appalled to discover how little he'd earned writing one of his books. To put this in perspective, he'd spent six months writing a book that had earned him the kind of money I could get for a month's worth of sick jokes.

That conversation came back to me in 1995 when I was thinking about trying to get a book deal. The beauty of writing books is that the deadlines are months away and you can fit the work around a demanding job. I knew Media Studies backwards but I also fancied making some halfway decent money off a book. I made a submission to BPP Letts, a publisher who had no track record in Media Studies and a vast tonnage of books in Smiths, Menzies and Waterstones. Nobody in their right mind was going to go looking for a book just because I'd written it. Then again, any GCSE student with ambition bought Letts' study guides. Within a few weeks I had a deal and I spent my last long summer holiday knocking out a book that Letts would be able to sell on the back of their brand. So, like Carlisle United in the early summer of 1995 I stood on the threshold of a more demanding league. We'd both proven we could perform in the easier climes below. Both of us had shown some flair and we'd pushed our levels of performance to the limits offered at that level, such as they were. The question was whether or not we could deliver. Knighton talked about ground improvements and a ten-year plan for premiership action. I'd told a publisher I could deliver them a book worthy of their reputation inside eight weeks.

As the new fixtures arrived I scanned the list for the all important 'romantic weekend.' In all the times I've booked such a weekend away around a football game I've never seen an away win. In the autumn of 1995 we were in Bournemouth. The town is so full of the elderly that many shop windows are made with bi-focal glass. The recreational drug of choice in Bournemouth is a chocolate digestive biscuit. The town doesn't begin to kick ass because most of the residents can't lift their legs high enough to connect with someone else's bum.

On that Saturday morning in Bournemouth Jane, Thom and I found ourselves surrounded by a convention of Rotarians in the dining room. The totally surreal sight was completed when I spotted another resident arriving in a Division One Carlisle United shirt. Rob Lees - for it was he - was a regular contributor to *So Jack Ashurst, Where's My Shirt*. He was also married to another wife in a million and Rob, his wife Sue, and I found ourselves standing in the teeth of an off the sea wind as Carlisle faced the kind of team we should easily have humbled if Knighton's plans were to mean anything. Some frantic and even handed first half football ended with us 1-0 down. Worse was to follow. Tony Elliot had been sidelined the previous season as Tony Caig had established himself in the team. I was a real admirer of Tony Elliot's goalkeeping. The guy was a crowd pleaser with a spectacular line in last ditch thrashing convulsions at the feet of opposing forwards. His ability to get down quickly and move with lightning speed through a crowded area was exceeded only by the entertaining tongue lashings he could dish out to napping defenders. During the championship run Tony Caig with his exemplary shot-stopping was - arguably - the right choice, but with the defence under test from Division Two's more mobile striking forces, Elliot had come into his own again. Caig's shortcomings at this time included an ability to hit his own corner flags from goal kicks and land the team in trouble. During the previous season Caig had exited a game following a full-on assault on a Scarborough striker. Caig was forced into this action because his 'kick' from goal had stalled in the stiff breeze, landed at the striker's feet and offered him a free one on one.

Elliot gave too much in the way of bravery at Bournemouth and ended up badly injured. So badly that they called for his parents on the tannoy and he left the game to put Lee Peacock in goal. Peacock is a striker who once scored an important goal against Carlisle, but that's another story. That afternoon in Bournemouth he was a passable keeper. I've seen worse displays from genuine goalies. We ran at Bournemouth, into them, round them and finally over them. For eighty yards we were deadly but we ground to a halt in the opposing box and got caught with a late break. From 2-0 down, there would be no way back that afternoon. After the game, with Carlisle sitting second bottom of the division and having nothing to show for so much effort, it dawned on me we were in the shit.

Michael Knighton was taking some stick from the support. It was well short of the outright hatred we'd feel for most of his reign but some events were already starting to worry the Blue Army. There were building works underway at Brunton Park but not much on the pitch. Reevesy needed a partner up front and one brain-wave was in evidence on the pitch at Bournemouth. Reevesy and Tony Philliskirk had formed a formidable partnership at Bolton. Their vague physical similarity and strong double act had seen the locals name them 'Bros.' Owen once made the telling observation that Bros made the right noises but didn't sing that many songs. Roughly speaking, it was at this level that football's Bros picked up their partnership. The idea was there but Philliskirk and Reeves couldn't rekindle the old magic. Three games, one goal, no magic on offer and Philliskirk was on his way to Cardiff. We'd signed him on loan from Burnley, making it bloody obvious that he was simply trying to 'bag' a few weeks at any club and he hadn't got past 'C' in the Groundhopper's Manual. If he stays true to form he'll finish his career at York on his fortieth birthday in a stunning finale which will see him and ten unemployed waitresses turn in another Bootham Crescent bonanza of stylish football. Don't knock it, you'll probably be in for more entertainment than I got from my team in the season after we won the Third Division championship.

Somewhere between Bournemouth and Peterboro I found my voice again. Having been there to cheer and admire the previous season, Carlisle had taught me about being positive. As my first book came out, and the offers to write more came in, my team and I had gone in opposite directions. I'd moved up a gear and coped. They'd moved up a division and hit a brick wall. Peterboro was the pits. A 6-1 defeat that left me shuffling in the pie queue at half time, sullen and speechless. We were four down by then and six down by the time we finally remembered which direction we were heading in. The scattered remnants of the Blue Army who'd made the trip gave it everything. 'You only sing when you're winning,' came out a few times and once we'd found the back of the net we chanted 'We've got a goal,' over and over again.

The real positive for me was David Reeves. In the face of the massacre he was back in defence, running in midfield and trying to make something happen up front. Captain Marvel, except that the only thing to marvel at was his positive attitude as we leaked goals. In all my years of following Carlisle I've seen nobody who could replace Alan Ross as a hero and example. Given that Ross got to me when I was impressionable enough to need a hero, his place in my affections has to be secure. There was no other player to whom I would have considered dedicating this book. By 1995 I was - supposedly - older and wiser than all that. However, somewhere in the teeth of that humiliation in Peterboro, David Reeves proved for all time that he too was a worthy hero. He still tried with the surging runs, only by this time they were starting well into our own half. He yelled encouragement to the team and, when we were 6-0 down and nothing mattered, it was Reeves who got on the end of a rebound as the Posh goalie parried Prokas' shot. 6-1. It didn't matter but in the same circumstances lesser men would have run around, collected their wages and shown no passion. Reevesy left us the following season and one article in a fanzine blasted him as a clumsy forward who would never qualify as a natural goal getter. Bloody harsh in my opinion. When Reevesy left I did, as I often do, conjure up an image of the departing player in my mind. When you lose someone quickly you often focus on one moment, one image. Strangely, the image that came to mind was Reeves in the away shirt at Peterboro with his sleeves rolled up, running and encouraging the team with everything lost.

This Second Division team was little more than the team that had humbled the Third Division, with a few new faces from the youth team. A level higher than the previous year, they were struggling. Some players had a nightmare that day in Peterboro, Tony Gallimore mistimed, misjudged and missed the ball completely. Tony Caig's positioning was desperate and his handling showed his shattered confidence.

Driving home from that pasting was like returning from the drubbing from hell that night in Dartford. Except, there was no way I would even consider walking away from this side. During the previous season, they'd shown me more domination and flair than I'd seen from any Carlisle team. Okay, they dominated the lowest professional flight but this team had pumped hope and affection into every Cumbrian with eyes to see. At least now we had a reality check on the dreams of the previous season. A few of us had wondered when Knighton's schemes would collide with the real world. By February 1996, reality was there in spades. There were other games to see that season, including home wins. But, for me, there are three defining moments. The first was that hard fought loss at Bournemouth which convinced me beyond doubt that we were going to have to fight for anything. The second was that 6-1 drubbing that showed which players had the fight and which needed to work. The third defining moment was the predictable sinking feeling I got driving out of a car park in Dartford after the season had all but finished.

This feeling came courtesy of Radio 5 who relayed the news we were all expecting. York had won away in Brighton to secure their own Division Two status. This game was played long after the rest because the original match had been invaded and called off as a result of a mass demonstration from the totally pissed off fans of Brighton. Those Brighton fans had a point, with a chairman who seemed hell bent on running the team into oblivion. The guy needed police protection in and out of the ground. We might have been doubtful about Knighton's claims but his physical well being wasn't in much danger from us in those days. Maybe from the vast tonnage of pies he appeared to be shifting, but not from the fans.

Knighton made noises about legal action given the position we were in. That replayed game at Brighton was - near enough - a formality. Brighton were hopelessly relegated, York were in the highest relegation spot and had escape within their hands. They won and survived in Division Two, at our expense. It may well have been that our new level, with the finances available then, was somewhere between the two divisions. We certainly weren't good enough to survive by right in the second. The Knighton tradition of major excitement at the end of the season was well established. We'd had the play offs, a championship and relegation in successive years. Knighton's threat to sue the league made the national press where his unsuccessful bid to take over at Old Trafford was - once again - trotted out.

At the same time the country was stumbling from crisis to crisis, economically speaking. There was speculation over whether the country could ever escape the boom and bust cycles. Strangely, none of these discussions ever extended to a consideration of boom and bust football. A style which appeared to fit the times and a style that appeared to be establishing itself at Brunton Park. So we started the 96/97 season back in Division Three. The smart money that year was on a rapid return to the Second Division. All of the bookies had us down amongst the promotion favourites. We started the campaign with some strength but less flair than we'd displayed two seasons previously. We also started it without some of the players who had made the previous promotion run a celebration of talent. Tony Gallimore had already completed a season at Grimsby by May 1996. By the start of the 96/97 season we'd lost others. Tony Elliot went to join Tony Philliskirk at Cardiff, Derek Mountfield was at Walsall and then eight games into his season we sold David Reeves to Preston where he could link up with Simon Davey. Davey had been at Deepdale from the promotion season. Mick Wadsworth was also gone, leaving Mervyn Day in charge.

We got replacements, notably the young Allan Smart up front in exchange for Reeves, but this new team had a bargain basement look compared to their predecessors. For all that, the campaign in the south east took in one defeat, at Fulham in late August. I missed this to go to my mate Bif's wedding and so I never saw Carlisle lose away from home that season. If one game stands out in my mind as defining of that season, it is the last ever visit to the Goldstone Ground. Brighton's plight was hopeless and they looked certain to leave the league that year before a last ditch draw with Hereford saved them. The same game condemned Hereford, a rural outpost and home of the SAS, to Conference football. We beat Brighton 3-1. It wasn't pretty, it was hard working. We went 1-0 down in an opening spell that saw The Seagulls running like headless chickens and suffering panic attacks when they got possession. This was an oddly effective tactic that penned us in for the first quarter of an hour. Put simply, we had ideas but we didn't have the authority to break out from the manic onslaught being staged by the worst team in the country. Some of the people who could have offered us that authority - Davey, Reeves, Mountfield - were literally in a different league by that time.

The goal scorers that day summed up the best of what was on offer. After Paul Conway had blasted a few seagulls out of the sky with a sitter of a chance it was the bulky frame of Stephane Pounewatchy who headed the first goal. What Pounewatchy was doing at Carlisle was a debatable point. French born and black, he wasn't exactly in the great Bill Green/Don O' Riordan/Derek Mountfield tradition of no nonsense defensive generals who'd cut their teeth in the no nonsense British game. Pounewatchy was ludicrously good for the level at which we blooded him. The second goal that day came from Warren Aspinall, thinning on top, grey haired and gap toothed - Warren looked like your dodgy old uncle who'd come round for a summer barbie and spent the whole afternoon feasting his eyes on your little sister's chest. His physique didn't exactly scream 'athlete' to the world, but that afternoon he fought and bundled a run through the Brighton defence that turned the game - the best goal from a Carlisle player I saw all season. Well into the second half Allan Smart managed a gangling storm on the opposing goal that gave us a fleeting reminder of Reeves at his best. This team had a bizarre mismatch of skill and sweat with hot spots of each. An image to sum up the whole situation was the plight of Rod Thomas. Marooned in no man's land for long periods he would still dazzle with runs only to find nobody had read his move. Injury prone and often making appearances off the bench Rod played - off and on - all season and didn't score once. In his first two seasons at Carlisle he'd hit the back of the net fifteen times.

We were like a misfiring racing car, storming when we were on form, fragile enough to fall apart in seconds, and forever capable of veering out of control. We never looked like the side of two years before and still we managed to crawl into the top three. As the halfway point of the season approached I'd seen enough of the Third Division to know that the widespread desperation at other clubs was our greatest asset. By this point I'd stopped worrying about football.

My Dad was ill with what - at first - appeared to be a kidney problem. He'd had a diagnosis of possible cancer before Christmas and had a kidney removed the day after New Year. His 'recovery' was slow and beset by problems, by which point it was obvious that he wasn't really getting better. By this time my work and family took up, near-enough, every waking hour. It was hard to get anything like the time I'd had during my mother's illness but I was at my Dad's one Friday in March when it appeared that his one remaining kidney had given up. We went to hospital where he headed off for tests and I got a taste of the lonely desperation it is possible to feel when you leave someone so close at the mercy of doctors and find yourself faced with the cold comforts of a hospital canteen. My dad had been through the same desperation when he'd had to leave my mum in the care of doctors.

As the sky darkened outside, Lesley and Rich arrived. My stint up north was supposed to give them a weekend off but we were all gathered to hear the doctor tell us that the one remaining kidney had also been stopped from functioning by a tumour. The options - major invasive surgery or something less than three days to live - had been given to my Dad. He didn't have to tell me, I knew right off that he'd opted to die sooner without the grief and indignity. I drove him home where he was magnificent. Reading the directions on a bottle of pills he told us they weren't to be taken with alcohol before washing them down with a good red wine uncorked to celebrate the occasion. At best, we had days to say anything that really mattered. I was able to say everything that I wanted and share the time with my Dad. Two days later, with Jane having come up from Maidstone, the remaining kidney was working again and something had obviously gone wrong with the imminent certainty of death. My Dad had made an art of the supposed final days. He wasn't going to die right away but he was obviously ill. The things we'd 'known' only days before were replaced with uncertainty. This was a mixed blessing. Deep down - I think - he knew he wasn't going to get better.

He told me a story once, when I was young enough to believe in the truth of everything he said - a story about a Chinese family. He told the story a few times as I got older. By which time I knew it was a wind up. I also realised that he liked this story a lot. A little Chinese boy is coming home from school and as he passes through the crowded streets he sees a man pushing a wheelbarrow. There is an old man sitting in the barrow. As he gets closer he realises that the man pushing the barrow is his dad and the man in the barrow is his grandad.

'Where are you taking Grandad?' asks the boy when he gets closer.

'He's too old to work anymore,' says the dad, 'and he is starting to get sick. I'm taking him down to the bridge. I'm going to tip him in the river.'

'I love grandad,' protests the boy, 'he's funny and he tells me stories.'

'But we can't afford to keep him,' says the dad, 'and grandad can't work to keep himself anymore.'

Eventually, against the boy's protests, the two men head off to the river. The boy thinks about losing his grandad as he walks away home. A few paces later, something occurs to him and he turns round to shout, 'Hey Dad, bring the barrow back, I'll need it to tip you in the river one day.'

My Dad had a sense of humour that took in the grim aspects of life. During that weekend when we thought we were going to lose him at any point he made a performance and celebration of his imminent death. There was a hint of artistry about the whole thing. Although he was ill, he still wasn't totally an old man. He was seventy, but his mind was much younger than that. He was still the same person who had told me the grimly funny story about the Chinese boy all those years before. All my Dad got from a mix up that had briefly fooled the doctors into thinking his kidney was surrounded by cancer was a few more weeks of life. They turned out to be a mixed blessing. He got more ill, less capable and less like himself. In those weeks his life lacked the quality he'd known before. It took a few weeks for us to know for sure that he was dying. In truth I'd known it all along.

We got more time and, although fitting it in next to holding down a job was demanding, there were treasured moments in those days. There were also strange moments. One of the strangest came the day Carlisle went to Wembley for the second time. Two years after our first appearance we were back in the Autowindscreens Shield final and this time the opposition were Colchester United. Both finalists were from Division Three and with our league position bobbing around the automatic promotion zone we were favourites. Colchester were eyeing the final play off place; in the end they missed out on this by a single point. For me, the Wembley trip was a strange day. I'd talked my mate Steve into coming along. Steve had been to the same final two years before when we lost. In 1997 I also talked my mate Michael along. Michael had been working with me for two years by this point. In 1995 the Autowindscreens Shield final had filled Wembley Stadium. In 1997 there were less than 50,000 there to see the game, including, apparently, many more Cumbrians than people from Colchester. It's always difficult to tell. On one side of me I had south eastern born and bred Steve. On the other I had Mike, more 'English' in his tastes and outlook than I could ever hope to be, though the son of black Jamaican immigrants and - therefore - never very likely to pass for a Cumbrian. However we mustered this crowd, our end was as packed and noisy as it had been two years before. Only five of the 1995 team were back for a second attempt at the prize. Caig, Hayward, Conway, Walling and Rod Thomas. Rod only got into the action off the bench. Five of the 1995 side had been sold. We had Rory Delap, a young defender/midfield player who had established himself in the side that season and who provided the most entertaining moment of the first half when he demolished a corner flag and put the game into five minutes of inactivity before a Wembley official ran the touch-line to massive cheers with a replacement. It was a non-event of a game. Our great scoring idea, the pace and power of Allan Smart, had limped out just after twenty minutes to be replaced by the pace, lack of height and injury prone body of Rod Thomas. Rod faced the rotund blubber monster that was Colchester's Peter Cawley. The shaven headed executioner at the heart of the Colchester defence kept us out for most of the game although neither side looked like scoring. When Roderick fell foul of the repeated attempts at execution, Matt Jansen's jinking runs were thrown into the fray in the first period of extra time. Jansen was a phenomenal prospect but - like Delap - still learning the game at this point.

It was a strange experience all round for me. These were days in limbo, knowing my Dad was so ill and struggling to see anything else as important. To make matters worse that day at Wembley it was obvious that this team were not the equals of the line up two years before - neither was the 120 minutes of football that preceded the shoot out. Up front we had ideas, but little else. Dave Currie's first touch ball killings were now finding an easier life in Scarborough whilst Reeves' commitment was clattering through defenders in a Preston shirt that weekend. Lee Peacock hadn't the pace, penetration or vision to trouble Colchester too badly. At the end of the season we would sell him to the matchless footballing machine at Mansfield where his sublime scoring talents would net five goals in his first season.

A whelter of conflicting emotions ran through me in the first 120 minutes. I'd got the adrenalin pumping hard enough as the seconds ticked down to the shoot out. And it got even more tense, as the shoot out went down to the wire.

Colchester shot first and scored. Up stepped Paul Conway and equalised. Colchester scored again. Owen Archdeacon missed. 2-1 to them. They scored again - 3-1. Deano's cool was not dented. He slotted an easy strike into the back of the net 3-2. Nineteen year old Karl Duguid stepped up for Colchester, and Caigy saved his middling attempt. Duguid wandered off and burst into tears. 'Sumo' Aspinall buried the ball with the strength of ten men. 3-3 and everything on the last kicks. Peter Cawley, bald blubber-monster, bad attitude on legs and scourge of the Carlisle crowd all afternoon, choked on his shot and Caigy got in a stop, 3-3. One kick left and it was Steve Hayward stepping up. I saw the clean strike, saw the net bulge, heard the roar, registered that one of those screams was mine, and briefly forgot every concern in that troubled period of my life.

In that moment, none of the previous 120 minutes of average football mattered, never before had Carlisle United won a final of this magnitude. 45,000 people, Wembley Stadium and a sea of bobbing sheep in the crowd. Inflatable sheep, woolly sheep placed on top of pork pie hats and customized t-shirts with Sean the Sheep pledging an allegiance that his Welsh creator would be unlikely to support. There was a lap of honour to parade the prized beer tray and a deafening exchange of mutual appreciation with the team. For those moments the scale of the achievement didn't matter. We came, we saw, we conquered and we did it against a southern team on southern turf. A Cumbrian dream, it had been a long time coming.

On our way home through Victoria Station, Steve headed off to get some food. I went to ring my Dad. It all poured out of me, the shoot out, the demolished flag, the sea of green, blue and sheep. He kept asking me to describe different things. What Wembley looked like inside, that roar when Captain Marvel Hayward had buried the decisive goal.

When I was a kid I remember my Dad going places and coming back to tell me what it had been like - parties I wasn't allowed to, events he'd organised, things he'd seen. I'd picture the scenes in the way that impressionable children do. Years later, when Thom was old enough to imagine the same things I'd tell him stories. One night he wouldn't go to sleep and I lay on his bedroom floor and told him about my train home from London being diverted to make way for a Eurostar. He didn't even know what a Eurostar was. He just knew fast trains and slow trains. Still, he drifted off to sleep mumbling, 'A fast train was coming, and daddy's train had to go on another track,' over and over again. To him, and me as a boy, the big world was made up of things we could only imagine. Now, in April 1997, I was describing one of those great scenes to my Dad and he wanted the whole story. Happy, I think, that the moment had meant so much to me and - just possibly - glad that he'd lived long enough to see my undying love for this team allow me one such moment in my life. It was strange and poignant, describing things like this to my Dad, almost as if he was the child. Strange that he, like his own son and his grandson, was asking for more details, wanting to live the scene in his mind, and share in the magic. He was seventy years old. He had a few weeks to live.

It was an odd reversal, like a scene from a movie. As if to underline this point, the strangeness of the moment took an unpredictable turn. Glancing around for Steve, with some welcome food I looked right into the eyes of a flustered Charlotte Rampling. Quite obviously late for something important, she glanced around and strode over to platform one where, presumably, a train was waiting for Paris.

My Dad didn't make it to seventy one. He died as a warm summer took hold on Cumbria and a few days later we walked down the road behind his coffin to the church we'd always been able to see from the house. In his final hours, he slept peacefully away as a sliver of moon climbed up over the fields outside. The last time I spoke to him we'd talked about the Conservative humiliation in the elections, an event he had enjoyed to the maximum. That was one long night when the constant dull pain and his prolonged wakefulness had been a positive blessing. He stayed awake to see it all, Portillo's hopes of leadership wrecked with his lost seat. Martin Bell taking Tatton with an anti-sleaze landslide and the sheer mind numbing magnitude of the massacre gradually making itself evident. From that first weekend of impending death in March he lived with most of the loose ends tied up. We talked and said the things that mattered. He was happy with many things. He'd seen his children married and settled with partners who had become close to him. He'd seen another generation of the family born. He knew that we would be secure into our futures.

He had many more things to live for and, until that final illness, my Dad was not in any typical way, an old man. He'd take pleasure in winding up a policeman keeping a watchful eye on hunt demonstrators. In his final year he enjoyed the wild inventiveness of an Ash b-side I taped for him. He'd take sides with Owen against Jane and I. In the final weeks of his life he would take pleasure in those victories which got him away from his failing health. Like an election massacre or my descriptions of Carlisle's first ever Wembley victory. My Dad lived just long enough to be dependent on others and that was never his wish. The one person on whom he might just have been happy to be dependent had died over ten years before, and he never really came to terms with losing her.

We all took some time to put our lives together but by this time they were busy and demanding lives. The kind where legislating for a death in the family equates to a set amount of leave in the corporate rule book. I took time when I could to get up home. The signs of some healing were there when I managed to get interested in the following season. After Wembley, whilst my Dad went downhill, Carlisle had earned third place, and automatic promotion from the lower flight for the second time in three years. The pre-season friendlies blooded some new talent and showed the extent of the underlying desperation in the state of the clear out. Steve Hayward, who had brought composure and some direction to the Wembley team was now at Fulham. The most exciting face of the new intake was an inexperienced defender called Ross Milligan. Well, he looked great in the pre-season run out. A few games into the real campaign and none of the new faces - signed or brought forward from the youth ranks - were looking that impressive. Up front Gareth McAlindon and Scott Dobie both got a lengthy run out. Youth team forwards, they managed three senior goals between them, all by Gareth.

The fall off in class between the championship team who had lost at Wembley and the third placed team who had won the same competition suggested that this new adventure in Division Two could be more traumatic than the previous campaign. The fact that we were prepared to sell the un-dentable composure of Dean Walling to Lincoln City showed the real level of ambition. Deano still played well and the dispute that led to his departure was, apparently, about the length of a new contract. In other words, there was no doubt he was still good enough for us, we just wouldn't put any real commitment his way. The departure of so much talent - Reevesy, Hayward and Deano - showed the short term thinking we'd come to hate in the next few years.

I took Thom along to his first game in August as we started the season against Southend with a 1-1 draw. Thom was four years and ten months, much younger than I was at my first game, and he was frightened by the wall of noise echoing from the low roof at Roots Hall. By the second half, when we scored, Thom was chasing a little girl round an empty row of seats, enjoying a day out in the hot sunshine. Allan Smart scrambled the goal that gave us a point and put us in eleventh place in the totally meaningless league table that followed the first Saturday. League wise, that was as good as it ever got.

A few weeks later I heard Michael Knighton implicitly blaming everyone from his players to the departed Mervyn Day for the previous season's performance. 'We limped across the line,' he said before going on to share his vision of a team that were so clearly better than anything in Division Three that they should have bettered their 1995 performance. I didn't recognize the team on the pitch from Knighton's description. On the pitch we were replacing lucrative sales with untried new talent or old salts who had seldom seen the higher reaches of the footballing pyramid.

We were signing players like Billy Barr. I've got nothing against Billy Barr personally but his track record was a solid performance at Halifax and a couple of seasons with Crewe. A couple of seasons before Barr's arrival, the well travelled professionals in the ranks had included the likes of Reeves and Currie who'd performed well at a much higher level. Billy Barr's dizzy heights were in Crewe, a little club, performing miracles at the time under the management of Dario Gradi. Their 6,000 capacity ground hosted First Division football, when they got relegated to Division Two, they fought right back into the play offs. In his best days, Barr was a player for such a club. David Currie's best days were at Nottingham Forest where a crowd equalling Crewe's average gate would have been a cause for panic. Like Billy Barr, ace goal getter Ian Stevens had briefly dropped to non-league football during his career. Already past thirty when we signed him he had spent most of the season to May 1997 netting seventeen goals at Shrewsbury. The turnover of players and the frequency of loan signings appearing in the team was one sign of the creeping problems. The other was the results. Mervyn Day eventually gave in to the inevitable and we began a period in which the media and fans would tell everyone that Michael Knighton was managing the team whilst he would insist that John Halpin and David Wilkes were responsible.

Given what we know now it seems fair to see the Second Division season from August 1997 to the end of the nail-biting season that followed as one long campaign. A campaign distinguished by the selling of the best players, the frequent appearance of loan signings and unproven reserves, and the certain knowledge that the real talent would depart sooner rather than later. The tragedy of these sides wasn't the lack of class, it was the nagging uncertainty and the sense of powerlessness on the terraces. The satisfaction I got in those seasons owed a lot to Thom and his growing love of the matches and the atmosphere. Knighton's blue and white army did me a perverse favour as they spiralled to the bottom of the Second Division. Thom found his own voice on the terraces, with five year old cries of 'Come on Dad, they're useless.' I'd feign wild anger and then buy him some chocolate at half time. In this way we built a bond that made football a thing to be shared. When the weather cooled Thom wrapped up and came along to Gillingham and Fulham, by which time he'd seen us draw once, lose twice and concede seven goals. Fulham had come up from the Third Division in May 1997, one place above us. The following year they made the play offs and we went back down. A result that helped seal both of those achievements was fought out at Craven Cottage near the end of the season. Thom had never seen five goals in a game before, he got the football bug that day. That game was fast, open exciting and packed with incident. Peter Beardsley played brilliantly in a white shirt, seemingly unaffected by long-term bullshit talk about him coming to manage Carlisle.

He may still come, who knows, all I can tell you is that he played brilliantly for Fulham that day and brilliantly for Hartlepool when he was 38 the following season. On both occasions we had cause to regret his skills. We didn't get Beardo but we acquired Nick Wright from Derby, Andy Couzens from Leeds and the on-loan Ronnie Wallwork from Manchester United. These players had ability. Wright was blinding against Northampton in another losing encounter at the Sixfields Stadium. But, time and again, the uncertainty undermined whatever there was to cheer.

In a full-on 90 minute encounter the team I saw lose to Northampton would probably wipe the floor with the 91-92 squad. We fought hard and the young players we'd drafted in knew the value of a first team place. But always, behind it all, was the unknown. Matt Jansen was absent at Northampton because he was 'training' with Manchester United. Given his skill and our league performance we had to be resigned to losing him, and Delap, in the near future. Like Stan Bowles before them, they shone given half a chance. Unlike the Carlisle teams of old we couldn't keep talent like this until the end of the season because the gap between ourselves and the others was now a great yawning chasm.

At twenty Matt Jansen joined Crystal Palace. He'd turned down Manchester United twice in favour of more lowly clubs. On arrival at Selhurst Park - he got half an hour of Steve Coppell's undivided attention.

'Good to have you here, Matt,' Steve began. 'I've got plans for you and they start on Saturday. By First Division standards it should be an easy match so I want you to get out there in the first half, express yourself, show the crowd what you've got and we'll have you pulled off at half time.'

'Pulled off!' yelled Jansen, 'Pulled off! Fucking hell, that's a result. All I got at Carlisle was an orange.'

Crystal Palace was a step up in class because our class was a memory. Watching Carlisle free-fall from the Second to the Third Division and stumble along the bottom for a whole season brought back the dark days of 1992. We had moments like a great 45 minutes, at White Hart Lane where we managed a 2-1 lead over Spurs in the Coca Cola cup. The whole team played brilliantly, Jansen was superb. We lost the game and the return at Carlisle, but we lost well.

Thom finally saw Carlisle win against Brighton in the Third Division with a second half display that turned a 1-0 deficit right around. The 3-1 win included a storming Steve Finney strike and a Damon Searle free kick that shook the goal posts to their foundations. We'd taken some other friends to that game, a habit I'd begun to develop. So many things were competing for time when in January 1999 I got a phone call from Steve Wells, a legend amongst music journalists. Working as a publisher's editor he'd been told to get anything he wanted from 'that pile of shit over there.' In the pile of rejects he found *Raiders of the Low Forehead* - my sicko rant of a novel previously known as *Taste the Paste* and *Sex, Food, Violence.* Steven wanted to meet up as soon as possible. Time was tight for us both so I talked him into watching Carlisle away at Southend. We saw Carlisle scramble a hard fought win in a game that could have gone either way and talked business on the train. It was the best day's work I'd had in months. On the pitch the 'stars' of this team were striker Steve Finney, who'd been in and out of teams at Preston and Swindon and David Brightwell, playing out his career after years on the books at Maine Road. We'd signed Brightwell from Northampton, his slow decline had reached Carlisle's standard. I pointed Tony Caig out to Steven as the only real class left. With weeks left to the end of the season Caig went to Blackpool for £5,000. He was out of contract at the end of the campaign and certainly a better goalie than our position - one off the bottom of the whole football league - would indicate. The justification offered was that we would have got nothing for him had we allowed him to go when his contract expired. So we needed the money then? A couple of weeks later Carlisle United reported profits of £1.4 million.

Caig's replacement was Richard Knight. Knight was nineteen years old, overawed by the task in hand and painful to watch. His promise eventually amounted to a lengthy spell for Oxford and the odd run-out at Hull, Macclesfield and Colchester. Knight was recalled to Derby to cover injuries. In a move that would later tax the understanding and charity of other teams - especially Scarborough - we invoked a clause in the league legislation and signed another on-loan goalie after the transfer deadline. We could do this if we were without a goalie. There were those who saw Knight play who'd argue we were without a recognised goalie even when he was on the pitch. So we acquired Jimmy Glass, a journeyman keeper who'd once spent a season playing outfield because of a wrist injury.

To put this in context, consider barely two years before, the Wembley win - the last thing we genuinely achieved in the Knighton era. Of the thirteen men-who played at Wembley in any part of that game little more than two years before, only one, central defender Will Varty, could possibly have played for

Carlisle on 8 May 1999. The other twelve had gone. Varty, to give him his due, was one of our better players in that desperate season. Predictably, we rewarded his abilities by loaning him to Rotherham, a team for whom he played on the afternoon that we fought for our survival. The following year, as we fought again for survival, Varty was a fully fledged member of a Rotherham squad fighting out a promotion campaign.

So, to the game that brought us - briefly - back to national prominence. We were not great. Not even passionate, given the circumstances, and we rode our luck. As one paper would later put it, it was 'mediocre stuff... played by men of poor touch and indifferent fitness.' Out on the Yorkshire coast Scarborough missed a sitter of a chance that could have saved their league status. They didn't think it mattered. We were one goal behind before David Brightwell equalised with a thirty yarder that actually did justice to the seriousness of the situation. With the time running out and no real prospect of a goal, many eyes were on Knighton in the director's box and the 'fat greedy bastard' chants were ringing round the ground. Four minutes into injury time, I mean, four minutes in! we got a corner. Everyone went up, including Jimmy Glass, the loan signing goalie from Swindon. Graham Anthony flighted an accurate ball over the penalty box, Scott Dobie's header was pushed out by Plymouth goalie Jim Dungey and Jimmy Glass got his boot on the rebound. He buried it, walloped the bloody thing like it was a goal kick and the net bulged. The place went mental. That moment, that perfect moment, had cleared the troubles for the time being. Like Hayward's penalty strike which had taken away a burden for me two years before, that Jimmy Glass goal, briefly took over seven thousand Cumbrians into ecstasy. Glass was mobbed, the pitch was covered and, eventually, Plymouth kicked off. Ten seconds later, the ref blew for time.

The press made a meal of the whole thing - Carlisle were national news for one day. The hero - without question - was Jimmy Glass. The club shop started a lucrative run on red goalie shirts, the press quoted Glass's few words on the subject with reverence, and there was serious debate about whether he would sign in the longer term. I'm typing these words with my Jimmy Glass souvenir glass in view. A man who had been denied first team football for almost four seasons was, briefly, one of the most famous goalkeepers in the country. Jimmy Glass's moment of fame was a media dream. 'It fell to me, wallop, goal, thank you very much,' he said. Asked if he was planning to stay at Carlisle he wouldn't commit. 'I'll tell you this,' he said, 'some very funny things happen in football.' Too bloody right they do. For starters, Jimmy Glass gets to be a national hero for a day. I found a newspaper picture of Jimmy Glass, arms outstretched, chased by pitch invaders, stuck across my computer screen when I got into work a couple of days later. Like so many others before, it just seemed to be his moment. Fame like this, would appear to be chance and yet, in reality, there is often more to it.

There were some strange coincidences that weekend. Graham Anthony, who took the all important corner, had signed for Carlisle from Plymouth Argyle, the team we were playing that day. He had also played for Swindon, the previous home of our 'hot' striker of 1999 Steve Finney. Swindon were also the team who - technically speaking - employed Jimmy Glass on the day he scored that goal. Spooky co-incidence? Well, not really, more a statement of where we were. By the summer of 1999 Carlisle United offered a hopeful career break for those players stuck in the reserves of middling First Division clubs - clubs placed somewhere around thirtieth in our league structure. This book opened with Carlisle United performing well, placed around thirtieth in the league structure as it was then. So, by 1999 we were reduced to fielding the quality of players we'd have been happy to offload in the late sixties. To put this further in perspective, Watford won the last competitive game of that season, the Division One play off final. They were financially prudent and under the direction of Graham Taylor, a proven motivator of journeymen and a blender of disparate talents. Watford's play-off victory gave them a second promotion in a row. Their scorers that day - Allan Smart and Nicky Wright - both signed from Carlisle after playing well against Watford. Taylor had worked wonders to get Watford back in the top league. Bob Stokoe or Alan Ashman couldn't have done it better. By 1999 we weren't good enough - on or off the pitch - to hold on to these players. The Blue Army knew who to blame.

One year before we stared the abyss full in the face, we were relegated from Division Two. In that year Carlisle United made £1.4 million in profit. Our income from transfers, including the sales of Matt Jansen and Rory Delap, was £2.12 million. Our response to this income included spending £100,000 on new players. These figures and the income of the directors, including our chairman, were published in the press in May 1999. They were well known to the crowd at that stomach churning game. For substantial chunks of the game the chants of 'one fat greedy bastard' replaced urging on the team. The target of the abuse was, of course, our chairman, Michael Knighton. What I would have made of those chants as a ten year old at my first game, I don't know. I'm glad I didn't take Thom to Brunton Park that day; glad I didn't have to explain why those people thought the man with the moustache was taking all the money. What does an image like that do to a child's wish to support a football team?

We had a hero in Jimmy Glass but think further and you realise that any Carlisle hero that day would have been an unlikely hero. Richard Tracey, a teenager blooded in the heat of the Carlisle free fall, hit the woodwork in search of the goal that would save us. He too, would have been newsworthy, and he too would have been an unlikely hero. Ask the crowd that day about their football heroes and they would - in all probability - have mentioned the men who have run through these chapters scoring goals, stopping the opposition in their tracks and pleasing crowds into the bargain. I'm sure that many in the crowd at three o'clock would have told you there were no heroes in the team they were about to cheer on. We won, largely by chance. We had nothing we could rely on. Jimmy Glass had seen us lose 3-0 to Scarborough a few weeks before his moment of glory and almost headed back to Swindon.

The last time a Carlisle goalie with so few games to his credit made the national news it was for the wrong reasons. Jon Blott played twice for Carlisle in 1985 - I saw him at Craven Cottage, a game we lost 3-2. He was a reasonable goalie and went on to join the police. When it was discovered that his police career went side by side with serious sex crimes the national press got interested. Carlisle United made the news pages that day as well! Blott's was an unlikely story, the kind that makes a blaze of news for a day. A freakish story. As freakish perhaps as the on-loan goalie who wanders up the field with nothing to lose, gets himself on the end of loose ball and creates history.

Glass said it all himself... 'Wallop, goal, thank you very much!' Think about those words, they tell you it was chance, and nothing more. There were other great football moments at the end of that season that were down to skill and self-belief. Nicky Wright's opening goal for Watford in the play-off final was a stunning overhead volley. Graham Taylor had made a journeyman team believe in themselves to the point that Wright simply went for it. Interviewed after the stunning closing minutes that saw Manchester United beat Bayern Munich to become kings of Europe, David Beckham said he'd seen the Champions League trophy on its way down the steps and already tied with white ribbons. That drove him on to drill in the passes that led to two killing goals.

So in the summer of 1999 we had only luck between ourselves and the non-league nightmare we'd hardly dared to consider. Michael Knighton promised us it was all a blip. Few of us believed a word he said.

'Smile,' we said, 'things could get worse.' Then we did smile, and things did get worse.

13 Andy Dibble, Michael Ingham, Peter Keen, Peter van der Kwaak, Barry Thompson and Luke Weaver

Mentioned for the first time in this chapter:

These are my opinions not facts. Others - especially those mentioned below - are likely to disagree.

Paul Baker - He'd played for us once before, in a team that suffered consecutive relegations in the eighties. It was news to me that he was still alive, still playing and still willing to commit his time and effort to Carlisle.
Peter Beardsley - Okay, we've mentioned him before. Not the manager.
Johnny Blom - A classic striker in the great Carlisle tradition. You know: Eric Gates, Gary MacDonald, Tony Fyfe, Christopher Dias.
Peter Clarke - In the great Stephane Pounewatchy tradition, a classy defender who gave up the higher aspirations - in his case at Highbury - to showcase his skills in front of two thousand on a freezing January night in Carlisle.
Nigel Clough - Not the manager.
Neil Cooper - Coach who took on the challenging task of making good things happen on the pitch at the turn of the century.
Andy Dibble - A goalie used in the 99/00 season.
John Durnin - Veteran forward who - like Steve Soley - moved to Brunton Park from Portsmouth.
Steve Halliday - Bargain basement goal machine, a welcome sight as the dark clouds gathered in late season 99/00.
Paul Heritage - A goalie not used in the 99/00 season.
Tony Hopper - In and out of form and in and out of favour. Central defender who lasted several seasons and found himself on the books at the turn of the century, whilst most of those blooded with him were plying their trade higher up the league.
Michael Ingham - A goalie used in the 99/00 season.
Peter Keen - A goalie used in the 99/00 season.
Peter van der Kwaak - A goalie used in the 99/00 season.
Rob McKinnon - The physique of a late period Joe Laidlaw, the skills of a late period Eric Gates. In a word, 'desperate.' He played for Scotland you know.
Brian Mclair - Not the manager.
Keith Mincher - The manager, briefly. Rumoured not to exist.
Nigel Pearson - He managed us to league survival, 98-99.
Matthew Pitts - Signed from Sunderland 1999. Useful striker of the ball with a work-rate that suggested he cared and a first touch that suggested his only hope of seeing Premiership action on the pitch was to train as a ref.

Gavin Skelton - Looked like a head on collision between a baby and journeyman boxer. Moved from the youth ranks to show a passion for the game that warmed the crowd, starting in 1999.
Steve Soley - Free-running, free scoring attacking midfield playmaking genius. Also spent a lot of time being crap.
Shaun Teale - Experienced defender. Decisive, effective and - generally - the equal of Third Division strikers.
Barry Thompson - A goalie used in the 99/00 season.
Luke Weaver - A goalie used in the 99/00 season, easily the best news of the season on the pitch.
Stuart Whitehead - Defender who made his debut for Carlisle in the 'Jimmy Glass' season. Better than some in the team. Then again 'some' included Rob McKinnon.
Martin Wilkinson - Go easy on the man, he's managed Carlisle United.
Graham 'Tot' Winstanley - Mentioned in chapter 1. Classy defender from classy teams of the past.

On 4 June 1999 I delivered the manuscript for *Singin' The Blues.* I already had the deal for *Raiders of the Low Forehead* and the plans for the new novel included more titles as Stanley Manly. In the following months I wrote two novels. The second of which - *Tokyo Bloodbath 2002!* - concerns a team from Workington, even worse than Workington Reds, who go on to represent England in the 2002 World Cup. As someone used to the ins and outs of Knighton era Carlisle, I had no problem imagining that football and the totally improbable went hand in hand. Things were looking bright for a few weeks at least. When it comes to writing for a living I tend to trust money in the bank and nothing else. The same - more or less - is true of football chairmen although in their case you can also trust points on the league table.

When Carlisle's promised revival fell flat on its face in the first weeks of the new season it was - probably - predictable that the writing work would go the same way. The first publisher of this book shelved the thing for a year to make way for titles on Hearts and Wolves that would raise the profile of his company. Understandable and sound from a business point of view but it left me writing a second final chapter to follow the one you've just read. In the end it worked out well. His company built up distribution and a website and *Singin' The Blues* came out in August 2000, selling out before Christmas. It was frustrating to the extent that the publisher didn't want to risk printing more copies but for a few weeks we out sold Harry Potter in Carlisle, result!

I could see the situation for what it was. Similarly the Blue Army could see the small amounts of good news around as the millennium dawned on us. These were evident in the desperate football of Exeter City, Shrewsbury Town and Chester City. A cold comfort for sure, but one the Blue Army had come to understand all too well by this point. We hadn't the security of watching Aldershot fold in mid-season or Newport County running off the pitch at half-time into the waiting arms of their concerned mothers who'd supply them with a loving Wet Wipe and a change of trainer pants. From our side - there was a touch more skill, enough aggression to leave Adolf Hitler incontinent with fear and a seemingly endless procession of new faces. Andy Dibble, Michael Ingham, Peter Van Der Kwaak, Peter Keen, Barry Thompson and Luke Weaver to name a mere half dozen. Now we've named those six, we've dealt with the new 'goalie.' For the sake of thoroughness we should mention Paul Heritage, another goalie on the books that season who played a starring role on the treatment table.

Such endless parades - of course - can go in two directions. Out the other end with little ceremony went Nigel Pearson, a manager who - with little to work with on the pitch and precious little time to achieve anything - had secured our league survival. Back down the M6 after 270 solid minutes and one magic moment went Jimmy Glass. The journeyman who shot us to league survival with ten seconds to spare. His career would take further turns - in and out of favour at struggling Swindon - Glass would turn down a move to Chester City on the transfer deadline, citing his affinity with Carlisle. The rest is a good story if you haven't bought and read *One Hit Wonder* you're missing out.

We landed goalie Luke Weaver, later to be abused on message boards for years but - briefly - brilliant. His skills all but won us three away points at his old club Orient in December. The only thing he didn't do was score the solitary goal. That fell to Matthew Pitts. Pitts had come from Sunderland, he - along with the half dozen new goalies - found himself in a squad that - with three exceptions - dated back no further than 1997. Forgetting for a second, Jeff Thorpe, Richard Prokas and Tony Hopper this was a team built on loans, trials, youngsters who'd failed their first auditions higher up the league and some dependable older heads on the way down.

Speaking of older heads... I was talking to Al Woodcock who ran the Carlisle United Online website. The one we now know and love as CUFC Online. It was the autumn of 1999 when he broke the hot news that would temporarily solve our striking crisis.

'Paul Baker, is he still alive!'

I knew damn well he was, he'd been at Hartlepool the previous season. He turned in a fair enough performance the first time I saw him after his return, at the Sixfields Stadium, Northampton. Baker was no stranger to struggling Carlisle. His sweaty and combative performances had been consistent through two free-falling seasons of successive relegation in the eighties. He was qualified for what he found at Carlisle. His role took in coaching, which was just as well, given the attrition rate of anyone charged with decision-making. Neil Cooper's coaching career at Carlisle followed in the great 'blink and you've missed it' tradition of Martin Harvey. However, this was as nothing compared to the legendary Keith Mincher who came and went in the summer of 1999. Anything you read about the man is likely to be pure speculation. Officially he left owing to unavoidable commitments abroad. Unofficially, his reason for departure appears in the one place Carlisle United have truly dazzled in the 21st century, the rumours pages on the internet! There - you may discover - some people doubt that he ever existed. Safe from prosecution and fired by frustrations, the internet was buzzing with Blue Nightmare rumours. Some of the entertainment was simply standard imagination-firing stuff. Like the fearsome skills of Swedish striker Johnny Blom, that would soon sort out the problems up front! Hell, the press releases and internet stuff made Blom sound great. We'd been here before, notably when Eric Gates' matchless experience, international pedigree and quality skills were mooted as the solution to the early nineties goal famine.

Elsewhere it had become really exciting. Mincher's management career was one orgasmic aspect, though on second thoughts, I've had orgasms that lasted longer than his stint in charge, and - sexually speaking - I'd count myself pretty normal.

Mincher's management career was celebrated on the rumours page. It was eclipsed for entertainment value by the management careers of the guys who were gonna come and sort us out. In cyberspace, you couldn't move for Carlisle United's new managers. Like King Arthur and his army waiting, asleep under the ground, until the moment when disaster threatened to overwhelm us all, Peter Beardsley, Nigel Clough and Brian Mclair were - apparently - ready to pit their tactical skills against the grim realities of the struggle for league survival.

Someone else - allegedly - on the way to sort things out was twenty stone, no-nonsense, 'die of shame you scum-bag,' telly star Roger Cook. Before the muck-raking end of the tabloid press suggested that the 'truth' wasn't all it appeared to be in Cook's programmes, there were regular stories suggesting that Cook's encounter with Michael Knighton might be screened at any time. Hell, Cook had taken on the most feared enemies of all. This was the man who once claimed on television that Martin McGuinness had served as the IRA's chief of staff and, near enough, challenged the man and the organisation to take him to court if he was wrong. On this evidence, the man's bravery/suicidal tendencies knew no limits. I'd often found myself watching Cook with admiration, such a reaction tended to be followed - on my part - by thoughts of how I'd like to live a long and healthy life and would - therefore - not fancy his job, even if it went with a salary of Knightonesque proportions. If Cook was regularly to go where others feared to tread - ran the logic - then surely, this tendency would, eventually, put him face to face with Carlisle United's larger than life chairman. Well, all we can do is... wait.

Years later I heard second hand that *The Cook Report* had been on the receiving end of a load of information from football fans, the Blue Army amongst them. They'd done some investigations for a programme that would look at the fact that any power-mad, self-important piece of shit could acquire a lower division football club. It came to nothing - apparently - because the clubs in question were far flung, leaving the show with a massive bill for gathering information. It was also highly likely that one or more self-important piece of shit would jump before the show was screened and - in any case - *The Cook Report's* future was less assured than Carlisle's at the time.

Whatever, since 1999 we've fielded poor teams and great rumours on the internet. We'll be in the Scottish league soon, Brunton Park will be bulldozed for houses or a supermarket. There's some entertaining bollocks out there. Some other bizarre 'rumours' have been backed up by observation. Like the one in 2000 about Martin Wilkinson watching games from behind glass in the east stand, relaying instructions by phone to the director's box and driving halfway round the ground at half-time to give his team talk. Whatever the truth of this arrangement, there was busy late-season traffic between the director's box and the forlorn figure of Paul Baker urging his men on from the touch-line.

And the 'men' in question! The stars of the new crop had come from the usual routes. Steve Soley and John Durnin were out of favour at First Division Portsmouth - a club that could claim some affinity with us, blue strip, lonely geographical location, glory days a fading memory, you know the kind of thing. We took the pair of them and watched them struggle to put shape into an outfit who were chasing clear air half the time. Peter Clarke, a defender who'd moved from Arsenal, got plenty of appearances in the first team and impressed on several occasions, sometimes for entire games at a stretch. The youth angle was best demonstrated by Gavin Skelton. A lad with heart in the admirable mould of the great Richard Prokas himself, Skelton threw himself at everything and won the crowd over, even when he failed to make a telling touch on the ball. Skelton's shaved head reminded me - strangely - of Baby Crockett, an overgrown toddler who starred in late sixties kids' comics. Skelton had potential, that much was obvious when I first saw him in an uneventful 0-0 draw with Grimsby in the Milk/Coca Cola/League/Does anyone really care that much about this competition? cup in August 1999.

We took some stuffings away from home and I got pissed off badly. Add a rail fare that offered a few pence change from fifty quid, a train fire that held up everyone and the small matter of a 5-0 stuffing at Sincil Bank, Lincoln and you've got the makings of a trauma that could lead a man to abandon football following in favour of dragging round the D-I-Y stores on a Saturday. A lesser man than me, that is. Hell, I'd grown hard to it by this point. That Lincoln game wasn't even the worst performance I saw that year. That honour has to be disputed between the final match of the campaign and the 80 minutes of complete and unadulterated, shapeless shuffling shite that provided the 'entertainment' for a fraction over three thousand supporters as Carlisle went down 1-0 at Brunton Park to Macclesfield. The Macclesfield performance was all the worse because we started that game as if we meant it. The first ten minutes were okay. But, the writing was on the wall when Pitts squandered a begging chance in the opening skirmishes. Macclesfield - it must be said - were friggin' abysmal. I'd returned to the paddock by this time, mainly because the loneliness in every other part of the ground was crushing. When I first went to Brunton Park there was a standard chant of 'You'll never take the Warwick.' Looking at the bare expanses of concrete visible at that end of the ground as the century turned, the Warwick could have been taken by a pensioners' outing. The fact was, few people could be arsed to take a position on the Warwick and the whole ground echoed in a sad, empty, mockery of better days. With crowds sometimes plunging to within sight of a paltry 2000 the reminders of the darkest days of past nightmares were all too close.

They were all too close on 15 April 2000 as Macclesfield rattled in the only goal of a desperate game. Our stars: Pitts, Soley, Halliday and Durnin were squandering possession, running about in disorganised impersonations of a tactical master plan and clattering the odd challenge into the opposition when it all got too much. On this final score at least, we were matchless. By Easter we were out there on our own as undisputed caution and dismissal champions of a skilfully challenged lower flight.

And still the improbability of it all pushed the envelope. A winning streak as the winter finally lost its grip had seen promotion chasing teams humbled. The best travelling performance within striking distance of my patch had seen Peterboro take a manful stuffing at London Road on a Tuesday night in March and, we were worth that win. A more typical performance in this era was the manner of the victory in a tense encounter at Chester City's compact and bijou residence, the Deva 'Stadium.' Outplayed for skill, we retaliated with 'commitment.' For the most part the results were predictable; Steve Halliday and Stuart Whitehead were ordered out of the action in the final ten minutes. Naturally enough, down to nine men, totally outplayed, short of anything approaching a winning idea in the opposition half and running well into injury time, we broke away and scored a spectacular winning goal, our first shot on target all afternoon and it came from Scott Dobie's boot twenty yards out.

Knighton's press conference patter was surreal: 'The fans love matches like this. They pretend they don't, but they do.'

'I thought we played better after the sendings off so maybe we'll start with nine men in our next match.'

'This club is the epitome of the roller-coaster ride that football is all about.'

'There's never a boring season at Carlisle.'

By this point two things were evident. First off, the desperate balance sheets and pointless, panic driven football on the pitch at Chester and Shrewsbury were slowly turning the tide. Regardless of beating Chester we could still be caught. Sure, this wasn't the worst team I'd ever seen, but this was a team struggling against the rest of the division. The year Mike Graham had back-peddled his way into my nightmares we weren't threatened at all. In 2000 nobody was going to fold in mid-season and save us.

A measure of the distance between Knighton's stream of sound-bites and the gut feelings on the terraces was there for a few dozen of us to hear in the paddock as the last game before Easter played itself out. A guy in front of me in the paddock screamed out loud. Maybe, taking Knighton's comments after the Chester game, you could claim the screamer was pretending not to love such a match, epitomising the glorious roller coaster ride that is football and reminding everyone that our season was anything but boring. You could claim that. Then again, you could say that after the best part of a season's torture, the most consistent spell of desperation in the club's history and the lack of anything resembling salvation on the pitch that afternoon, the screaming blue had simply had enough. He explained himself. He screamed because we'd made two substitutions and Rob McKinnon was still on the pitch. I agreed with him. As I had eight years before, I picked on the most athletically challenged member of the first team and noticed his blunders.

As the season wound to a close I could see McKinnon and in my mind his porky frame was symptomatic of everything that was so wrong with the team I couldn't help but love. McKinnon took some fine abuse that afternoon against Macclesfield, as he did on the odd occasion he managed to last a complete match. 'Experienced' to the point that his contract negotiations probably revolved around his assurance that he could 'do a job', McKinnon had grafted his glory years out at Hartlepool and Motherwell throwing in a totally incomprehensible loan to Manchester United in which he had failed to make a first team appearance. By the end of the 99/00 season, chunky Rob was showing that same love of pointless running, passes into nowhere and yard-short chases of opposing players that had characterised the final months of Mike Graham's career. Say what you want, McKinnon wasn't boring. His frequent slips could reduce a supporter on the edge of sanity to that ear splitting: 'ARGHHHHHHHHHHH!!!!!!!!!!!!!!!!!!!!!!!!' we have all heard from time to time. That's what the guy in the paddock sounded like, before launching another tirade on the head of Paul Baker as our player-coach tried again to instil some shape into his men. I envied the screamer that afternoon. At least he could muster the pumped up fury to scream. Since the demolition afternoon at Sincil Bank, Lincoln, I'd been reduced to burying my head in my hands and groaning on a regular basis. My other odd habits - like two Scotch pies a game, as many Kit Kats as I could handle and unnecessary trips into record shops on my way to away games were another clear cry for comfort. Screaming would - probably - have saved me money that season.

I guess I should count myself lucky. My Dad had to venture into Asian undergrowth and see men hit by bullets to share in the screaming depths of life's roller coaster. All I had to do, by comparison, to see men reduced to terrified screaming wrecks staring their own mortality full in the face and losing their grip on reason in the face of such terror, was to pay £8. I got this experience with the added bonus of leaning against a crush barrier and munching my way through a Brunton Park scotch pie. Great pies, at least something is as good as it used to be at Brunton Park. I got a reality check the night of the Macclesfield game when I went to a school reunion in Wigton. It was a great do, I spent ages talking to people I'd barely known at school. We'd all lived a bit, could talk kids, mortgages, divorces and the rest. The one guy rumoured dead turned up alive. When we got to talking about what we did these days I got the same response a few times, 'What, you're still going to watch them!?' Nobody else - it seemed - still cared about our 'local' team.

By this time our 'season' was the final few games. We were better placed than most. We still had eight games remaining when some of the others had six. Our final games included two six pointers, the massive result and desperate display against Chester City being the first of these. This final run in also included more home than away games and some encounters against teams who - in all probability - would find themselves mired in mid-table mediocrity with nothing to play for by the time we lined up against them. So, there was hope. And - like the sight of Richard Prokas finally replacing McKinnon in the Macclesfield game - we could relate to this and feel positive, now and again. Then again, this 'hope' said a lot about the desperate depths to which we'd now sunk. The turn of the millennium side were fractionally better than their predecessors and they showed their commitment in that collection of cautions. Not exactly entertaining and barely qualifying as football some of the time, it could still get us worked up. I'd become hardened to the horrors now. This was a new experience, battle hardened and taking a perverse pleasure in the depths to which this experience could drag me. The lack of skill on the pitch left my imagination running riot. Just how and why - I wondered - did Rob McKinnon find himself on loan at Old Trafford? Did Alex Ferguson drag his improbably talented teenage army into a room, line the Nevilles and Dave Beckham against a wall and say, 'Look lads, there's no guarantee of anything in this life. You only get back what you put in. So practice those ball skills, make yourselves special. Because if you don't you'll end up like...

AT THIS POINT ALEX DREW BACK THE CURTAIN TO REVEAL A CHUNKY BODY IN THE PROUD RED SHIRT

'.......Rob McKinnon.'

NEVILLE, NEVILLE AND BECKS: 'ARGHHHHHHHHHHHH!!!!!! !!!!!!!!!!!!!!!!!!'

Six hours later, as the dusk turned to darkness on the training ground, the few staff still around finally ejected David Beckham after the young star had practiced landing over 400 free kicks right on top of a ten pence piece.

Maybe it was simpler than this. Maybe chunky Rob stood in the centre of the training ground as a couple of dozen of the highest paid professionals in the country jogged round and round his ample frame.

Or maybe, somewhere in the distant past, around the time that his country called upon him, Rob McKinnon was a good footballer. Well, anything is possible. Eric Gates played for England, deservedly. He 'played' for Carlisle, desperately. A DNA test would have revealed both versions of Gates to be the same person. Those of us reduced to paying money to watch the ageing striker might have told you otherwise.

By this point, my team and I were heading in different directions in terms of performance. After a year in which I'd hardly got a moment to myself it was time to do something about the situation. 1999 had opened impressively for me, the writing had thrown a few opportunities my way. This book and the chance to see *Raiders of the Low Forehead* published were only the start. By the time the new football season kicked off Stanley Manly - the nutter who wrote Raiders and bore a striking resemblance to me, thinly disguised with a cloth cap and smouldering fag - was planning a live appearance, considering further novels and branching out into journalism. Under my own name I was working on a range of other stuff from treatments for TV shows to some more music journalism. The day job had finally seen the start of a pet project I'd been working on for years, our professional writing course had taken in its first group. This work was great, but it was also a problem. The scale of the whole thing was impossible, and getting worse.

I'd tried a few things, getting other day jobs with the same flexibility wasn't easy and full-time writing jobs were out there offering exciting six month contracts with the vague possibility that there might be more work. In the end I figured what I wanted in terms of cutting down the day job and went into work in the first week of 2000 prepared to negotiate. It didn't come to that, I asked for what I wanted and got it. The only tough condition was keeping quiet about the whole thing until a few negotiations had been completed around the rest of the college. By this time Stanley had done his first gig, a London launch party for the media and anyone else who could scrounge an invite. Not the greatest performance of my life, but another dimension to the writing life and access to several phone numbers I'd have struggled to attract in any other way.

By Easter 2000, I'd come through some dark days of exhaustion and found something to aim for. Carlisle, by comparison were crawling along the bottom for one more year. The regular news updates I downloaded every night talked about reserves wanting to get into the side, plans for the future and what could be achieved. The action on the pitch talked about struggle and desperation.

The Peterboro game was - probably - as good as it got in the south east. 2-0 winners over promotion contenders we were worth the points even if we hardly dominated. John Durnin's goals were clinical, inspired and special and, on the night, that was about the difference. Elsewhere in the south east, notably at Barnet and Lincoln, we managed some shape on the odd occasions we found ourselves in possession. The Peterboro win was part of a sequence that saw us climb from the bottom to a lofty 22nd place. But whenever things began to look hopeful we managed to squander these chances. On Easter Monday we needed a points gap to take the pressure off the end of season run in. Away at Southend - a team marooned out of touch with either end of the struggle, mathematically safe but hardly a 'class' side, we had a perfect opportunity to take a result home. We deserved the 2-0 humbling we got and Peter Keen - in goal for the injured Luke Weaver - was the only thing that kept the score line respectable.

Our captain - David Brightwell - had made just over forty appearances in eight and a half seasons on the books at Maine Road, Manchester. He followed this with a slide down the leagues and a smattering of loan spells before finding his level at beleaguered - Nigel Pearson managed - Carlisle. His moment of glory, like almost everything else he'd achieved - had been overshadowed. The one true moment of sublime footballing skill the day we beat Plymouth to stay alive in the league was not Jimmy Glass's short-range burying of the ball, it was the long range strike from Brightwell that equalised Plymouth's lead. That - it would appear - is the story of Brightwell's career. One of a pair of brothers at Maine Road he was overshadowed by his brother Ian, used less and sold earlier. In the Carlisle defence, a year later than his fleeting second of Blues glory, Brightwell was outmanoeuvred by Shaun Teale, another old head on his way down. Teale had turned out regularly for Aston Villa and still had the touches, positional sense and clinical efficiency to show the level of skill he'd once commanded at will. In the Carlisle defence his skills had to blend with a level of panic and disorganisation that left everyone in danger of punting the ball into space.

At Roots Hall, Southend, Brightwell and Teale marshalled the back line as best they could. Their respective performances said everything about the state of our plight. Teale, by and large, cut out passes, foiled runs on goal and punted loose balls into the path of our breaking midfield. Brightwell sliced passes and looked ineffective. During what passed for a promising move our thwarted attack watched the ball as it was booted back to Brightwell. With a similar position and situation to that massive strike against Plymouth he sliced it clean into the crowd as we groaned in desperation.

The following morning I was checking out the league tables, looking at the promotion and relegation issues that would have a bearing on my trips to away grounds and I found myself saddened at the drop zone positions of Welling and Sutton United in the Conference. I'd taken up research against the day I might need to navigate the lower reaches on a regular basis. Where exactly was Forest

Green Rovers?

Predictably, it came down to the last Saturday again. Three teams, Chester, Shrewsbury and Carlisle, kicked off knowing they were fighting for survival. Jane and I had booked the 'romantic' weekend away in Brighton months before. I'd hoped the game would count for nothing. I took Thom, and found myself apologising to him. It was one of those - 'If you could have seen what I saw at your age, Son' - kind of conversations and, as a rule, I'm not that kind of Dad. Then again, the picture of 'Tot' Winstanley in the programme that afternoon didn't help.

They put donkeys in with race horses sometimes. The idea is that the simple and unconcerned demeanour of the donkey will keep the highly-strung creature calm in the face of the hormone pumping terrors to come. In truth, I needed Thom with me that afternoon in Brighton. Choosing to be responsible for him was - in the circumstances - both a selfish and sensible act. The brain-blunting 'what if they lose' thoughts were running riot by one o'clock that afternoon and the gut churning nerves had taken hold before I even saw the Withdean Stadium. It was an athletic stadium with a makeover suggesting the team didn't want to stay but thought they might have to. It was hot, really bloody hot. The whole thing was challenging a seasoned football fan's grip on reality before the kick off.

Talk in the crowd soon spread the news that a lot of the team had been clubbing into the early hours. The more the pressure screw had turned since that lucky win over Chester, the worse we had crumbled. For the second time in as many seasons a Carlisle team playing for their very survival squandered possession, struggled to find a shape let alone a tactical idea worthy of the name and tested the nerve of the people who still cared. I was so nervous I held on to the conversations with Thom. He was the one familiar, trustable thing in that unreal place. The concerned parent in me could think some strange thoughts. Having taken him to that desperate display I could only feel protective. I hoped at that moment that he'd never understand, at any point in his life, how much it helped me to have him there.

The whole game passed in a blur of moment to moment despair. Our passing was hopeless, the attacks - for the most part - desperate runs against a well-marshalled defence. Peter Keen was easily the best player we could muster. He pulled off one spectacular save. I groaned, held my head in my hands, stood and held on to little more than hope. When we heard that Shrewsbury were winning the enormity of the situation was crushing. For sanity, I could at least explain it to Thom.

We were going down. We didn't look like scoring and we needed a miracle. We got it in the shape of the Peterboro goal that condemned Chester City to non-league football. A year before Peterboro had scored against Scarborough, a goal that allowed Jimmy Glass to shoot himself into history. Now they beat Chester

City, and shot us into marginal survival. The margin, a better goal difference. You could say our salvation on the strength of a Peterboro goal for the second season running confirmed our 'spooky' team status. In reality it was coincidence. In the end it came down to our minus 33 against their minus 35. You could say that a 600 strong Blue Army celebrated the achievement. It was relief, nothing more. Hell, I felt for Chester City that day. They had seen certain relegation at the midway point that season and then staged a revival that put hope of survival in their hearts. They came close to scoring in their final match - something we didn't manage. Above all, those Chester fans went to their game able to believe that their team could do it. Something that was, frankly, in short supply for us at Brighton.

I got one magic moment for the collection, but I had to wait until that night when the paralysing fear had loosened and the reality of survival had sunk in. With Thom and Jane in tow I was wandering past a bar on the seafront when I saw the baseball cap that read, 'Knighton is a c***.' There is a stall on the Palace Pier at Brighton that allows you to pay for the motto of your own choice on a baseball cap. The blue sporting that cap had been in front of me during the game and we'd exchanged opinions on the horror show we were watching. That night, he and some like-minded people, had put their money where their mouths were. His mate had shelled out for a sister motto, 'Knighton is a t***.'

14 Paul Simpson

Mentioned for the first time in this chapter:

These are my opinions not facts. Others - especially those mentioned below - are likely to disagree.

Jonny Allan - Striker who started with us, didn't get established and became a fan favourite at Halifax and Northwich Victoria.
Ian Atkins - Passion and graft in a tracksuit. Another manager who'd seen the rough end elsewhere and came with a realistic idea of what was happening. Loved for these qualities even when his teams couldn't win.
Ryan Baldacchino - Fast, tricky forward with mop of blond hair and skinny physique suggesting he'd have been better cast in a daytime soap opera.
Chris Billy - Stiff-running and stuttering midfield genius who combined passing, passion and visionary passes with stomach churning mistakes. Prone to flapping his arms in gestures that looked like panic, even when the pressure was off.
Mark Birch - Atkins era defender. Signed for ten grand at a time when transfer fees seemed to be banned at Brunton Park. Went on to Gretna and glory.
Roddy Collins - He talked big, he strutted around his technical area in a sharp suit, the results were patchy. Loved and hated in almost equal measure. A manager we're unlikely to forget.
Tom Cowan - No nonsense, tough tackling Scots defender. He'd seen action at Sheffield United and Rangers. Signed from Dundee, probably fancied the better weather in Carlisle. Why else would he sign during our record run of defeats?
Stuart Elliot - Young defender who appeared incapable of going beyond six months with anyone. A real star against Orient away, typical of the talents Roddy Collins would use and discard.
Craig Farrell - Useful striker signed from Leeds at the back end of 2002 with a nifty line in snatched shots and forcing himself through tight spots in opposing defences. Then again, goals of that kind were the only option for most of his time at Brunton Park.
Richie Foran - Irish goal-machine who would, eventually, hit the net 29 times for us. In a word, 'excitable'.
Matty Glennon - Quality shot-stopper and fiercely brave goalkeeper. In and out of Carlisle teams from the back end of 2000 and in and out of the club.
Kevin Gray - Looked like a wrestler, ran that back line like a sergeant major and just edged it over Lumsden as player of the season in the Conference for my money.

Mo Harkin - Wycombe, Carlisle, Nuneaton, Crawley (where he played against us twice), Forest Green. Check your local paper, he's coming your way soon!
Karl Hawley - Diminutive muscle bound striker. A good first touch, an eye for goal and special talent at missing sitters. Leading scorer 04-05.
Carl Heggs - 'Striker' possessed of a first touch that went further than many shots. Despite clear limits to his abilities Heggs became a cult hero to Cumbrians and chalked up a couple of notable achievements for a Carlisle player.
Tony Hemmings - Looked like a proper athlete. Ran around, used his strength to win the ball and never scored in a whole season.
Chay Hews - Five games for us. None for anyone else you've heard of.
Derek Holmes - Old fashioned centre-forward. Scots born, star of Bournemouth's reserve team until we signed him to replace the departed Andy Preece.
Danny Livesey - Defender, a Christmas present from Bolton in 2004 when he agreed a loan deal on 24 December.
Will McDonagh - Another Rod Squad import from Ireland. Midfield, misfiring but willing to work when it mattered. Ended his one appearance in his final season with a red card against Grimsby.
Brendan McGill - From yards away looked about twelve. Nippy winger with the ball glued to his feet.
Peter Murphy - Irish defender/midfielder signed during the early days of the Rod Squad. Sometime captain. Programme notes: 'Comfortable on the ball, Peter is happy to pass or take players on.' The problem was when he did these things we'd often end up tearing our hair out.
Adam Murray - Signed from Mansfield in 2005, straight into the first team and play-making for the inconsistent forward line.
Glen Murray - Workington, Barrow and then the full-on glamour of Conference level Carlisle United. A striker capable of making the play in the last third.
Andy Preece - Stylish and classy veteran striker, signed at the back end of 2003 by Simmo who knew what he was getting. Helped turn around the nightmare start to 2003/04. The following year he humbled a few Conference defences before leaving to take charge at Worcester City.
Brian Shelley - Rod Squad Irish defender who'd known our boss when both were at Bohemians. Defender with a defender's instincts. The official site claims 'surging runs forward' are his trademark.
Paul Simpson - Local boy, long rumoured to be on his way. Eventually arrived as player in 2003. Appointed caretaker boss on Roddy Collins' departure and permanent boss soon after prompting the development of a love/hate relationship in which his dogged qualities gradually won over many.
Magno Silva Viera - Stylish Brazilian loaned from Wigan as we got used to

Conference football. Hat-trick hero at Aldershot in September. We loved his jinking runs and flair in front of goal. What he made of Cumbria after the Copacabana Beach isn't recorded.
Brian Wake - Inconsistent and enigmatic, even the football reference sites can't decide if he plays in midfield or up front. Acquired under Roddy Collins. Scored nine times in his first season, including two hat-tricks.
Kieren Westwood - Agile goalie with storming length on his kicks, blooded in the Conference where he spent most of the season on the bench.

The curses favoured by many were hurled at games, put onto message boards and anywhere else that might help us tell it like we saw it. I could reel off season after season in the painful and seemingly endless final days of the Knighton era. Looking back it seems to me that the next few seasons were one long turgid parade of limited teams, poor results and dashed hopes. The real drama wasn't on the pitch, and anyone who cared knew it.

The pundits had us down year on year as prime relegation candidates as the Conference beckoned. We could roar ourselves into believing on the terraces but all we really had to cheer were moments. Fuelled by the Blue Army and the efforts of a few players and backroom staff Carlisle United achieved a little in spite of the leeching qualities of its overweight owner. A man by this time apparently trusted only by blood relatives and - by his own admission - the most reviled individual in Cumbria. Give Knighton his due - he got one thing right.

I knew people involved in businesses in Cumbria who wanted nothing more to do with Knighton. It seemed Carlisle United owed money everywhere. The message boards were filling up rapidly as the world and his dog finally got on line. The venom started with what people would do left alone for five minutes with our fat controller and soon progressed to dirt digging intent on finding out where he lived, where his businesses were registered and where his family could be cornered. Knighton became well acquainted with the local constabulary mainly through repeated requests for protection. Many rank and file fans suggested the local constabulary should be asking pointed questions about the Brunton Park books when the fat one phoned them.

Damn shame about the football, the rest of my life was going well. The first edition of this book came out, shifted a shitload in no time and got me into the Cumbrian media. My colleagues in Dartford thought it hilarious. Especially

~~~~~~~~~~~~~~~~

AUTHOR'S NOTE:

The facts and figures in this chapter are drawn from a variety of sources. With regard to the details of the final days of the Knighton era I'm indebted to *One Hit Wonder* by Jimmy Glass and Roger Lytollis and also the journalists who took an interest at the time, especially David Conn of *The Independent* and his article *Fans Fury at Knighton Threat to Close Carlisle* published on 27 April 2002.
~~~~~~~~~~~~~~~~

when it emerged we were outselling Harry Potter. Admittedly, the Potter book had already been selling for a few weeks, and admittedly this feat was only achieved for a month in the city of Carlisle but... result!!! By December a bookshop in Carlisle rang me at work asking for another three hundred. The publishers had run out and weren't printing any more. In the end the bookshop bought up every copy in Kent and tried to buy some from *Sportspages* in London, however they'd sold out too. Fourteen weeks, every book sold!

On 12 August we played Halifax at home and I did a signing in James Thins. I shifted a few dozen books, ran into some old friends and some really good people. One woman dropped off - as a gift - a programme of the first game I'd ever attended. The wife and daughter of Alan Ross came by to thank me for the dedication and the comments about their man. I wondered what they made of the swearing and the rest of the stuff in the book but it clearly meant something to them that I'd made the effort. I started to choke up discussing Alan Ross on Radio Cumbria. I was living the dream, but then again my dreams aren't what you'd call normal. I didn't pay for the second game of the season, I sat next to Derek Lacey and added expert comments as we lost to Orient. Radio Cumbria ran a competition to answer a question and win a copy of the book. My first attempt at setting a question - 'which fat greedy bastard would you most like to kill?' - was turned down as unsuitable. They were laughing in the studio when they turned it down though.

By this point the new management of Ian Atkins was beginning to show itself. He'd seen the rough end at doomed Chester and almost pulled off a miracle at our expense so he knew the score. A sign of things to come was his acquisition of Carl Heggs. A skilfully challenged striking machine, Heggs combined the classic qualities of a comedy star - ever willing, not always able. Before and after Carlisle, Heggs played 'non-league' football. He ran, fumbled and dragged himself back into action to run again as I watched him in those early games. He didn't get on the score sheet until 12 September. Despite this, a section of the crowd adopted him immediately. Heggs was one of those honest crowd pleasers, in some ways a throwback to the great Stan Webb himself. A fool maybe, but our fool, and he cared. Atkins liked his players experienced, realistic and dripping sweat the whole time. If Atkins could have cloned his younger self eleven times he'd have had the perfect line up.

At Orient, with me in the commentary box, we were stuffed by an outrageous penalty decision. With CFM Radio mocking the legendary Derek Lacey to his face and trying to sneak an interview with Atkins I took it on myself to wander into the dressing room and grab the boss for his comments. Radio Cumbria were - after all - paying good money for exclusive access in this direction. I hadn't entered the tunnel before I heard Atkins swearing. He 'fucked and bastarded' his way up the stairs before repeating the same attitude, minus the swearing, as Derek held a microphone to his face. A lot of my worries about the team vanished at that point. Whatever damage Knighton was doing, we had the right man in the dugout. Atkins had criminally limited resources, but he'd push them to the limits, no question.

Improbably we hit tenth place at the start of September 2000. Atkins' well-travelled warriors included Ian Stevens, back for another stretch up front, Tony Hemmings, a solidly built black forward player who wouldn't manage a goal all season and Mark Birch a young defender. There was something special about Birch... he'd cost us money. As a rule we preferred them for free. Birch came from Northwich, Hemmings came by way of Ilkeston and Chester. There were no stars in this team. Atkins did his best. So did most of the bottom flight, predictably, they dumped us well in the shit. We were in the bottom five at the end of September, sank slowly in the following weeks and hit rock bottom by the first week in November where we stayed - more or less - until the last few days. Luke Weaver's confidence slowly shredded itself before our eyes and Atkins brought in the solid no-nonsense shot stopping of young Matty Glennon, a keeper who instilled some belief in the back four. Elsewhere the old heads and unflappable graft of the veteran strike force finally did the job. With suggestions of summer already in the air I shouted myself voiceless with a few hundred other desperate Blues at Southend in April. Ian Stevens scrambled a goal and that scrambled us a point. The following Wednesday at Lincoln we managed the same result thanks to a Heggs' strike. We were safe. Torquay or Barnet would go down. We had half a week to enjoy the fact that nothing could prevent us kicking off in the same league the following season - the safest finish we'd known since 1997. Atkins duly got the credit.

By this time supporters' moves had led to the formation of an independent trust hell bent on getting some influence in the boardroom. They held a huge meeting in the Sands Centre before the final home game. We kicked off at Brunton Park in front of almost nine thousand where we basked in sunshine, watched a goal-less game and listened as Atkins addressed the crowd. That morning at the trust meeting he'd been slapped on the back so many times he was - allegedly - bruised from shoulder to shoulder. Heggs, scorer of the saving goal, his last in the professional ranks, had also achieved lasting fame - the first Carlisle player to have a website dedicated entirely to himself. Sadly 'Who Let the Heggs Out' appears no more on the internet, but we all saw it, and laughed along. These heroes helped us, but nowhere near as much as seven defeats in nine games that marked Barnet's run in. We drew our last four games, scoring twice.

There was one massive game that season. Having humbled the awesome firepower of Woking and Kidderminster to get to the third round of the cup we finally got a break, Arsenal at home. It sold out, I was one of thousands who didn't get a ticket, but it did make *Match of the Day*. Arsenal got a lesson that day. Okay, the game was predictable, we both tried hard, they took a 1-0 lead, shut up shop and allowed us to play a bit. We couldn't turn them over, they - probably - could have raised their game if we'd come close and the pundits did the usual 'brave performance,' 'fighting spirit' bit in describing us. But they got a lesson alright. For a long time pundits had faced Arsene Wenger with the same question. When one of his skilful stars gave in to human instinct and mullah'd an opponent the phlegmatic Frenchman was generally asked his opinion. With his usual thin lipped expression of complete emotional control he'd manage the slightest of shrugs and say, 'Ah, but eet iz a game of football, zey 'ave ze pasśion.'

Arsenal were already leading, Patrick Viera was ambling through midfield, probably already thinking about the next Premiership game and Richard Prokas caught the inspirational Arsenal skipper. WHAP!!!!

Midfielders from Penrith 'ave ze passion' too. There is one superb newspaper photograph. Viera is eating grass, Prokas strolling away. Prokas, by common agreement, is unlikely to appear on University Challenge. The one place he displays genius is in the seconds after one of his legendary challenges. His somewhat unconventional facial features arranged into the look of a surprised child. 'What, me sir?'

What Prokas was doing on the pitch when the final whistle went is between the ref and his conscience. Reduced to watching it on TV I still turned away for a second and muttered, 'Ooh, fuck.'

There were 'fucks, shits, bollocks and bastards' and worse flying around terraces and message boards. The real action was away from the pitch. When you put the facts down coldly on paper they look logical. There is a sense of real events bringing about changes. It didn't feel like that to me. An exiled fan is powerless to start with, reduced to message boards and long journeys to get that all important reality check. Under Knighton's chairmanship we all felt this way. If you read the message boards you got the impression he talked crap the whole time, cared about nobody but himself and would sacrifice our club.

By the end of 2000, he'd resigned as chairman. We weren't celebrating, he still owned 93% of the club. Resignation wise, he had no choice. In September the Department of Trade and Industry banned him from directing a business for five and half years. Mrs Knighton was also banned for two years. Their crimes? Well, they'd run St. David's a private school company into bankruptcy with debts of £474,000. With their company going tits up they'd paid their own holding company, a creditor of St. David's, £203,000. Not a smart move when other creditors were - pretty much - being ignored. The Inland Revenue - owed £288,000 - failed to see the funny side. The whistle was blown and the Knigtons were prosecuted. When Carlisle United took the field against Arsenal the club had only two directors, Andrea Whittaker who'd been secretary of the club at one time and a certain Mr M. Knighton, as in Mark, son of Michael.

Mark Knighton was barely in his mid-twenties. His father described him as,

'A bright boy with ideas.'

I knew somebody who'd worked with Mark in relation to the printing of Carlisle United programmes.

'Is he a bright boy?' I asked.

'He hasn't a clue man.'

Mark Knighton certainly had ideas. That was another story. Eventually a leak to the press would reveal a mobile phone bill from Carlisle United apparently showing repeated calls between Knightons, junior and senior. But, of course, the fat one couldn't run the business any more. Those calls must've been corkers:

Michael: Hello, Michael Knighton here.

Mark: Dad!

Michael: Son, what a surprise.

Mark: How's the weather in Heads Nook?

Michael: Oh, you know, broken clouds with a chance of showers later on. How's the weather at Brunton Park?

Mark: Well you know, broken clouds with a chance of showers later on. Funny that eh?

Michael: Yes indeed.

Mark: Bye dad.

Michael: Bye son.

And if you believe that you'll believe Carlisle United will be in the Premiership inside ten years. It is, of course, possible that the elder Knighton knew damn well his son had ideas because he was feeding the ideas to him by mobile phone. That's possible, it was widely suspected, and never proven. Had it been proven FGB (as fans called him) could have faced jail, the terms of his ban disallowed him from being involved in the management of a company, 'directly or indirectly.'

It got worse.

Early in 2001 Knighton 'sold' his shares to a company called Mamcarr. There'd been rumours of a sale and negotiations had certainly been going on. Insurance magnate Brooks Mileson was one name in the frame to buy the club. His interest continues to the present day. Mamcarr, by contrast, seemed to come out of nowhere. They/it was registered in Gibraltar where a few hundred pounds can buy you a company and complete anonymity. The public face of the new ownership was Stephen Brown a fat guy with a moustache who could have been Mr. Knighton's brother. Jimmy Glass would later recount a great Stephen Brown story in his book *One Hit Wonder.* Glass was guest of honour at the Arsenal cup-tie. Brown was fixing to announce his 'take over' the following week and already had his feet well under the table. Asking our saviour if he wanted a drink Brown headed behind the bar at Brunton Park and pulled a half of lager himself. It seemed a little eccentricity at the time. Looking back it was an insight into Brown's real identity.

Very quickly some worrying facts came to light. Brown's recent employment included working as a waiter in a curry house. He announced his acquisition of Carlisle United after driving in his rusty Vauxhall Cavalier from his local dole office where he'd just signed on.

At the time I was writing lad-mag columns as Stanley Manly. Every month Stan would put forward some common sense proposal to make the world a better place. One month he advocated diverting all cigarette tax into stem cell research and bringing back coupons in fag packets. Inside ten years we'd be attending some forty-year-old smoker's 'Last night of the lungs' party. The smoker would buy his or her cloned new lungs with twenty years worth of coupons. Like Mark Knighton, I had ideas. Sometimes I'd shut down the files after a couple of hours of writing down my brainstorms, log onto Carlisle United Online, read the latest update and think, 'I could never make this shit up.' It had to be Carlisle United Online - the site that would later become CUFC Mad - and the other unofficial sites. Nobody in their right mind trusted the stuff on the official site. The unofficial message boards were livelier, more honest and more prone to dropping the real revelations.

Sightings of Stephen Brown in his rusty D-reg Cavalier were - briefly - a common occurrence. He was trundling all over the place. He didn't seem to spend much time at Brunton Park. This enigmatic and secretive creature apparently did know something about Mamcarr. David Low, a management consultant working with Mamcarr talked to the *Cumberland News* stating that those behind the operation would reveal themselves 'sooner rather than later.' We're still waiting. Ominously, responding to a question on why they had chosen to remain anonymous he said only, 'It's a decision they have made which they are entitled to make.' One thing widely known about Mamcarr very soon was that the letters in the name suggested something sinister.

MAMCARR = Michael, Anne, Mark, Chevonne, Anna, Rosemary, Rory - the entire Knighton family.

I took that interpretation from *One Hit Wonder,* Jimmy Glass's autobiography. I've heard other variations suggesting one of the As stood for 'And' or 'Alf.' Michael Knighton is the son of Alf.

Arghhhhhhh!!!!!!

MAMCRAP? A lot of people thought so.

Eric Martlew, Carlisle's MP was asking questions in The House and demanding a full Department of Trade and Industry enquiry. Fact after worrying fact emerged. Knighton's holding company, CUFC Holdings, had borrowed £362,000 from Carlisle United, a club, by its own admission losing £25,000 a week. Worse still, the day after the fat one quit as chairman, CUFC Holdings secured a loan of £960,000, mortgaging Brunton Park as security. The 'bright boy with ideas' who was half of our board of directors had a strange approach to running a football club. David Low insisted the finances could be sorted out if fans - already organising boycotts - returned. A doubled average attendance would mean profits. Everyone believed Knighton was still running the show, the boycotts got stronger. I'd been staging my own protest, the one and only time I'd been in the east stand I was interviewed by Border TV. I wasn't paying to touch the monument to Knighton's glory. I cut down my travelling to home games.

No wonder we found it hard to concentrate on football. The Blue Army were in good company - The Football League were also worried about who was in charge. Stephen Brown was on his bike, or his rusty Cavalier. He had failed to show he had the capital to deliver his end of the takeover. He had, it appeared, pulled similar stunts, turning up at football and rugby clubs in Scotland claiming to have millions, enjoying their hospitality and attention as he prepared to take over. Knighton senior claimed Brown had taken him for a mug. Others suspected but never proved that the two might be in something together. Brown has never spoken - his whereabouts concerns United fans to this day. As we stumbled on to salvation and Ian Atkin's bruised back, the accounts for the previous season were being prepared. We'd lost £537,000. In the process we'd paid £30,000 to the departing Knighton despite the fact he was still earning 'consultancy fees' from us. Negotiations came and went, Mileson and another contender, Irishman John Courtenay were both in the frame.

There had been false dawns before and consistent complaints that when deals had been agreed they collapsed because of unreasonable last minute surprise conditions thrown in by Knighton. Why would a supporter continue to give time and money to this club? On 13 July 2001 I printed out a post on the Carlisle United Online message board, I read it last thing at night every day for the next week. It ran to three and a half pages. At one point it said, 'Being proud of supporting Carlisle is about being proud of being part of the most wonderful part of the country. You cannot generate these feelings for another football team, because it is not the game of football alone that drives us. I love supporting Carlisle because I love Cumbria.'

The last time I'd been so choked up about Carlisle United I'd been at Radio Cumbria trying to put into words what Alan Ross had meant to me. I lost the name of the guy who posted those words on the message board, but I've never forgotten what he said. Looking at the replies he got, I wasn't the only person touched by his words.

The battle at Brunton Park raged on. As the previous season's losses were reported the one real asset on the pitch - Scott Dobie - went to West Brom for a bargain £150,000. Atkins had brought in some loan signings to help us survive - they were all refused longer contracts. Four more players - Carl Heggs, Lee Maddison, Steve Soley and Steve Halliday - were sacked by the board, supposedly because they were earning too much and the boycott of season tickets made their wages too great a burden. As pre-season training got underway Ian Atkins had only five experienced professionals. Finally, the man who'd achieved the impossible quit. Predictably his account of the events differed from the club's official version.

Consider these facts about Ian Atkins: he was banned from signing new players until a week before the squad kicked off in 2000/1; he wasn't paid until halfway through the second month of his stint; his accomodation was never sorted out and he lived in a hotel the whole time, 200 miles from his family. Nobody from the club publicly thanked him for taking a team - composed mainly of cast-offs from elsewhere - from six points adrift to league survivors. I could go on about how I felt. The truth is, his departure, like everything else was a symptom of the real problem. At the start of the next campaign I was sat in a broom cupboard in Dartford, the local BBC 'studio', talking to Radio Cumbria.

'What do you think about Roddy Collins' plans?' I was asked.

Our new Irish manager was talking big, as in, 'I'm a winner and nothing is going to stop me,' kind of big.

'It's not about changing managers,' I said. 'Nothing is really going to change until the club is sold.' Three sacked players were reinstated although it later emerged that the plan to clear them out had been in place for a while. Carl Heggs opted for redundancy and tried - without success - to become a Northampton Town player. United didn't want the players back, but they couldn't legally sack them. The Professional Footballers Association amongst others had got involved. The PFA knew Carlisle well by this point. They'd lent them money to pay wages. Some of this money was still outstanding.

The boycotts, patchy and informal the previous season, took hold as we stumbled out of the starting gate in 2001/02. We didn't win until 18 September and it was mid January before we won two league games in a row. In October we'd played a Saturday home match in front of 1849 fans. Our game competed with a live England match on TV but teams in the Conference still pulled bigger crowds that weekend. Less than 1500 saw the home demolition of Barnet in the first round FA Cup replay on a Tuesday night. I didn't go to a home game before Christmas. But I still felt the same when I did see Carlisle. A couple of performances I did see that year - Orient and Southend - stand out as typical of the season.

At Orient we took on the ref as well as the home team. What the bastard in the black was on I don't know but we were well into the second half before he gave a 50/50 decision our way; the Blue Army erupted in cheers. Luke Weaver played another stunning game against his old team. Elsewhere the team showed new faces. Roddy Collins would eventually tax the memories of all but the most devoted fans with a turn round of players, loan signings, trialists and imports from Ireland featuring strongly in the mix. He liked company did Roddy Collins.

Steve Halliday had gone to Doncaster and come back inside a few months. Along with Steve Soley he had the touches and the awareness of what he was up against to grind out results. Orient were better than us and spent a long time making the point. We held on hard. Jonny Allan, a striker barely old enough to shave, got a run around and looked useful. Stuart Elliot, a defender who would eventually go through nine clubs without establishing himself anywhere, also rose to the tough challenge. It was early days for Collins. Now it's obvious that a consistent feature of his management saw the likes of Allan and Elliot showing clear promise and then failing to make progress. Stokoe, or Ian Atkins (had the latter cared that much about youngsters) could probably have got more out of them.

Still, Collins strutting around the technical area was a sight we loved. 'Roddy, Roddy give us a wave,' was a regular chant. He'd throw up an arm, usually after a good twenty minutes of being set upon by the Blue Army. We'd go mental and five minutes later we'd start the chant again. Well, it made a change from thinking about the future of the club or pretending we could control anything beyond a few passes through the middle of the field.

There was a top moment at Orient though. With the game grinding on to 0-0 the predictable second half substitutions started and something resembling a full-sized floor mop in a red shirt appeared on the touchline. 'What the fucking hell is that, what the fucking hell is that?' erupted behind me. Orient's Chris Tate duly trotted on, by which point the roar was: 'One Jimmy Saville, there's only one Jimmy Saville.' Class. We'd supposedly been in the market for that creature a few months before.

Roddy's misfiring army battled through a poor season but managed to stay above the drop zone for the most part. Strapped for cash, full of disparate talents and always battling the problems off the field they still managed a greater comfort zone than the previous three managers had enjoyed. We owed something to the desperation of others, notably Halifax who were condemned to Conference football by 1 April. We owed a lot to the few experienced pros we had, Soley, Halliday and Stuart Whitehead. Whitehead remained, just about calm enough at the back to make a difference for most of the season. Given the problems, that was an achievement.

Roddy's signings made a mark. If one player typifies Roddy's time in charge it has to be Richie Foran. Foran was supposedly the player with the worst disciplinary record in the whole of Europe for 2000/01. We signed him the following September. Between then and the last days of the 2003/04 campaign, by way of a loan to Oxford, he'd collect 29 goals and four red cards in a Carlisle shirt. Foran made a mark alright - on defenders' legs, in their faces, anywhere where his elbows could connect being a speciality. Roddy liked his football physical. If we couldn't top the league on championship points we could run away with an unbeatable total of disciplinary points. Roddy's teams reigned unchallenged in this area for months on end.

Watching Roddy's teams was like finding yourself in a car with a roaring five-litre engine and a faulty transmission. The power and strength went unquestioned but hooking it up to get forward movement was chancy the whole time. We were great, sometimes for a full ten minutes but less gifted teams with plodding tactics could grind us down. If the Orient game was typical of the fighting spirit and frantic search for the right combination that defined Collins, the game at Southend was typical of the best bits of Roddy's reign. We lost but we lost well. We were sickened by a last minute winner for the home side. We'd fired and fought away at them, Tony Hopper scored with a spectacular overhead strike. Foran stopped fighting long enough to net a typical goal. That was Richie's best play. Whatever Foran did in life was likely to involve hunting and killing things. His goal at Southend saw him burn up a few yards of turf, connect with a fast ball into the box and flick it goalwards with a well marshalled home defence reduced to helpless spectators. He was in there like a commando and they didn't see it coming. On this evidence we had flair and Roddy had some of the right ideas. He'd told them to go out and express themselves and - to be fair - his team did that. But tactical masterplans seemed to elude Roddy. We had moves, other teams had strategies. Roddy's spectacular results with Bohemians in Ireland showed he knew something about motivating teams but the quality of his ideas simply didn't translate beyond the bottom third of the bottom flight.

The real result, though, was finally on the way.

In January 2002 John Courtenay announced: 'I am pleased to announce that Michael Knighton and myself have agreed a deal for the sale of the club on principle, subject to heads of terms.'

By early April they'd rowed in public. At a bizarre press conference the club claimed Courtenay hadn't produced evidence that he had the cash to take over. Courtenay countered claiming Knighton had seen the evidence but hadn't produced the paperwork to sell the club. The fans supported Courtenay. Particularly when on the same day it became known that a £30,000 cheque towards the £100,000 agreed with Shelbourne FC for Richie Foran had bounced. Knighton could splutter phrases like 'Just a technicality' all he wanted. Big guns were lining up with his ample frame in their sights. Knighton blamed the supporters - again! - threatening to take the club out of the league. Football League officials pointed out he'd missed the deadlines for this. If you're planning on destroying a football club please remember it's 31 December to give notice of quitting the league and 1 April to confirm it. Got that? Okay. Knighton, apparently, hadn't. We were glad; nobody doubted he'd have done it. He was desperate. Reliable reports suggested £3,000 a week was going from the club to service a bridging loan whilst the overall level of debt was around £2 million. To top it all Knighton said he would appeal the DTI ruling from September banning him from directing a business.

As Carlisle stumbled to seventeenth place in the division the club's financial chances ran out. In June the Inland Revenue issued a winding up order in search of about half a million they were owed and Carlisle United went into voluntary administration.

Damn shame, my life was going pretty well apart from that. I was knocking out scripts including a few radio plays. I'd been nominated for a couple of big awards, including the Best Single Drama at the Sony Awards and my work had helped a digital station win one Sony Award. I could make up stories well enough, but nothing like the stuff that was happening at the club I loved. The best thing about being my own boss part of the time and shifting the writing was the way I had some control over what I was doing. One unseen advantage when I'd opted for this route was the way the good feelings it created helped put the football nightmares in their place.

I wrote up a storm in the summer of 2002 whilst John Courtenay fought his way onwards and eventually - by 26 July - to ownership of Carlisle United. Like everything involving Knighton it seemed there would have to be a sting in the tail. There were loads but two stinkers stick out for me: firstly when the finances were revealed it came to light that Knighton's company had taken well over £200,000 in management fees during the fat one's last year at Carlisle and young Knighton had borrowed thousands of pounds interest free from Carlisle United.

'Bastard,' I muttered reading that on the internet. The way I saw it that was my fucking money, and that of thousands like me. Secondly, the club's history had been destroyed. Photos, programmes and a century of memories vanished from Brunton Park. Put it this way: Carlisle United don't own one decent photograph of Alan Ross. I know because I asked them to supply one for this book. How can there be any excuse for that? Some of the missing treasures were found in a skip outside the ground as the Knightons departed. As an act of spite it struck me as tragic, pathetic and beneath contempt.

In June Jane had rung me at work. She was in Holland and in tears. 'I've done it,' she said, 'the chairman said it was the best exam he'd ever seen.' In the weeks before this Jane had talked me through presentations on the theory of psychotherapy. Her reasoning - pretty damn sound if you ask me - was that if she could make a Cumbrian understand the main points of psychotherapy she was definitely going to make sense to her examiners. Now she was qualified and I couldn't put into words how proud I felt.

She knew a thing or two about mental states. Later that summer I asked her about Knighton's behaviour. 'He's got problems,' she said. Not exactly a clinical diagnosis and just about the kindest thing I heard anyone say about him by then. It's three years later and I still struggle to feel anything simple about Knighton. I've gone from hatred for his actions through wondering what kind of mental storms pass for thoughts in his head to just wondering... why?

If you've read this far I hope I've at least made the point that I'm older and wiser than the kid who first wandered into Brunton Park all those years ago. Age and experience might have given me the ability to see several sides to a problem but where Knighton is concerned I'm still a jumble of emotions.

Older and wiser maybe, the thought of that man still gets me emotionally. I doubt it was Knighton at the Oxfam shop. Whatever happens to him in future, I struggle to imagine him ending his days as a poor man. His creditors maybe, but not him. The most rational I can be now is to think that his last half decade left me with the feeling of going to family gatherings where some embarrassing alcoholic would burst in and spoil everything. That unpredictability and the sense of everything being a drama was the one real constant, well that and the relegation battles. I'd never felt more distant and powerless as a supporter. But I still felt the rush when the team, trailists and youngsters in their ranks, ran forward.

Roddy Collins had fallen out with the board leaving Billy Barr as caretaker boss for the final weeks of the previous season. By early August Roddy was back. In a season that would be immortalised with an Irish television documentary - The Rod Squad - he set about showing what he could do. Young flair players - like Ryan Baldacchino and Brian Wake - were in. Others, Will McDonagh and tricky winger Brendan McGill got a chance to stake their places. I saw more games. A few stick out in my mind from the league season for different reasons.

Southend away - again - because it was another pitched battle in the great tradition of Roddy's wars. The second league game of the season. It was my first sighting of Baldacchino and he flew down the wing, often trading passes with Lee Maddison. We wasted a lot of the final balls. But that combination kept threatening until Maddison was crocked so badly his head needed stitching. My throat had taken some punishment too - it was that kind of game. Brian Wake replaced Lee, signed from Tow Law Town, a home of football excellence that also produced Chris Waddle, Wake showed some midfield class. As the season before, we were outgunned for tactics, but we fought harder and made the flair plays count. With the final whistle less than five minutes away Will McDonagh scored. Hardly a class goal, but it was worth three points and eleventh place in the league.

The following Saturday away to Lincoln we hit eighth place with our second tight 0-1 in a row. It got personal. We had three players, including Foran, sent off. John Courtenay got caught up in a spat with the crowd. The whole thing ended in court although Lincoln faced no prosecution for the anti-Irish ranting from their crowd. The on field battles were taking their toll and the treatment room was busy. Meanwhile Stuart Whitehead played out of his skin at the start of the season to show a real captain's example. The brief climb into the play-off places was a false reflection of the situation. We fell into the drop zone soon enough. Jane, Thom and I had the usual 'romantic' trip away that just happened to take in a Carlisle game. In this case Cambridge, a real fight on the pitch which we lost to a disputed goal. Disputed because once Matty Glennon had fumbled the save the assistant ref decided the ball was over the line. It wasn't, I got that much first hand because the Carlisle United team coach pulled up at our hotel and I got some quality time with the people I'd just watched. John Courtenay was brilliant. He talked common sense, valued fans and grinned and accepted it when idiots like me wanted a picture with him. Oddly the next home game was against Oxford. We took all the luck we'd been denied at Cambridge and won. This time with a scorching long strike from nippy little Brendan McGill. Having taken the lead we hung on with ten men for most of the game. McGill's goal was topped for class by another of Roddy's Irish contingent. At Orient Brian Shelley broke out of defence, waited until his back was flat on to the Blue Army in the stand and unleashed a thunderbolt from over thirty yards that screamed into top of the net. His only goal in a Carlisle shirt. Shame we conceded two.

The usual roaring engine and dodgy transmission approach was in evidence. We'd come out of administration in October, just too late to see off an approach for Stuart Whitehead from Darlington. We had limited funds and a manager who, presented with the bargain bin, would empty it. Shelley and McGill's goals were the high points. Well that and the fact that Exeter and Shrewsbury were obviously every bit as crap as us. Roddy wanted to please us and be loved in return but as we bounced around the bottom half dozen patience was wearing thin.

In the end we bought a reprieve, just. I didn't go to the evening kick off at Shrewsbury. They had to win to keep their survival hopes alive. I got the prediction right on the message board, sort of. Where everyone else was posting potential scores I reckoned there would be less than 22 men left at the final whistle. I'd still imagined it wrongly. It didn't occur to me that the 21 men walking off at the end would include the whole Carlisle team. For once another crew had topped us for bad attitude. Brian Wake's hat-trick had seen us win with the odd goal in five, we were safe. The final home game against Bournemouth was another stress free zone. Just as well. We lost by two goals and played like we didn't give a shit.

We did have one sublime day that year - another defeat- but what a day. Having humbled the stunning talents of Stockport County, Wrexham, Bury and Shrewsbury Town we found ourselves at the Millennium Stadium, Cardiff on 6 April playing Bristol City for the LDV Vans Trophy. The trophy and the sponsors had changed since we won a big beer tray donated by Auto Windscreens at Wembley it in 1997. Thom was ten now. We travelled down on the train, drank in the mighty crowd and the big match atmosphere, and he got himself a blue and white jester's hat. Despite himself Thom had become a

Carlisle regular by this point. We'd found a real father and son way to be together. We'd tried a few others. We could - just about - manage equality in Play Station football but only if he was Costa Rica and I was Brazil.

The roar inside was massive. Over fifty thousand, mainly from nearby Bristol, but enough Cumbrians to get that rush of pride running from the second I stood at the top of the steps. I got talking to John Honeyman, a GP from Wigton who'd seen both of my parents through their final days. As he looked after my parents he'd struck me as a decent man, more than just a doctor. The kind of person you should find in Cumbria. Meeting him in Cardiff was like touching the best of Cumbria, in the middle of fifty thousand people. Everyone was up for a great day. It had been a long time, too bloody long, since something had felt this life-affirming and this good. We were the underdogs of course. But we'd enjoy it whatever. The first half seemed unreal. More of an exhibition match with fast, passing, stylish football but no full-blooded assaults on goal. We had some chances, Wake was caught offside connecting with a perfect pass. Inside the last ten minutes Richie Foran flashed a shot just past the post. The 2-0 beating we took wasn't as bad as it looked. They were Second Division, favourites by a mile. They took the first goal well. It was Lee Peacock, our ex-striker who once deputised in goal at Bournemouth, who put them one up. Matty had saved brilliantly at full-stretch from a first attempt that looked like a goal, Peacock pounced on the loose ball. We leaked a second with the final seconds running out because we were pushing into them in search of the equaliser.

Roddy had looked brilliant that day, strutting about in his match-day suit, looking up at the crowd. That summer we signed Paul Simpson, a seasoned pro with a track record taking in Derby and Manchester City. Simmo had come from player-coaching Rochdale. His arrival had been rumoured for a long time, mainly because as a Carlisle lad he looked such a likely bet to finish his career with us. By the end of August he was player-manager. Roddy's barmy army had staged the worst start to a season we'd seen in 46 years. By the time Simmo took charge we had one point and the League Cup campaign had come to grief at Walsall.

Al Woodcock's requiem for Roddy on the internet was a masterpiece, 'You get the feeling Roddy Collins would have made a great winner... he was a fantastic presence at all times.' True. On the other hand he managed us for 92 league games, 25 of them he won. Four league defeats in a row marked his final weeks. If Roddy had delivered we'd have idolised him. When his teams flashed and - let's be honest - sometimes when they staged full-blooded physical assaults we'd roar and grin. He couldn't convince anyone he had a full grip on the situation. The lack of a tactical masterplan was only the start. There were scenes of action in World War 1 that turned over fewer bodies in the same length of time. Mo Harkin and Chay Hews anyone? Well Roddy thought they had something. You'd be struggling now to remember something about them.

I wouldn't want Roddy back but I'll treasure the memory of him strutting around at Cardiff for years. If only he'd been a real winner. If only...

I read an Augusten Burroughs book called *Dry* recently. If you think some of the stories here are grim you should try it. For the most part it's a true life account of how he battled through alcoholism and eventually stopped worrying about it by becoming a crack head. There's a story he heard second hand recounted in the book. A man is horribly injured in an accident. The worst injury is the loss of both arms. Seeing the poor creature wheeled into a ward in clear distress a nurse takes pity, closes the curtains and gives him the least expected hand job of his life. And that - more or less - sums up a lot of the 2003/04 campaign for Carlisle United. Roddy's stumble from the starting gate wasn't the half of it. Forgive the repetition but... it got worse.

Struggling to pay off debts the team had a makeshift look. Paul Simpson couldn't really go shopping until November when the financial restrictions were totally lifted. The administration had hit us harder than most clubs. Where most pay a substantial portion of their debts we'd had to cough up the lot and a sum not far short of half a million to pay off the administration costs. Some new stars were on show before November, notably experienced midfielder Chris Billy, signed from Bury. Billy's passing and vision were a cut above some of Roddy's raw Irish recruits. His ungainly running action and tendency to move his arms up and down in the heat of a midfield battle made him look like a terminal stress case. It did nothing for the nerves of the paying spectators.

It got worse. Simmo's first win as manager came from a tough and far from pretty scrap, to a 3-2 beating of his old club Rochdale on 13 September. He didn't win again in the league for over three months, taking just one more point before beating Torquay on 20 December. I saw the one more point. Another scrap of a game in Southend. They really should have won but we held on for 2-2. Fourteen games without a league win, a club record, a dozen league defeats on the bounce, sixteen points adrift at the bottom of the table, five points in total before Torquay. We'd finally done it. We were Newport County or Doncaster. We were that team people spotted in the table before asking, 'Who's gonna get the other relegation spot?' If - like me - you kept going, kept paying and kept shouting you'll know what it took to support that outfit.

It was - of course - hopeless. Simmo had to go. The chants on the terraces said so, the message board said so, I even said so in my column on CUFC Online. He hadn't a clue. Shame, he still had the moves as a player.

Remember the guy with no arms and the nurse? Honest, it was like that as far as I could see. We all knew it was hopeless. But still, in the middle of the inescapable pain there were moments. Little orgasmic explosions. Simmo came back from injury away at Cheltenham in November. Simmo's strength in the midfield freed Billy to look up and place his passes. For twenty minutes from the start we bossed them around, ending in Simmo picking up the ball twenty yards out and crashing a screamer onto their crossbar and down into the net. Shame they came back, scored two and beat us. It was Simmo again away at Cambridge in February with two more goals and a man of the match performance. Shame it only earned us a point. Somewhere in the fight for survival a guy behind me in the crowd shouted with a fury that brought a few of us up short.

'Arghh, McDonagh, what the fuck are you doing on the pitch?'

We were back to finding the worst culprits and making them personally responsible for everything that was wrong with our lives.

What McDonagh was doing was trying to cope. Simmo had inherited a bargain basement team with several untried talents and a smattering of dazzlers from the Irish league that Roddy had believed would qualify as flair players at this level. Roddy had wanted a team that could play like Brazil. Simmo's dour realism came from a different direction and the squad looked confused. But you could just about see intelligence at work, even in the worst moments. Where Roddy had told the likes of Brian Shelley to express themselves, Simmo forced tactical formations on the squad. The forward running referred to in Shelley's programme notes wasn't often seen on the pitch. It was a battle all the way. Even the victories - like a 2-3 win at Scunthorpe - were built on grit, sweat and a mass of bodies goal side the whole time. Blooded in management at Rochdale, Simmo was realistic. He saw the gaps and plugged them as best he could. It was percentage football the whole way but he tried to turn it round.

The Blue Army thought they'd seen every agony and humiliation known to supporters. Now we lived a new experience. Carlisle couldn't even die properly. Teams marooned at the bottom allow the support to shuffle through the motions to the end of the season. Without hope, you learn to cope and think ahead. In mid-December we knew it was hopeless. No team could turn this round, but starting with the defeat of Torquay we did begin to turn it round. Five points from 21 games were followed by 39 from the next 23. If we'd managed that second half performance over a whole season the resulting points total - 78 - would have put us fifth, three points ahead of Mansfield. Speaking of Mansfield, with the road rapidly running out, we faced the play-off contenders in the third last match of the season, held a 3-2 lead into the last minute and then faced a penalty. By this point the reality had changed. There were four teams - us, York, Scunthorpe and Orient - within sight of the drop. If we kept winning all the way we could survive. On the other hand, that Mansfield penalty was relegation in a single shot. Glennon saved it, we breathed again.

Every win was a shot of adrenaline. It was also a shot of agony. So near to safety, but we had to keep winning. Most dying teams, just laid down and died. Now, with two games to go we were sitting in our highest league place since the start of the season, 23rd with York below us. Thom and I took our seats in the east stand for the game against Cheltenham. We needed a win, followed by the real problem, an away win at champions Doncaster on the final day. In the warm May Day sun with around 9000 packed in, the desperate situation seemed unreal. It had seemed unreal to someone I met earlier that day. I bought a disposable camera, not wanting to risk my own in case things got ugly that afternoon. Paying for the camera in Boots I told the girl, 'I'm going to get some pictures at the match.'

'Oh,' she said, 'are Carlisle playing at home?'

Playing at home! It was more than that. We were fighting now, stringing moves, chasing the play. This was a team that could win. The first half goal was a typical full-on scramble. An Andy Preece shot, deflected by a defender under pressure and Brendan McGill sneaking in to tap it goalwards. We'd got them confused. Simmo skied one from a good position in the second half, we made other chances but the tension was there in everyone. With five minutes to go they mounted another attack, something that had become more frequent in the second half. Kayode Odejayi rose to head it home. Matty, brilliant for most of the season, hadn't a chance of reaching it.

As we lined up to battle again it was Will McDonagh with his head down, turning to his team mates, clenching his fists and roaring, 'Come on!'

What the fuck was he doing on the pitch?

Trying to cope, but now it was impossible. Simmo's heroes had fought themselves almost to survival but the final whistle on 1 May 2004 made sure we'd celebrate our centenary by kicking off in the Conference. Thom and I were on the pitch with everyone else. I saw one guy in floods of tears. Others were choking them back. In a way I envied them. I wouldn't do that with Thom there. I was more stunned than anything. Numb. It was someone turning off a life support system. 'Look, he's fought as hard as he can but there's no hope of recovery here.' You'd nod silently, say, 'I understand... but he put up such a fight,' and spend years coming to terms with the confused feelings. At the time it felt like the death of a relative who'd lingered a long time. Inevitable but tragic. The truth is, it still hurts like the death of a relative. It'll always hurt me that it had to come to this. So much so because the team that played out that 1-1 draw didn't deserve it. This was a good team. A team in play-off form who lost because they made the odd mistake on the day. This wasn't Newport County or Doncaster, pathetic for a whole season. But, a season is a marathon, not a sprint. We went down because we didn't get as many points as Scunthorpe and Leyton Orient. Damn shame, one victory definitely achieved that season belonged to Simmo. Loads of us had said he wasn't up to the job and had to go. We were wrong and he'd proven it with 39 points in 23 games.

It was a close season like no other. The club changed hands again. Fred Story - six feet eight inches of former rugby star and Britain's 938th richest man, side by side with Simon Cowell - was the new man. A no nonsense builder with a dour practicality, it was another culture shift from the ceaseless promises of Knighton and the jovial crowd-pleasing approach of Courtenay. The Blue Army swapped posts and observations on what was coming. We'd annihilate everything in the Conference, we'd be trapped there for ever, nobody would come, we'd be part-timers inside a year. All this and more seemed possible for as long as it took to read a post.

I needed some reality checks. Outside of Carlisle United things had gone pretty well. By that summer I was juggling a load of projects. Some writing, some consultancy and a few salaried jobs. I was chasing more work and getting chased by others in return. My website was up and running and as a result a few odd bits and pieces had been offered. I had regular employment as a writer. One thing I'd learned is that just dropping yourself into a new situation is a good way to learn what skills you really possess. Carlisle were now going to have to learn in the same way. By this time I'd also got a new insight into my love for Carlisle.

Since he was eight Thom had been training and playing for Bearsted. From the start he'd gravitated to the goal. When Carlisle surrendered possession, leaked a goal and started at each other looking for someone to blame I felt frustrated. When Thom went down at some kid's feet I learned to cope with fear. It all started in the under nines. Bearsted were a poor side with no experience. They'd take a beating, come off the pitch and start messing about with the remaining water in their bottles. Bottom of the league and thinking it a laugh. Well, it was the taking part. As the managers finally made themselves understood the results turned round and we managed a season like Carlisle in Roddy's only full term, gaining league survival with a last ditch fight. Midway through that season we conceded our first penalty. Some of the team went mad, Thom calmly walked into his goal. 'He's going to save it,' I thought. And he did. Shame they scored off the resulting corner. On a sloping pitch with parents standing on the goal posts to stop them blowing away in a freezing wind Thom pulled off a sudden death penalty save to win a cup-tie. His hands were so numb he didn't know he'd kept the ball out of the net. The following season Bearsted fought into a play-off place, only there were no play-offs for the under tens. As Carlisle hit suicidal form in late 2003 Bearsted under elevens stormed to the top of the first division and had premiership promotion and the championship in the bag before they lost a game. It was a good job Thom broke sweat in training, he spent entire games without making a proper save.

In the face of Carlisle's capitulation Thom's fledgling football career was a good means of keeping things in perspective. At Carlisle I was watching professionals who had a choice. I still felt churned up watching them but I had a kind of security. If Knighton couldn't kill this club, nothing I could imagine was likely to kill it soon. When Thom faced a penalty or went storming into a crowd of players or made a mistake I felt the bond any parent would. But with him there was more uncertainty. Would he be in the squad the following season, would he want to be? The more he understood of this the more we found a way to be together. At Southend in the relegation season we chatted to Tony Elliot before the game as he coached Matty and Peter Keen. Thom watched Matty laying into defenders and stopping shots. Like me many years before he was watching a professional do the things he dreamed of doing himself and he was getting a feel for this club.

As the Conference fixtures offered themselves Thom and I faced a bonding experience we'd never known: a season in which we were promotion favourites, a season in which we were playing loads of games within easy reach of Maidstone. The last time this had happened Thom couldn't spell 'Carlisle.'

So we could accept the inevitable and live with it. I wanted some good moments, the next season - at least - offered them up time and again. In August Thom and I bought away replica shirts. At the second home game I had the first of the moments I wanted desperately. I closed my eyes, let the warm sunshine fall on my face, drank in the sounds of the game, turned to the right and decided to remember the next moment forever. The scoreboard said 4-0, Farnborough Town were the nil, we were barely half an hour into the game and Karl Hawley's hat-trick was already up. Their keeper looked like he was auditioning for The Comedy Store and we had another hour to play.

7-0 in the end, as we sang, 'Can we play you every week?'

Time and again Thom and I would turn up to grounds we'd never visited before, park almost in the shadow of what passed for a stadium, exchange a few words with friendly opposing fans and find ourselves back in the car with the engine running in time for the classified check on Five Live. Okay, I'm a sad bastard to think this worth celebrating. But there are thousands like me. We did this time and again because the south east is full of Conference sides. 2004/05 offered Dagenham, Woking, Crawley, Gravesend, Stevenage, Canvey Island, Aldershot, Farnborough and Barnet.

We had some great moments. Away at Canvey there were free Easter eggs for the kids and a home side hell-bent on self-destruction. By the time Carlisle were attacking their own fans in the second half we were 3-0 up, they were down to nine men and Ashley Harrison, Canvey's reserve keeper was on after the first choice had been dismissed for handling outside the box. 'The green stuff Harrison, get it on the green stuff.' A blue was baiting him as Harrison tried to steer a goal kick to his own side. Harrison was up against more than that one comedian in our ranks. Canvey's two strikers looked like they could have joined Brendan McGill shopping for clothes in Mothercare. Their midfield was his only target and with nine men opposing us Simmo had put five across the middle and decided to play an exhibition game in the second half. After a couple of attempts that crossed the touchlines Harrison got a clearance to a Canvey player. 'Oh Harrison, you are a fuckin' star!' said the joker as we laughed.

Elsewhere it wasn't so funny. Two away defeats to the only goal of the game in February saw Dagenham hugging each other to celebrate three points and Woking leaving the pitch to celebrate dumping us - the favourites - out of the FA Trophy. Dagenham in particular was a bad one. Well into the second half the big idea involved hoofing balls over the top out of midfield to the fast running Magno Viera and Craig Farrell. Farrell was a Leeds reject, Viera a stylish star player from Brazil via Wigan. They could both perform. Farrell had been leading scorer in his first season with us, Magno crashed a hat trick into the Aldershot net in September '04, netting over a dozen goals in the season. At Dagenham their supply was cut off for an hour. We went a goal down and Simmo threw on the muscular presence of Karl Hawley and Glen Murray's ability to go wide and cut in. We got more chances but still lost as the few Cumbrians there stood and shivered.

We bobbed up and down the play-off places as Barnet streaked away with the title. Barnet's 3-1 win at Brunton Park in front of the biggest Conference crowd of the normal season - 9,215 - did them a real favour. When Thom saw us win he finally got a taste of those feelings I'd had at his age. That belief that you could turn up expecting a win. Then go home recalling the skilful moments you'd seen on the pitch.

But it wouldn't have been Carlisle without the misfiring and frustration. My life was well on track so it didn't keep me awake at night when we lost. I could see the bigger picture. Fred Story and Simmo came from the good old Cumbrian school of practical, surly, hard work. Fred's building connections were what we needed as Brunton Park took a biblical soaking when Carlisle flooded. At one point we were set to make history by playing an English game in Gretna, Scotland. In the end it didn't happen. We did - however - rekindle old memories by playing at Workington. Simmo and Story were building slowly, too slowly sometimes. Peter Murphy - praised in programme notes as a stylish midfielder - crashed a screamer into the Stevenage net. They scored two in return and as Thom and I wandered out one blue was up against the perimeter wall waving his tickets - rail and match - and screaming for Simmo's attention. The message: he'd spent a shitload of cash to be there and he expected more in return. Some things were still seething away from the pitch as well. The messageboards were alive with claim and counter claim about the relationship between the new chairman and the supporters' trust.

The play-offs was the least I expected and we duly qualified with the luxury of going through the motions in our last game. We'd come within a couple of hundred of the attendance record for the division. I'd seen us win 5-0 away and 7-0 at home. We'd discovered a few new stars and clocked up an average attendance of over five and half thousand. The next closest - Exeter - was below 3,400. We'd turned in some poor games but we'd also played well. The message boards hinted at the usual conspiracies and dark motives behind the scenes but out front things looked better than they had in almost a decade. For me the best thing of all was the chance to show this to Thom. His life was now more complicated. Five days a week at the local grammar school and facing premiership under twelve strikers at weekends. But, there were plenty of Saturdays for us to watch Carlisle together. Not a bad season. And we still had the play-offs. Two games against Aldershot starting at their place on 2 May.

Honestly, we were crap away at Aldershot. The miracle is that we didn't lie down and die in that first leg. They could have had two or three. They only got one. Simmo had reorganised the front end around the midfield talents of Adam Murray who'd forsaken regular first team football at Mansfield for us. Against the clinical defending of Aldershot, Murray struggled to get the final ball through to Magno. It was painful to come this far and watch Aldershot rain shots in on Matty's goal. Matty pulled off a couple of good saves, they missed a few sitters and the best chance we saw in the first half was Peter Murphy lobbing just over the bar from 40 yards when their goalie had been forced into a desperate clearance. Desperate clearances were becoming our trademark and when Matty - put in danger once more by the defence - punted one directly to their striker Dwain Clarke the ball was fed out wide to Nick Crittenden who'd had the Aldershot fans yelling all afternoon and Matty's desperate retreat was made worse by a lob going over his head and in off the post. We feared being buried but just held on until Simmo saw sense, throwing on Brendan McGill for some width. We didn't deserve it but we got two chances to level. Peter Murphy blasted in and their keeper saved with his head. In the final minutes Tom Cowan skied a free header with the keeper out of position.

So it was going to be a tough fight. Spare a thought for the exiles. There was an important meeting on 6 May. Nobody warned me. Every tosser on the planet decided to get together, pick their own patch of the M6 and have an accident. I crawled up the M6 and fought down the panic. By the time I got into Cumbria the road cleared and two thoughts did battle in my head. One said, 'I can just make it.' I had about 45 miles to do in as many minutes. I also had to park and run in. The other thought said, 'If they nick you over 100 you lose your licence. Instant red card.' I kept it between 95 and a ton, roared up the road and saw a Merc - clearly doing about 105 - hammer past me with junction 43 in sight. Everyone in the Merc wore a Carlisle shirt. I ran the last half mile and got a break. In the ticket queue a bloke was offering one C stand ticket. Everyone around me was in twos and threes. I snapped up a precious seat.

There were almost eleven thousand in there, waves of noise bouncing off the walls. I forgot the last 370 miles and drank it in. What a game! Billy was on fire, crossing for Cowan to miss another header with the goal at his mercy. Running the midfield with his typical stuttering and stiff runs and - when it really mattered - getting on the end of McGill's cross for a 2-0 lead after Danny Livesey had headed us one up from a corner. It flowed from end to end. They hit the post, so did we. Chances came and were missed. My head was in my hands over and over again. I felt my throat getting sore from the action. They scored in added time, we missed a good chance to steal it. Extra time went past in a blur of heart stopping moments. We went close off a corner, they blasted over. They had corner after corner in the second period but nobody scored again.

Penalties:

They scored

Lumsdon put one in low and to the left.

They scored.

McGill tapped one he should have battered, their keeper saved it.

They scored.

Glen Murray did the same as Brendan McGill.

'Oh no,' groaned the guy next to me.

'We were down on penalties at Wembley that time,' said a voice from inside me. Honest, it wasn't me. I was somewhere out of my body at the time.

3-1 down, they shot to win the match. Matty was sideways, airborne and just able to touch it onto the bar. We were a fingertip away from disaster. Matty crouched, roared and punched the air. So did 10,000 others.

Viera blasted one into the top right as if he were on the training pitch.

They shot for the match again. Crittenden who'd tortured us a few days before choked, offering Matty an easy save. He roared again.

Peter Murphy blasted us back to 3-3.

Sudden death.

Gary Holloway, a peroxide job who'd wound us up with some blatant dives in the previous game made it look easy 4-3.

Billy did the same 4-4.

Something was seriously wrong. My legs started to crumble. I wasn't standing on solid ground anymore. 'Fuck,' I thought. As the crowd went mental I went cold. It was a tea-party in my head. Voices shouting. I thought about Jane, Owen and Thom. I didn't want to keel over in this crowd. 'I'm not going down until I know how this ends,' I thought. I felt fine, it was just my legs. I looked around, the bloke next to me was worried too. Then - in a lot less time than it's taken to explain this - I got it. The whole stand was vibrating. 'Relax,' I said to the guy who thought he was having a heart attack, 'It's the stand.' You couldn't blame us. Brunton Park hadn't seen anything like it in years. We'd forgotten it could be this way. Jimmy Glass was different. A miracle in a generation of pain. This was the real thing.

They lined up the next one. Jon Challinor went bottom right with determination. So did Matty Glennon. Matty's hand was there before the ball. The Warwick erupted over the wall. The rest of us went mental. Shame it wasn't over. It took a couple of minutes to convince some on the pitch there was still a match on.

Danny Livesey lined it up, put it where Matty had been a couple of minutes before and found the back of the net.

Y-Y-Y-Y-Y-Y-Y-Y-E-E-E-E-E-E-E-E-E-S-S-S-S-S-S-S-S-S!!!!!!!!!!!!!!!!!!!!!!!

Bring on the Britannia Stadium.

The Britannia - it has to be said - felt like a proper stadium for a proper final. After a season of pleasant if threadbare grounds this was more like the real thing. Thom bought himself an air horn on the way in and once things kicked off he was blasting away with the rest of the Blue Army. The surge of energy coming from the stands didn't let up for two hours. We'd taken about 10,000, Stevenage less than 4,000. In the first half that was the difference. They choked and struggled whilst we played football. Simmo had it right this time. Glen Murray and Derek Holmes the combination up front, the rest of the team probably the nine that most of us would have picked. On the smaller Conference pitches we might have struggled more but in the first half at Stoke, McGill was finding the width, Billy and Lumsdon were providing the service and Derek Holmes and Glen Murray were connecting with enough accuracy to leave Stevenage Borough tracking back in desperation. We roared them on and after 23 minutes Tom Cowan got in a perfect cross, Peter Murphy rose and buried it. We had a few desperate moments later in the half but we were running the game.

Stevenage, outgunned, outshouted, outrun and - basically - out of it, got a tongue lashing in the interval. They threw on three subs in the second half, chased and forced us to defend. Kevin Gray's solid determination, a few desperate clearances and Matty's hands and - once - Matty's left leg deflected the danger. I could pretend I took it all in but I'd be lying. It went by in a blur of nerves, screams and a wall of noise. Only twice did I hear the faint noise of their few thousand over us. We'd had chances in the second half - Holmes had snatched a shot, Magno Viera had missed another and when they went up in a last desperate attempt to level it in added time, we broke and could have buried them there. We earned a free kick, 94 minutes in by my reckoning. Chris Billy spoke to the ref, the ref nodded. We took the kick, straight into the stand, Billy roared at us, the noise from our crowd was deafening and the Conference was history.

We stayed, we cheered, we lived every moment. Eventually, Thom and I pulled up at the Stafford services on the M6. A couple of tables of quiet Stevenage fans were over by the window, wanting nothing - it seemed - to do with anyone. The blue shirts, much more numerous, were strutting around. I grinned and exchanged words with a few. We looked the usual odd assortment of blues in exile heading south from a game. We got talking to one couple from Warrington. The victory had shot us all full of hope. Now we had the reckoning. They bemoaned Kidderminster's relegation depriving them of an easily reached league game. We all hoped Macclesfield would win their play-off, leaving us Lincoln, Southend and Northampton within striking distance. The curious roulette game of the exiled supporters would play itself out in the next fortnight. But we were on the way back to the league. We should never have left in the first place. By late June, we'd have our new fixture list..

And for Thom and I there was more. There had been no faking his reactions. He'd suffered through the nerves with the rest of us, his replica shirt, jester's hat and air-horn adding to the power of the Blue Army. In this season more than anything, he'd found his voice in the crowd. He wasn't going out of curiosity anymore. We talked on the way up about the tactics, the likely pairing up front – which we both got wrong – and what this one game meant to us. As the car headed on into the night Thom fell into a fitful sleep. We'd see how he was in the morning. With luck we'd be home by 2am. He was due on the pitch to train with his team at 10am. Bearsted FC is well run, but the budget is tight. Their colours are white shirts, blue shorts and blue socks. Throughout his time as goalie Thom only had the one shirt, a padded goalie shirt with his squad number – 1 – on the back. My generation 'trained' by playing football. It's different now. Demanding fitness drills go before the tactical plays and, finally, a practice match ends the session. It's hot work when the sun is out, especially running through the fitness drills in a thick goalie shirt. Thom solved the problem by wearing his white replica Carlisle away shirt, only putting on the padded one for the practice match. From a distance he looked like the rest of his white-shirted team. But, sat on the touchline watching them train, I'd catch sight of that shirt.

Thom slept and I thought. In the faces of the Carlisle team that had come to celebrate with the crowd there'd been a few who'd made their mark in the Conference. Watching the speed and fury of a game you think of them as men. Up close and leaping about in front of us it had struck me how young Kieren Westwood, Magno Viera and Glen Murray really were. Their delight wasn't to do with escape. They'd been no part of the disaster of the previous seasons. They shouted back at us because they'd made their mark. They'd achieved something. They shouted because when it works, it really works, football can be *that* good.

I ran the game through my mind as we covered the miles and one picture kept coming back. As the team had gone wild, popping champagne in front of our part of the stand, I'd noticed Fred Story. Fred stands out in a crowd. More – I think – than he wants to sometimes. Ten years before as we prepared to win a championship on the pitch at Colchester I'd seen Michael Knighton crouching by the bench, his fat backside pointed at the fans. He waited for the whistle before running on to bask in the glory. As the team celebrated at Stoke and threw champagne over each other Fred stood back, looked at his players and clapped them, and the supporters. Fred's a Cumbrian. I hoped, really hoped, he saw it like I did. I hoped he felt it, right there inside. Like many of you must feel it. This club, our one professional league team, is part of us. We dream, we live, we share and we belong – partly – through what it means to us. For a while there, we almost lost it.

15 Fred Story

Mentioned for the first time in this chapter:

These are my opinions not facts. Others - especially those mentioned below - are likely to disagree.

Zigor Aranalde – Classy Spanish defender. Lanky, skilful, deadly with a punt forward and capable of scoring goals. The Blue Army responded with chants of; 'We love a Spaniard.'
Dennis Booth – Assistant manager under Simmo and a great performer in the loud, barking and animated tradition of stars of the Brunton Park touchline.
Michael Bridges – Former premiership striker, troubled by injuries and out of favour elsewhere, signed by Simmo in November 2005, brought some class, classy goals and scouts from bigger clubs to our games.
Simon Hackney – Skinny and skilful midfielder with elusive-swerve capability and accurate shot. Featured in the Conference, came into his own as a super-sub in League Two.
Raphael Nade – From the Ivory Coast to Carlisle via Woking, a striker who scored freely in the great championship season. Mostly whilst on loan to Weymouth.
Alan O'Brien – Forward loaned from Newcastle, started with a goal in a home defeat against Bristol Rovers,
Mark Rivers – Must've seemed a good idea at the time, signing a League One forward who'd trotted out with Crewe and Norwich plenty of times. Not exactly bad but scored his best goals for the reserves.
Anthony Williams – Signed in summer of 2005 when Matty Glennon's existing wages and the club's estimation of his worth couldn't be reconciled. Starred on the message boards pre-season when supporters of Grimsby Town congratulated us on signing the worst keeper they'd seen in years.

We all live in a Fred Story house
A Fred Story house
A Fred Story house.
The Blue Army

League Two offered a few good away games in the south and some workable options of getting up north to see dependably bad visitors to Brunton Park. The traditional pre-season skirmishes started on the internet, along with the speculation about where we'd end the season. There were the predictable moves in and out of the squad. However much we all thought we knew we still couldn't help watching the transfers for signs of how serious the coming campaign was likely to be. Out went Matty Glennon, still pulling 'Rod squad' wages and under threat from the blinding brilliance of the improving Kieren Westwood, Matty couldn't agree a new contract with us but could get himself a regular berth at Falkirk. He went on to a bizarre season where he had a habit of turning up on television just before *Match of the Day* sprawling in hopeless attempts to stop Celtic and Rangers strikers in the token clips of SPL action shown on the national news. When Falkirk's bank balance plummeted to the same level as their total of points Matty – who'd become something of a favourite with their support – was off-loaded to St Johnstone where he pulled off a Jimmy Glass moment, punting in a sloppy clearance from a last minute corner to secure a vital goal. The 'new Matty' was Anthony Williams, who became a legend to the Blue Army before he'd punched a ball in anger, through our message boards. There were a few Grimsby Town fans out there who couldn't wait to tell us what a disaster the chunky Welshman was. 'Worst fucking keeper I've ever seen,' being one of the more polite posts I read, and that from a long time supporter who probably went back to the days when swearing in public was a sign of really bad character. Outside of Grimsby his CV boasted Hartlepool, Macclesfield, Gillingham and Stockport, suggesting the man had a fondness for cheap housing and the nearby presence of pubs full of honest working men. Warming up in the bright sunshine away at Wycombe as a mighty Blue Army got into voice for the new season Williams looked like some throwback to the FGB era days of Durnin and McKinnon where a solid frame and a fondness for an after-match drink were prized.

Based on this signing and some checking out of bookies' predictions I threw my matchless football knowledge into the message board discussions. We'd finish mid-table I reckoned, eighth if we were lucky, probably somewhere about twelfth. The older heads were counselling 'caution' and 'consolidation' for the coming season. We were back, we'd survive, getting it right off the field mattered most at this stage. There were plenty out there – it seemed – who agreed with my assessment.

Wycombe were likely to be a good test. Not exactly the most fashionable club in the land. Thom and I duly battled round the M25 and found ourselves in front of a wall of noise as the Blue Army got started on a deafening season. We almost scored three minutes in when Derek Holmes came thundering in to try and get on the end of an Adam Murray lob. On ten minutes the 'worst fucking keeper I've ever seen,' pulled off a decent save, deflecting a goal-bound header round the post. With Carlisle defending in front of the Blue Army these were edgy moments. One season away from this level and we honestly didn't know how good we were. We had a couple more moments of desperate defending before another new face – Ziggy Aranalde – produced a moment of skill that sent us wild. Spanish by birth, 'Ziggy' had torn up the turf for Walsall over four and a half seasons, played twice for Sheffield Wednesday and seen one red card in the process and turned 32 months before he joined us. A pedigree like that means either: 'thanks for the dosh, I'll run around the way Eric Gates did,' or 'I know the value of first team football, I'm here because I want to be.' Just after the quarter hour Ziggy took a throw in, got the ball again from a pass back, slipped a lunging Wycombe challenge and picked out Derek Holmes with a stinging ball in. Holmes managed more athleticism and twisting than we'd seen the previous year and buried it in the one spot their goalie couldn't reach.

'Y-E-E-E-S-S-S-S!!!!!'

The sun was shining, the birds were singing and we'd just taken the lead against a side that were worryingly good. Simmo's new troops still looked a little disjointed and out of sorts but the signs were good. Ziggy in particular impressed us all from the start. Even when the results weren't coming in that early part of the season the chants of 'We love a Spaniard,' were sung from the heart. Wycombe got back into it, we cleared a couple of determined shots off a corner before they fluked an equaliser in the first half. Scrappy goal, but they deserved it and Williams was showing himself better than the nightmare keeper we'd feared. Carlisle attacked towards the Blue Army in the second half and we had the best of the 45 minutes. Adam Murray fluffed a shot from a great position, Peter Murphy put bruises on the Wycombe wall when he drilled a free-kick in from the edge of the box and Holmes struggled to get control on a back post header after McGill had sent in a stunning cross. We rode our luck too, Williams' save from a scorching volley on the hour was out of the top drawer and Ziggy, having shown us he was here to sweat, damn near assaulted one of their players who had the front to slip the ball past him. It was an early season, feel good sort of game, but the ref was still generous to show the yellow card. Simmo put himself on for the last few minutes and almost pulled off a pass to start a match winning move. At five o' clock we had a point, it'd been a better game than we'd expected and there were a few smiles and jokes about as we trooped out into the crawling traffic.

The mid-table predictions looked about right, in the meaningless excuse for a league table that gets printed on the first weekend we were tenth, way ahead of Wycombe but that was our 'C' against their 'W.' By the end of the month losing at home to Northampton we'd dropped to thirteenth, a few more points and we climbed. Thom and I trundled round the M25 on a Friday night in early October to the magnificent Kassam Stadium, Oxford. The ground is three quarters magnificent, three great sides and a wooden fence behind one goal allowing punters going to and from the multiplex on the other side of the car park the added thrill of dodging balls as they drop from the night sky. There are doubtless many youngsters in the area kicking about with quality leather footballs. There may also be a few disgruntled sorts trying to argue out of paying the excess on their car insurance to replace the smashed wing mirror that resulted from Oxford's inability to hit the target.

We'd got ourselves into a comfortable father and son routine now, Thom didn't much care about the legends of the past. Simmo's ability to blend a squad had given him the chance to know and appreciate the crew who'd fought us to near-survival in the league and fought their way out of it at the first attempt. They would never be 'his' team the way Alan Ross and his team-mates were mine but this was a team he knew and appreciated. Okay, the faces changed but not so fast as they had in previous years. And along the way we had some adventures. The three sided ground is always good for a laugh and we settled in amongst an impressive turnout of the Blue Army, near to a well turned out tweedy type who wouldn't have been out of place discussing a day's pheasant shooting. We'd just started attacking our coffee and kit-kats when the tweedy guy spoke up: 'Fuckin' disgrace that!' Trust me, it wasn't, it was a good run with some poor anticipation that had left our new loan signing a couple yards short of the ball. Within minutes it was obvious the guy had a hatred for Alan O'Brien that ran deep. O'Brien, a pacey forward loaned from Newcastle was making his second and final start for us, he'd play three more games off the bench. I'd missed the home defeat against Bristol Rovers where O'Brien had scored the only goal but why this well-turned out Blue got his dislike of the new boy I had no idea. Thom's eyes were wide and he was struggling through the chocolate because he was stifling a laugh.

O'Brien – it must be said – had a shit game. He started off running all over the place, was generally in the wrong position for balls punted forward and spent a fair amount of the game cutting inside and – towards the end – changing wings in search of action. A couple of good passes along the way and one blinding run off Keiren's rapid throw out in the second half didn't really make up for the lack of involvement overall. If you wanted to be charitable you'd liken his game to the first days of Peter Beardsley before the rest of the team cottoned on to his class. If you wanted to be harsh you'd liken him to Jean Claude Pagal, clearly playing a classy and stylish game in his head but struggling to get into the mindset of the bottom flight. Five minutes from time Simon Hackney replaced him.

Overall, we blew hot and cold, deserved the 1-0 beating we took and hurled some abuse at Billy Turley, the Oxford goalie, once banned for testing positive for cocaine and once – allegedly – a transfer target for Carlisle. The goal that sunk us was a sickener of Aranalde timing his challenge badly for once and poor marking leaving the opposition with options to spare. Right under the noses of the Blue Army as well. Attacking the wooden fence end in the second half and Peter Murphy, Karl Hawley and – worst of all – Chris Billy squandered some decent chances. Almost at the death Derek Holmes beat Turley but headed against a post. Thom and I were up for all the attacks, burying our heads in our hands and urging the team on. We were still enjoying the endless tirade of filth and insults from our well turned out neighbour in the quieter moments and whenever O'Brien looked like getting in on the action.

Queuing to get out of the car park later we could be philosophical. We'd done enough to deserve a point, sometimes we'd made bad mistakes and the marking on the only goal was a disgrace. Aranalde despite being easily beaten by that telling run had a decent game. Above all, it was obvious that Simmo was trying to build a squad worthy of the division and ambitious to escape. The wise heads posting on the message boards seemed to have it about right, we were twelfth. Where the previous few years had got us used to entire squads changing and a confusing list of jobbing footballers we had a fairly secure pool of players, the word 'consolidation' had appeared often enough on the message boards earlier in the season, it seemed about right.

I'd been consolidating a bit myself, I had enough projects on the go to keep myself really busy. Having decided to get back to updating this book and placed the story on the news page of my web site I'd been fielding a few e-mails about when it would appear. Not – as it turned out – for the start of the first season back in the league and not for the final date that would have given us a reasonable chance at the Christmas market. Damn shame: that date 29 October brought an early Christmas to Brunton Park. Stockport County did a passable impersonation of Farnborough Town from the previous season, complete with comedy goal-keeping error for the third goal. In this case Carl Ikeme – on loan at Stockport from Wolves – misjudged a lob, connected with the top of his hand and deflected the ball into his own net. By this point we were well into the final minutes of the first half, Karl Hawley's stocky frame fought off damn near the whole Stockport defence to pile in a low shot for the opener, he got it easier for his second, Simon Hackney weaved and flew down the left wing, Hawley took a pass and flicked it up for Holmes to head home from the right side of the box, after the comedy error we still managed another before half-time. Raphael Nade, signed from Woking after giving us a few moments to regret in the Conference, found Holmes just inside the box and big Derek hammered it home. Bloody amazing, what the thought of a 4-0 lead at half time will do to the taste of an average coffee and biscuit. What really mattered about this performance was the dominance and the sense that we wanted it badly. Hawley brought up his hat-trick in the second half heading in off a corner and slamming home another textbook shot in the final moments. With almost seventy minutes up Alan O'Brien came on to jink and surge a bit but he couldn't get on the score sheet.

I'd claim this match as a turning point. Okay, Stockport were a stuttering excuse for a footballing side, something they'd prove over most of the season and Carl Ikeme – on loan from a Coca Cola Championship side don't forget – was so unspeakably crap in their goal he'd be despatched back to Wolves in double quick time and spend the rest of the season playing out unimportant games in front of echoing and empty stands with their stiffs. Also on his way was Alan O'Brien who returned to Newcastle as we continued searching for the perfect combination. For the rest of the season his main source of cheer would be a broken bone in Michael Owen's foot that briefly brought about speculation he'd have more chance of first team football. The departure of the widely abused Graham Souness seemed to revive Newcastle's fortunes. It also marked the end of O'Brien's first team football after four sub appearances for the Geordies that season. So, all told, 29 October changed things for some individuals. For Carlisle United there were some positive signs. We sat sixth in the table that night, our big win had turned the goal difference to plus 4. More to the point, we'd taken apart a poor side, kept the pressure on when the game was won and fielded the odd player – like Simon Hackney – still on the fringes of regular first team action. Put simply, we had a squad putting pressure on first team places, more useful talent than we could squeeze onto any area of the park and the ability to string together top class moves. The second goal, Hackney riding challenges, slipping it to our leading scorer who opted not to go greedy but flick the ball to his partner, in a better position, said it all. Whatever Simmo and Dennis Booth were dreaming up on the training pitch, it was good stuff. The results of the reserves, also humbling most teams unfortunate enough to find themselves on the same pitch, were another sign that the 'consolidation' talk of the early season might not be misguided.

The mark of successful teams is the way they win games, even when they don't dominate. Torquay away, had everything. Referee Gary Lewis turned in a performance others went on to describe as comedy. Hawley's first goal looked a mile offside. We held a 3-2 lead when the ball was driven at Danny Livesy in the 78th minute. When Gary Lewis saw a penalty, the Torquay fans couldn't believe their luck. It got more bizarre. Westwood dived and got behind the ball, their fans – placed well enough to see – didn't give the tell-tale instant roar that signals a goal, but the ref awarded it. We got a free kick on 83 minutes, in the fall out from awarding it Leroy Rosenior – one of Torquay's three managers that season – was banished to the stands. Maybe Rosenior knew what was coming. Kevin Gray got his head on the end of the kick, the net bulged, Kev ran in, grabbed the netting and roared at the thinly spread Blue Army, a blow up sheep flew out of the stand and hit the ground and the points headed north.

Another clincher of a game for me came at Rushden on a Tuesday night in early December. I'd picked up a tape in my local Oxfam – *Seven Habits of Highly Successful People* – for the journey. I'm guessing some pissed off punter had bought it at full price and chucked it away in disgust having failed to escape middle management. Whatever, so far as I could make out the seven habits of success didn't include 250 mile round trips to mid-week encounters at the bottom end of the professional game. Not that I was complaining. The same night Liverpool and Chelsea fought out a goalless draw in Europe, that early in the season their game was amongst the biggest treats on offer for the armchair fan. A few of us got a result before the kick off that night. Wandering in from the Rushden car park I was passing the players' entrance when a someone who'd arrived on the official Carlisle coach stuck his head out of the door and asked me over. Let's not go there in terms of who this was, it's enough to say the fistful of tickets he gave me – just over thirty by my reckoning – came in handy. Facing competition from live television Carlisle hadn't been able to give away their official allocation. Damn shame, the better entertainment was on offer in Northamptonshire that night. I put in a few good tactical moves myself by way of sprints across the car park staying out of sight of Rushden stewards and handing out tickets to incoming fans. What we got for free was well worth the petrol money. You could look at the two teams at opposite ends of the table and say our three points were always likely but that says nothing about the game. For fully half an hour they were fast and dangerous. What matters at this late stage is that the disciplined heart-breaking machine Simmo was fashioning out there on the park had stepped into gear by this point and for the first time that season I, and a few others, shuffled out muttering words like 'championship' with no sense of dishonesty. We were fifth, but that night we were brilliant and the class of the first team performances was becoming consistent. A measure of how bloody good we were was there in the opening half hour. Well, 32 minutes if we're going to split hairs about it. On balance they'd had better possession and more chances, the problem from their end, 32 minutes in, was our 2-0 lead. Predictably Holmes had buried the chance that fell at his feet from a poor defensive header and held off a challenge just after the half hour to flick a begging chance to Karl Hawley. However, the Blue Army were sat behind the Carlisle defence for the opening half and the move that I'll remember was big Kevin Gray launching his beefy docker's body into a full-length dive to head back to Westwood with Rushden hammering in on our goal and less than twenty minutes on the clock. Arnison had a blinding game, Westwood pulled off some cracking saves but that header from Kevin Gray, bloody hell, that was class, that was inspired. The man's built like a brick shithouse and that move, was graceful. You can look forever for signs and meaning in games and results, most of the time it's a pointless waste of time. But that moment for me was something of a milestone. Kev's header came at 0-0, we got the ball out and Holmes scored off the next move. Just over then minutes later Hawley's goal killed off the game for all but the few hundred huddled in our end. Kev's header matters as I see it because at that moment, we were in the zone.

Most of us will manage to do something well in life. The problem for most football fans is that we'll never manage to play football well. But there are always those moments when you're gifted at a job, funny around a table in a pub, shit-hot between the sheets, that kind of thing. Sometimes it just comes. Not because you think about making something work and not because you were born better than anyone else but because you're on it. We were taking a bloody onslaught in the opening twenty minutes at Rushden, they should have scored. They had pace, vision and commitment and they played inspired football. They'd come out with something to prove but at the moment Kevin Gray launched himself, they might have felt their hearts sinking. It wasn't a training ground move, it sure as hell wasn't the trick a coach would encourage in a chunky defender in his mid-thirties, it was just the thing that came naturally when they were about to score. Only a confident team would make a move like that look natural. When Kieren Westwood punted the ball upfield I laughed out loud at what we'd just seen, partly marvelling, partly relieved, I wasn't the only one. A minute later we were up celebrating a goal. By the end of the half Paul Arnison was having a pop from thirty yards and the few of us gathered in the Carlisle end were sure we'd made the right decision to come. Bollocks to Liverpool and Chelsea!

We started the second half defending well and controlling the game. From behind the Rushden goal our third looked like something from a football movie. Westwood's kick just kept coming at us, when the ball eventually hit the ground it was well into the danger zone, Holmes' head directed it down where it bounced, Rushden hadn't a defender in range and in a moment we all saw coming a mile off Chris Lumsdon stormed in to bury it, from twelve yards, with his head. It truly was a strange goal to watch, with much of the Blue Army fairly low to the pitch in Rushden's modest home Westwood's kick and Lummy's run coming towards us both had that odd quality, denying us the perspective to the judge the speed, leaving our senses struggling to get an accurate handle on them. At moments like that time seems, a little, out of kilter. Then again, it was business as usual when the ball hit the back of the net.

All of this suggested we had a team capable of good things but the really good news was there in spades long into stoppage time. Officially it was recorded as 90 + 1 when Michael Bridges got his name on a Carlisle United goal for the first time. By the time Bridges scored I'd already exchanged some words with a few of the Blue Army who'd spotted the backs of Rushden supporters in their executive boxes turned towards the pitch. They'd opted for the goalless draw in Europe. Big mistake, if they wanted to watch some team other than Rushden putting in a skilful move they should've seen Bridges' first for us. Hawley took a pass, played a great holding role, passed to Bridges who'd made a classy run into space, Bridges' first touch was pure class and the cool headed finish striking in past the advancing goalie was our starter for a series of such moments. He'd rack up six goals in his first ten outings for us. Put it this way; on the drive up there I'd been listening to some mouthy American on a tape telling me the habits of highly successful people including being pro-active and being able to see the end of a job before starting it. True enough, in the few seconds from the start of his run to the final strike of the ball Michael Bridges said it so much better. I had about 125 miles to drive home, I didn't mind a single one of them.

If any one thing said: 'we want to go up this season' it was the signing of Michael Bridges. Off and on a regular in the Leeds United first team, and someone who'd put in appearances for Newcastle and Sunderland, Bridges was Premiership quality before injuries and finding himself in the wrong squads with the wrong managers took a toll on his career. He could just about say 'mid-twenties' with a straight face when asked about his age when we got our hands on him. Thirteen outings, several of them from the bench, at Bristol City suggested he wasn't a total crock. Rushden was his first start and first full game in a Carlisle shirt and he'd brought a class and work rate we needed to take us from a good League Two side to a great one. This was what we'd hoped for by loaning Alan O'Brien. Bridges was clearly going to come with a bigger wage bill than O'Brien but, all told, that was probably good news. Apart from anything else I detected a shift amongst crowd discussions and message board posts after Bridges' arrival. Those suggesting Fred Story's position in charge of everything was a tactical move to unleash a nightmare of Knightonesque proportions were still around. The lingering mistrust between the supporters trust and the club was rumbling on and there were doomy predictions from other quarters. The willingness to put a player of Bridges' quality onto the pitch and commit to the risk in wage bill was the best answer Fred Story could give, well that and the goal tally, oh yeah and the rate we gathered league points from that point. Raphael Nade came from Woking, tried his best and did a few good things but he would never be a United legend. If his signing said we wanted to strengthen the squad, signing Bridges proved for sure the board and the manager were a double act. Nade would go on to free-scoring and adulation from the crowd, six goals in his first six games, on loan at Weymouth. Mark Rivers, another clubbable sort who boasted Norwich and Crewe on his CV wouldn't get the chance to stake a regular first team place. He'd go on to score a notable hat-trick, for the reserves. We'd go onwards and upwards.

Speaking of Michael Knighton his presence came creeping back into my life not long after the Rushden game. Given Knighton's fondness for threatening legal actions and my fondness for not losing my house in legal fees, I'll keep this to a paragraph of highlights. But... I got invited to a party linked to Jane's psychotherapy work. A couple of others at the same gathering had been involved at board level with a club we've played often enough. The unwritten rule at such gatherings is that the psychotherapists have some time chatting whilst their partners get together and try as hard as they can to avoid talking about their feelings, well at least if they're Cumbrians they do. I got chatting with the two who'd been involved in football. Given their dual experience of football and working with experts in mental health this was interesting to say the least. I got the lowdown on a few eccentrics, Owen Oyston, convicted rapist and footie chairman, the larger than life creature that is George Reynolds, convicted safecracker and sometime Darlington chairman. The gist of the conversation was that these men and others like them couldn't touch the very individual creature that is Michael Knighton.

Right on cue FGB himself burst back into our lives. The launch of his official web site prompted hilarity and hatred, generally in the same breath, from a Blue Army getting used to good management and a sense of stability. In its original guise it was a site so bizarre it bordered on genuine comedy. It prompted me into action with a once in a blue moon column for Carlisle United Mad. I couldn't resist it. Consider some of the gems of self-promotion in Knighton's account of his own life:

Let's start with the mission statement: *Characters like Michael Knighton might not be every one's cup of tea, but they are never boring and can be very entertaining ? whatever your views!*

Fair enough Michael; although that's so general you could apply the same words to Adolf Hitler. Not – of course – that I'm comparing FGB with the Fuhrer, there's a lot of differences, I mean, Hitler was slimmer and more charismatic – allegedly. By the way, the question mark in the sentence above, ungrammatical and seemingly pointless as it is, appeared on Knighton's site. Now let's get to Knighton's early days as a successful businessman:

The young, confident, hansom entrepreneur had stole a march on those better known big time international entrepreneurs.

'Had stole'. C'mon, there are twelve year olds out there who could tell you what's wrong with that. Incidentally, it's 'handsome' when it means good looking and 'hansom' in describing the cab, pulled by horses and – once over – a favoured means of transport. So far as I understood it, financial irregularities and lack of business spelt the end of St David's, the public school Knighton ran before dabbling in football. The ramblings on FGB's website did leave me wondering what they we're teaching the kids in terms of spelling. grammar and punctuation.

Later on Knighton revealed he had: *written over four books*,' including: '*a 200-poetry anthology.*' To the rest of us that would probably be: 'An anthology of 200 poems.' As for the writing 'over four books,' there was no Amazon listing to suggest anyone had published them. The only result I got punting FGB's name into Amazon was George Reynolds' autobiography, *Cracking It*. To be frank, with well over 100,000 new books coming out every year in the UK being an author is nowt special. With online publishers like lulu.com taking manuscripts from everywhere and threatening to put vanity publishing out of business for good we're now at the point where everybody, even the dirt poor, can write books. So FGB could have published his works. Maybe 'written over four books' meant he'd bought four exercise books and scribbled a few words in each. I got a good rant in on my column around Christmas, got a few e-mails back in the New Year suggesting others thought Knighton's re-emergence on the web hilarious and we all got on with the business of supporting a well managed and well run football club. After I'd taken his desperate literary style to task Knighton's site miraculously re-emerged having taken a good going over with a spell and grammar check. Despite the time I'd put in to pointing out the mistakes and despite his fondness for such transactions, the overweight one didn't get in touch to offer me a consultancy fee. Strange that.

We were loving the latest chairman though.

We all live in a Fred Story house
A Fred Story house
A Fred Story house.

For those of you buying the book for nostalgia reasons and no longer in the habit of coming to games that one is to the tune of *Yellow Submarine*. As the fiercely cold New Year dawned we were warmed time and again by the powerful presence of the Blue Army. Hell, there was plenty to sing about. Living in a Fred Story house suited us all. There was another chant to savour. 'Haw-ley, Haw-ley, Haw-ley, Haw-ley,' it felt good enough when the muscle-bound goal-machine, complete with a sprouting afro, buried another one but sometimes the chant was aimed in another direction. Never better than in the minutes before we kicked off at the Sixfields Stadium, Northampton. The team were getting their pre-match talk, Hawley was wandering behind the goal. That's Hawley, as in Hawley senior, Karl's dad. When I was thirteen I doubt such a thing would have happened. On a cold Friday night in Northampton it was bloody good to point out to my thirteen year old son that the Blue Army were chanting in praise of a black spectator. Some things – thank fuck – can change for the better in football.

For the record a 5-0 hammering of Rushden at Brunton Park on 18 February took us to the top of the league for the first time. The promotion rivals had been jockeying most of the season, surging and fading away like runners in a heat for an Olympic final. We'd drawn the previous game with Shrewsbury 2-2 and, frankly, hadn't looked much like champions. We'd slowly crept up the play-off and promotion places, stuttering like the rest, but, once we hit the front. We were the runner who slowly gets a vest width ahead, looks around, takes one deep breath, gobs out a monster greenie from his lungs and turns up the pace. What followed was a record breaking winning streak, seven league games in a row. We beat Barnet (2-1), Northampton (3-0), Darlington (5-0), Boston (4-2), Lincoln (1-0) and Grimsby (1-0). By this point we had a six point lead and a goal difference of plus 40. Northampton and Grimsby were looking at automatic promotion, others, notably Lincoln were serious play-off contenders. We'd shown the lot of them no mercy. When Bristol Rovers finally pegged us to a 1-1 draw on 15 April the finishing line was in sight, we had a five point cushion, a game in hand, a five match run-in and the comforting thought that Mansfield – fourteenth – that night were the highest placed team left on the fixture list. It was a good job that teams were surging and stopping in the other leagues, at least in the three divisions above us there was a little bit of tension and uncertainty about the destination of the manager of the month award.

Thom and I were there or thereabouts throughout the run. If I could bottle one night that season and enjoy it over and over again it would have to be the stuffing handed out to Northampton Town at their Sixfields Stadium, a magic night. For once the M25 and M1 were survivable, the pre-match feed was decent and we swapped the good natured banter of supporters of promotion chasing teams with some Northampton fans before the game. A wind into our faces meant Kieren was up against it in the first half, something he coped with superbly. Northampton were bloody good, ran most of the opening 45 minutes and made one desperate slip, gifting Hawley a chance he buried like a commando out for a kill. We gradually fought our way back in, pulled class move after class move and – on 74 minutes – got the ball to Michael Bridges. Bridges' first touch for control was so good it confused the home defence, the sweet lob from 25 yards out that followed was the best goal I'd seen a Carlisle player score live since Paul Conway ran from end to end over a decade earlier. In a word: 'classic.'

If I were looking for a word to sum up the season it would be: 'loud.' In the moments after that goal we were deafening. The Blue Army put in a superb performance, never letting up for a second. Every twist of the game greeted with a response taken up by the packed end. Some of it probably a bit harsh; the chants to opposing goalie Lee Harper of '1-0 and it's all your fault,' were eventually replaced by some choice stuff about his mother's chosen profession. If anything brought about the defensive error that gifted Danny Livesy the final goal it was the ceaseless flow of energy and noise coming from our packed end of the ground. On such nights it is a joy to be alive and supporting Carlisle. Let's get this in context. As we finally dropped the odd points later on it was Northampton, strong and consistent who surged up behind us, taking the fight for our championship into the last week. Whilst we'd fought unsuccessfully to stay in the league and grafted our way back in the previous seasons Northampton had narrowly missed out on two League Two play-off finals. That night they played well, mustered good support and believed they were worth three points when the ref blew for the kick off. We simply dug deep, came up with better ideas once the game had started and threw in the moments of skill – notably from Westwood and Bridges – that turn games.

We weren't too bad in the LDV Vans final at the Millennium Stadium either. Once we'd gifted League One play-off placed Swansea City an early goal we took them on equally, equalised and felt cheated when they sneaked a winner. I saw a set of stats claiming 53% possession to Carlisle and twelve shots on target to their eight. To be honest, whilst we wanted it badly on the day most of the crew around me treated it as a good day out. Thom and I had finally seen sense and joined the London Branch of the support, the mini bus picking us up half a mile from home and dropping us in a car park walkable from the stadium in Cardiff was a bonus. Frankly, I'd seen the future. Once the family is off my hands I'm sure it'll be chats in pubs and a few snacks before the game with others who'll discuss cracking Paul Conway goals, the nerve shredding nightmare that was Mike Graham's last season and Stan Webb's eccentric haircut. Either way, on the day of the final Thom and I made a big decision, we liked the way the London Branch handled things, and determined to become long-term members.

Thom had started making a few other big football decisions that year. In February he'd been cut up about something bothering him. After five years turning out for Bearsted he'd got enough things going in other parts of his life and – frankly – he just didn't like the football as much as some of the other options. He found a couple of other sports where he had more natural talent and there were mutterings about forming a band. By this point he'd spread from his keyboard to taking all of my guitars into his room at different times, stuffing his iPod with the noisier parts of my record collection and moving in on his mum's drums and percussion gear when he got the chance. Bearsted Under 13s had matched Carlisle, a solid start and an incredible run in the New Year. In their case nine wins on the bounce. Thom was there for the first five of those wins. At half-term he poured out his feelings and I rang the manager. I'd tried talking Thom into seeing out the season but when a thirteen year old makes his mind up...

Thom had joined a disorganised band of his mates at the age of eight. They finished most games in the first half of their opening season laughing, spraying each other with water and walking off the pitch without a point. Once the managers had instilled some discipline the team grafted their way to survival. Thom had stayed through good seasons, had a championship medal to show for one season and a man of the match trophy in his possession having won it in the final game of another season. He'd learned a lot about getting stuck in, had trained outside during the winters and shown a willingness to knuckle down and work over the years that suggested he had determination. In his final season he was sharing goalie duties with another keeper and coming on as sub during most games. In a tense collision with another championship chasing side in December the scores stood at 3-3 when Thom opted to kick out and try and start an attack instead of smothering the ball. In the resulting scramble we conceded a goal. He was gutted, but he was already wondering how much longer he'd stay. To his credit he set his own targets and didn't make a fuss about them. In fact, he told nobody until he'd achieved them. He trained hard, played out more games, made some decent stops including a corker that saved a vital win. In his final game he came out to the edge of the area for a one on one, tackled the opposing striker and got a decent clearance out to our midfield. So, he'd obviously learned something from watching Kieren Westwood. Having made his point he decided enough was enough. He joined a team of his mates and left a respected team in second place in the league who'd go on to fight their way to a cup final. He'd learned a few things from football, one of them the same lesson most of us learn, that we have to work for the things we want. To be honest, the first Sunday morning without a game felt like a bereavement to me. More so because I wanted to see how Bearsted's season ended and it saddened me to be spectating on the internet. I got in an extra long run and didn't enjoy any of it. But I respected Thom's independence.

It brought one thing into focus. He was in the Carlisle crowds out of choice. There was no pretence any more that he would learn vital lessons watching professional goalies line up their walls and bellow deafening wake up calls at the defence. Thom only had one problem as a Carlisle supporter, he was growing out of his replica shirt. Before the end of the season we had to visit the club shop. By the time Thom replaced his centenary away shirt with the 05/06 'championship' away shirt we were promoted. That much had been sorted when Hawley smacked in an equaliser at Mansfield in the final seconds. We had three games left, all against relegation threatened clubs. With the championship at our mercy it was time to take stock.

This is MarkT on the message board after the Mansfield game:

Are you watching?
Are you watching?
Are you watching, FGB?
Are you watching, FGB?

Just heard big Fred Story on BBCRC. What dignity in victory! What a firm grip of reality! What a contrast to the chairman the last time we were promoted from this division!

I couldn't tell you much about MarkT, but he posts sense. For me the best moment watching the promotion celebrations on television the following day was Story's down to earth approach to his achievements. A class line from Fred: *One of the strengths of this club is that the owner knows nothing about football.*

Right. One of the strengths of this club is that the owner has the brains to surround himself with the right people and trust them to get on with the job. Another of the strengths is that he listens to what they say. If Fred comes from the practically minded school of football chairman, that's okay with me. The man who knows nothing about football put an ailing club back onto a solid business footing and dug deep when the money for Michael Bridges' wages looked like a good gamble. On the pitch at Mansfield he was modest, Paul Simpson turned round, looked at the bobbing crowd of his own players busy – it appeared – trying to break every one of Dennis Booth's ribs and just said: 'They're mad, this lot.' Story and Simmo: hard working, modest, both well aware it was a team effort and everyone from the fans to the men on the pitch to the coach driver had done their bit. Story and Simmo: willing to work hard, get stuck in, not take all the credit. Decent lads, in a word: Cumbrians.

There were thousands of us singing it with pride in the loud season:

We all live in a Fred Story house
A Fred Story house
A Fred Story house.

On 29 April the whole family turned out at Brunton Park. The last time I'd taken Jane and both kids had been the opening exchanges in the Coca Cola/Milk/Worthless Cup in August 1992. On that occasion Thom got in free because he wouldn't be born for another two months. I was really, really nervous. We could win a championship, on the pitch at home. It had happened once in our history and the fact it doesn't appear in this book tells you how long ago it was - 1965 if we're going to do the statto bit. Great idea sharing it with the family. Bloody unfortunate we threw away the script and came up against Torquay under their third manager of the season, Ian Atkins. I'll take to watching soap operas if they ever make Atkins England manager but if full-on, in your face fighting for survival is what you want, you'll struggle to find a better manager. Torquay played fast, two touch, percentage stuff and headed in at half time with a 2-0 lead. Jo Kuffour, an Arsenal reject, showed some pace, skills and class in their attack. We, by contrast, dozed through a pedestrian opening spell. Almost thirteen and half thousand were packed inside, the biggest crowd of the season, and I could hear the few Torquay fans shouting from the Waterworks end. I couldn't hear the half time team talk but I could imagine it: 'There's our biggest crowd all season out there. They came to see you lot play and look at you...'

Whatever he said, we looked like we meant it after the break, Ziggy got one back and we put Torquay through the mill over the second half. So their travelling fans got the bulk of the goalmouth action feet away from their positions on the open terrace. We lost, but we lost well and the moment we'd wanted, posted about, hoped for finally arrived after 86 minutes when Simmo came on for Lumsdon to the biggest cheer of the afternoon. He put in a few good touches, almost got a good move started and was the first to turn and applaud us at the end. We almost staged a last second sharing of the points with Westwood, on the edge of his own half, punting in a long shot that skimmed the top of the net. The whole family invaded the pitch along with thousands of others. Along with a fair smattering of the Blue Army I walked to the Torquay support and applauded them, I even slapped hands with a couple on our way out. Shame about the result. Simmo got a less friendly reception at Rochdale three days later but we dished out a 2-0 defeat – Livesey and Murphy scoring – and near-enough sorted the championship. Only freak results, like a 16-0 hammering whilst Northampton won could stop us.

As it worked out on 6 May our opponents, Stockport, hit the woodwork and we blasted a few shots close in the final game. 0-0, it'll be discussed in future because Simon Hackney made way for Paul Simpson's last professional run out in the final seven minutes. The fairytale ending was possible, but Simmo didn't get the power or direction on the one free kick he took. No matter, it was enough of a result by five o'clock. Champions by three clear points, the best goal difference in the division, the most goals of any League Two team, and Karl Hawley leading scorer in League Two. For the purists all of Hawley's 26 goals had come from open play. Our average attendance was over 1200 ahead of the second team in that table and the same average attendance – 7218 – would have been good enough for eighth place amongst the League One teams. Aye, not a bad season. So much for the wise-heads, me amongst them, who predicted mid-table.

The reckonings had started in other areas. I'd been dropping in on a thread on a message board started by 'Blue_manc.' A blast at those still suggesting Fred Story was the wrong chairman, it read, in part:

Let us get some facts straight here.

1 - Fred Story has sorted out this club

2 - He may yet prove to be the best thing that has happened to our club... ever

3 - We would NOT be in a better position if Mileson had taken control

4 - Our club - for the first time in 10 years, is safe and secure for the long term

5 - Any attempt to wreck the relationship between CUFC and Fred Story is anti-CUFC. It will clearly and transparently harm the good of the club. Given what has happened over the last 3 years or so, Story could, and you could argue SHOULD, have walked. Left us to stew in our own mess and die. He didn't. We should be thankful.

I beg all true CUFC fans to get behind the man, the club, the team and continue to build for our success.

I didn't need convincing and judging by the replies, neither did many others. I'm in favour of the supporters having a stake and a say in the club. It matters, it's our club and it's bigger than any one person - fan, player or chairman. None of us can really own a club, or a part of a club because what it means in terms of the spirit, the ambition of the people and the place is impossible to isolate and give away. We can only keep the club to pass on to others. The fans need that stake because not all chairmen are like Fred Story, not all managers are like Paul Simpson and not all squads are like the players we assembled in that championship season.

The weekend of the last home match had turned over a few feelings for me.

The day after the game I'd seen one of my family knowing he was seriously ill. Watching the car pull away, knowing almost certainly some of us would never see him again, hurt us all. One of those moments that takes away the thoughts of the moment and puts you in touch with a bigger and more powerful reality. He'd accepted his fate calmly, with dignity.

As this was going on, my own working life had been keeping pace with Carlisle United. In terms of some of the projects now on the table I was in a different league to before. The day after the Stockport match I put in a couple of hours on my mountain bike, time to clear my head. Having picked the day's bright biking shirt from my collection of Carlisle replicas I set off up the North Downs. Since the first edition of this book came out, I'd given over more of my life to writing. It had gone well. I had a lot on my mind linked. This book to finish, again. Other projects to chase, some chasing me. There are times it's like a tea party in my head, but I like it that way. So much of it is about the future, that's the good part. I also had the thought that someone I cared about was dying and all of us would have to accept that. And I had the reality of what had happened since Thom and I sat in the sunshine at Wycombe to see the start of the championship campaign.

The obvious thing would be to see that weekend, championship secured, as some kind of closure, but to me that feels dishonest. Seasons come and go, we can no more change that than we can stop life catching up with the people we care about, and in the end, catching up with us. We can hope, work hard and keep the faith, sometimes we can get more in return than we expect. But none of it remains completely under our control. The end of a season is a break, nothing more. So I'd have moments to face over the summer, with any luck some good ones work wise, with good sums of money attached. Family wise we had the consolation that we could pull together when things hurt. As I hauled myself up the hills on the bike and managed to put myself into a hedge taking one corner too fast I was wondering how to finish this book. Some thoughts kept coming back to me.

I started out wanting to know about Carlisle United and get involved, for a time they were part of my growing up, all told that passion and that feeling of belonging has never left me. The illusion when we're growing up is that we can become part of it and control it, that's why we start to shout, that's where the silly rituals of lucky behaviour ahead of games come from. A lot has happened since I first started, some things have changed. In terms of saluting the arrival of Karl Hawley's dad in a crowd they've changed for the better. In terms of turning the game into an wildly unequal contest determined completely by massive financial power, I'd argue they've changed for the worse. If I'm out of date frankly I don't bloody well care. I just feel more honest crammed onto a terrace supporting Carlisle than I would crammed into a theme pub 'supporting' one of the giants of our game. I'm old enough now to know we can't control the football we watch more than we can truly control the lives we live. It's bigger than all of us and if that's what I've passed on to my own son, I'm glad.

So I had a lot to think about dripping sweat into the Blue home shirt on that warm May morning in Kent. But there was one thing to console me. Within a few weeks the final promotion and relegation issues would thrash themselves to a conclusion. Not long after that the new fixtures would be out. There would be trips to plan to Brunton Park and for those of us exiled at the wrong end of the country there would be dates in Northampton, Bournemouth, Brighton, Gillingham...

Epilogue - Why not Arsenal?

Marrying Jane was a good decision. But we don't always see things the same way. Bear in mind she's now a fully qualified psychotherapist. When we fall out, I'm on a loser. It's bad enough that she tells me what I'm thinking before I can get the words out. Worse when she tells me why I'm thinking it. I can't win.

In the face of her pointing out I'm stubborn, unwilling to change and likely to keep on repeating the same behaviour forever I can at least fire back with the same line, 'So, what? I'm proud to be a Cumbrian.'

Practically speaking, I could have made my life easier. Maybe by calling myself a football fan, sitting on a couch with my Sky subscription safely in a drawer and 'supporting' Arsenal. A new signing for Arsenal at the moment would, in all probability, be worth more in transfer fees than the eleven players who will take the field in Carlisle United shirts at their next game. Crudely speaking, an Arsenal player today could buy any one of the Carlisle first team and parade him as a mascot before a game. That's the gulf between my team and one of the best in the land at the moment.

Carlisle United isn't my whole life. Had it been that bad, I'd never have left Cumbria. But, I've never stopped going and I've been there when they needed me. It is matters of life and death, and only matters of life and death, that have come between me and this club. Along the way there have been distractions. Sex, drugs, rock 'n' roll and then the really good stuff, falling in love, getting married and having a family. Druggies are bloody cop outs the lot of them. They only get into that stuff because they can't take the life changing, emotion churning, adrenaline surging addiction that comes with the hard stuff in life. Like having a family, or supporting a football team. I'm in it for the duration. Nothing ends here, apart from this book. You might take the boy from Carlisle, but you'll never take Carlisle from the boy.

ARMY OF ME

Chances are you bought this book because you care as much as I do. If so, most of what follows might well be known to you. But if not...

THE WEBSITES (in alphabetical order)

Carlisle United Memorabilia: Split site one half offering every little artefact a true blue could want and the other offering up to date photographs from a fan's point of view. Adam Sheridan is a man dedicated above and beyond the call of duty, the least you can do is drop in and check out the result of his efforts. www.adamsheridan.co.uk

Carlisle United Official Supporters Club: Pretty much does what it says on the tin. Updates on the club. Updates on their activities. Lengthy coach journeys in the company of those also afflicted with an obsessive love of Carlisle United are a particular speciality. www.cuosc.co.uk

Carlisle United Supporters Club London Branch: Active, dedicated and capable of generating a lively mob for the longest of journeys. Many expats who've moved south for career reasons give the branch a selection of very able people. Predictably, their website is well informed and their fanzine *Hit The Bar* keeps faith with the old paper based format offering a level of match reports, opinions and news updates to put the fanzine editors of many bigger clubs to shame. www.carlislelondonbranch.org

CUFC Online: The biggest unofficial site, the liveliest message board, most of the news up to date and I drop in with a column once every six months or so. In other words I'm biased. During Knighton's regime this was the only place to get current views you could trust. www.carlisleunited-mad.co.uk

Juicer's Bluuuz: Statto heaven for Blues obsessives. Latest stats, permutations, current form league and many other options. I imagine lights burning into the early hours, wives and girlfriends falling asleep ignored and a dedicated army of United fans worldwide saying to themselves, 'So if we win by two clear goals and they only draw...' Since nerve shredding final weeks are a speciality at Brunton Park this site is strongly recommended for surfing in the springtime. www.apab45.dsl.pipex.com

Official Site: Worth a look now because it's big, it's bright and it cares about the fans. Has all the fixtures, current stats and up to date details on the squad. www.carlisleunited.premiumtv.co.uk

Reeves is Offside Again: Funny, informed and full of the larger than life personality of Dave Atkinson. Sadly Dave's life took a serious swerve off the rails for a while there, putting the site into inactivity. Should be back delivering the goods if you drop in now. www.kynson.org.uk/RIOA/

The 94th Minute: The web home of dedicated fan Lee Rooney (no relation as far as I know) a youngster who's devotion to the whole world of Carlisle is truly admirable since the vast majority of his supporting life has clashed with terrible teams, a chairman we hated and results that would have driven fainter hearts away. Good looking and lively site kept well up to date. www.rivals.net-94

United Trust: The organisation previously known as CCUIST. Independent supporters' trust forged in the dark days of dictatorship under Knighton and now fronting a plan to retain a regular supporters' voice at the club. Their site offers a downloadable constitution, information on membership and meetings and downloadable newsletters. www.united-trust.org.uk

THE AUTHORS

'You may say I'm a dreamer, but I'm not the only one.' Those still available are listed first. After that it's a random sort of round up. For more details check Adam Sheridan's site.

Darkly, Deeply,Beautifully Blue: The Journal of a Football Season. John Haworth (The Book Guild, 2005): The club's doctor lifts the lid on The Rod Squad period including the trip to Cardiff in 2003. Offers a few pithy insights into some of the characters we knew and loved.

One Hit Wonder: The Jimmy Glass Story. Jimmy Glass with Roger Lytollis (Tempus 2004): Punchy, honest and engaging account of the footballing life of Carlisle's saviour. From training on pitches that served as toilets for local dogs to battling compulsive gambling, Jimmy shoots from the hip. Also well informed on Carlisle's recent activities on and off the field.

McIlmoyle, The Legend of Brunton Park. Gordon L. Routledge (Arthuret 2004): Honest and unfussy account of the career of one of the all time greats. Lets the facts speak for themselves.

The Sporting Life: Chris Balderstone. Alan Porter (Elaine Humes 2002): Pretty much the same animal as the McIlmoyle book. Also recommended for cricket lovers since the man played at the highest level in that game and umpired as well.

England's Number One: Great Adventures of a Serial Soccer Yob. Paul Dodd, Iain McNee (P.I.G. 1998): Dodd talks about fights, drugs and life in Carlisle. The results are gathered in short, in your face, chapters. Appropriate given the subject matter. Personally speaking I couldn't put it down and finished it the same day I bought it. Still available and - therefore - probably boasting the longest shelf-life of any CUFC related book.

The Lads In Blue. Paul Harrison (Yore Publications 1995): Sold out quickly at the height of our mid-nineties optimism but long reported to be on the way back with a new edition. The definitive history written by a true fan, he's also an expert on the Loch Ness Monster. Respect! A further tome, *Come on Ye Blues* dealing with the years 1995-2005 is forthcoming.

Mick Mitchell: Football journalist and the most prolific author on Carlisle United. His *Proud to be a Cumbrian* features interviews with living legends including Rod Thomas and David Reeves. Mick's *Life With Carlisle United* and *Heroes of Carlisle United* are out of print but worth tracking down if you get the chance. The 'Heroes' book boasts a cheesy picture of the seventies legends posing with droopy facial hair and swimwear at Silloth!

The following are all listed as unavailable but recent enough to leave you with some hope of picking up second hand copies.

Blue Army: Ross Brewster (Cumbrian Newspapers Ltd 1995)

Carlisle United - Sixty Glorious Years (Lakescene Publications 1988)

AND FINALLY:

Knighton has stated his intention to write a book to 'put the record straight.' There have already been posts on messageboards suggesting it will be scanned and available for free download within hours if it ever appears.